RAILWAYMEN OF THE WELSH VALLEYS 1914-1967
Volume 2

Ex-GWR '4073' 'Castle' Class 4-6-0 No 4098 *Kidwelly Castle* heads south from Pontypool Road station with a Manchester-Plymouth train on 1 August 1959. *ColourRail*

Cover illustrations:

Front

Top left: Pontypool Road's '72xx' Class 2-8-2T No 7210 takes water at Talywain station with a train of empties from Panteg sidings to Blaenavon Big Pit on 14 January 1961. *Trevor Owen, ColourRail*

Top right: Pontypool Crane Street station and goods shed staff pose for a photograph on the up platform in 1914. *J. S. Williams collection*

Bottom: Ex-GWR '4073' 'Castle' Class 4-6-0 No 4098 *Kidwelly Castle* heads south from Pontypool Road station with a Manchester-Plymouth train on 1 August 1959. *ColourRail*

Back

Left: The South Bay at Pontypool Road station, looking north. *R. K. Blencowe*

Right: A Type 3 loco passes the site of Blaendare Halt with empties for Big Pit, Blaenavon, on an unknown date. *J. S. Williams*

RAILWAYMEN OF THE WELSH VALLEYS 1914-1967
Memories of steam working from Pontypool Road shed (86G)
Volume 2

Philip W. L. Williams

A Silver Link Book

© Philip W. L. Williams 2022

ISBN 978 1 85794 590 4

All rights reserved. No part of this publication may be reproduced, stored in a retrieval system or transmitted, in any form or by any means, electronic, mechanical, photocopying, recording or otherwise, without prior permission in writing from Silver Link Books, Mortons Media Group Ltd.

Silver Link Books
Mortons Media Group Limited
Media Centre
Morton Way
Horncastle
LN9 6JR
Tel/Fax: 01507 529535

First published in 2022

email: sohara@mortons.co.uk
Website: www.nostalgiacollection.com

British Library Cataloguing in Publication Data

Printed and bound in the Czech Republic

A catalogue record for this book is available from the British Library.

Copyright of photographs belongs to the photographers credited in the captions and acknowledged in the Introduction.

Bibliography

The following references have been used in the preparation of this book, in addition to recorded conversations with former railway employees and railway enthusiasts and written documentation supplied by them.

Drayton, John *On the Footplate* (Bradford Barton Ltd), page 59

Across the Footplate Years (Ian Allan Publishing Ltd)
Gittins, Sandra *The Great Western Railway in the First World War* (The History Press), page 62
Pontypool Free Press
www.aslef.org.uk>information>history

The Author

Local railway enthusiast Phil Williams was a contract structural engineer in the aerospace industry. His father's uncle, Harry Miles, was a Swindon-trained locomotive fitter at Pontypool Road in the 1930s. His family also have interesting links to the mining industry. His great-grandfather was Thomas Williams, the Colliery Engineer at Tirpentwys Colliery from before 1902 up to 1912, then at Crumlin Valley Colliery, Hafodyrynys, and the Glyn Pits, from 1915 until he died in 1925 aged 76. Phil's father's great-grandfather, Joseph Harper, was one of the 1890 Llanerch Colliery disaster rescue team; he worked at the British Top Pits. His father's uncle, Williams Harper, was the foreman of the wagon shop at the Big Arch, Talywain. A life-long friend was a former Pontypool Road locomotive driver Phil Williams, affectionately known as 'full-load Phil', who inspired an interest in railways from a very early age.

Contents

Introduction	6
Acknowledgements	8
Chapter 1: The Eastern Valley	10
1. Driver Tom Davis	10
2. Driver Derek Saunders	10
3. Fireman Charlie Reynolds	15
4. Railway enthusiast Rob Morgan	45
5. Fireman Gwyn Hewlett	53
6. Fireman Henry Williams	56
7. Fireman Terry Warwood	58
8. Fireman Colin Polsom	62
9. Terry Target	63
10. Barry Foster	75
11. Railway enthusiast John Williams	90
12. Railway enthusiast Terry Jones	107
13. Wagon Examiner Andrew Atkins	108
Chapter 2: Main-line memories	111
1. Driver Tom Davis	117
2. Fireman Derek Saunders	119
3. Fireman Gwyn Hewlett	132
4. Fireman Charlie Reynolds	135
5. Fireman Terry Warwood	141
6. Fireman Graeme Merryfield	146
7. Fireman Colin Polsom	147
8. Fireman Henry Williams	150
Chapter 3: Aberdare loco shed memories	153
1. Fireman Terry Wilkins	153
2. Fireman Phil Marks	156
3. Railway enthusiast Keith Jones	161
Chapter 4: A brace of Williams	163
1. Driver 'Full Load Phil' Williams: a tribute	163
2. Dave Williams's trainspotting memories	167
Chapter 5: Later years, 1965-1988	169
1. Pontypool Road shed closure	169
2. Vale of Neath: Crumlin and Hafodyrynys	175
3. The Top Line	180
4. Pontypool Road	222
5. South of Pontypool Road	230
6. Aberdare and Quakers Yard	243
7. Childhood memories	244
Index	247

Introduction

Publisher's note: This book was originally to have appeared as a single volume, but such was the quantity of material, both written and photographic, that it was decided to publish it in two parts. Sadly the author Phil Williams died suddenly in 2017 before Volume 1 appeared. Volume 2 contains what would have been Chapters 6 to 10 of the original book, but Phil had not supplied an Introduction to the second volume, so what follows is an extract for the Introduction to Volume 1 to give the reader some background to Pontypool Road shed and the people who worked there.

*

This book has been written to record the memories of surviving former Pontypool Road loco depot staff, Aberdare loco staff and local railway enthusiasts. I have spent four years recording and writing the memoirs of 22 people spanning the years 1914-1967, researching photographs and writing up their memories.

My interest owes its origins to a former Pontypool Road locomotive driver called Phil Williams, affectionately known as 'Full Load Phil', who was a near neighbour when I was growing up in the early 1970s, and was then recently retired. My father, John Williams, got to know him around 1970 and Phil would tell me stories about the depot and locomotives. He started at Pontypool Road in 1923 and retired in 1968. My father often asked him to contact Bradford Barton Publishing, based in Truro, to record his memoirs, but alas he wouldn't.

My father has been a life-long railway enthusiast, and from 1965 to 1982 photographed the Eastern Valley railways in their decline. Since 1969 I have been visiting the remains of such places with him, and thus the seed of interest was sown. Footplate rides on empty coal trains to Blaenavon, heading north from Coedygric Junction to Blaenavon Furnace Sidings with Ebbw Junction driver Gordon Secker, a ride on a 'Hymek' loco from Talywain to Coedygric Junction with driver Mr Richins of Griffithstown, or a ride on a weedkilling train from Coedygric Junction to Hafodrynys New Mine are recalled. My own steam memories are limited to the NCB Talywain-Blaenserchan branch in 1969-70, Hafodrynys and Merthyr Vale Collieries in the 1970s, and Mountain Ash in 1978. For Christmas 1977, my father bought me a sound cine camera, which was used to record local railway scenes from 1978 to the early 1980s. The sight and sound of a braked coal train from Big Pit, Blaenavon, heading south over the Big Arch at Abersychan in early 1978 in a fall of snow, and similarly the last train of coal from Hafodrynys New Mine on Sunday 1 April 1979, with brakes applied, passing the Mason's pub on Station Road in Griffithstown, are now lost forever.

Pontypool Road was a well-known depot in South Wales, and was located at the eastern end of the Vale of Neath Railway (VoN). The eastern end of the VoN from Pontypool to Quaker's Yard was constructed by the 19th century civil engineer and visionary Charles Liddell, for the Newport, Abergavenny & Hereford Railway, as its Taff Vale Extension, and was built to link

Introduction

with the Taff Vale Railway at Quaker's Yard, allowing South Wales coal to be transported to England and the Midlands. Crumlin Viaduct, designed by Tom Kennard, was the highest viaduct in the UK, the third highest in the world and, for its size, the cheapest ever built. During its construction Thomas Kennard lived in Crumlin Hall (later used as Crumlin Mining Technical School). On the Varteg hillside near Pontypool is a cast-iron memorial known as the Dog Stone, where Thomas Kennard accidentally shot his setter Carlo while out shooting on 12 August 1864. Crumlin Hall was in later years the name of GWR 'Hall' Class locomotive No 4916, and its namesake became the Crumlin School of Mines.

Pontypool Road shed was built in 1855, this fact being recorded on a roof supporting pillar located near the lathe in the north-west corner, cast by the City Basin Foundry[1]. The shed provided footplate staff for Pontrilas and Branches Fork engine sheds, the latter having branches with gradients of 1 in 22 and 1 in 19.

Pontypool Road today

Pontypool Road loco depot closed to steam locomotive operation on 31 May 1965, but remained open until April 1967. Today it is the site of a bypass, and the station has a reduced island platform, with the remains of a spur to the down carriage sidings. The station's bays were removed at Easter 1978.

In 2016 Panteg & Griffithstown station was removed for preservation by the Dean Forest Railway Society for future use on their railway. The alternative option for this building was for the Canal Trust to use it to re-line the canal bed as infill! Another local railway landmark now lost forever.

Panteg Junction exists as an up and down loop, the Northern Sidings are overgrown and silent, and Little Mill Junction uses a single spur to store track machines, on the former Monmouth line. The only surviving example of Charles Liddell architecture is the old original station building at Pontypool Road. In the Eastern Valley, the only surviving part of GWR railway line lies buried, since December 1935, beneath the Llanerch Colliery tip on the Branches Fork to Blaenserchan Colliery branch. Crumlin Viaduct has survived, in part, thanks to 50 yards of railings being used as car park fencing at Pontypool College in 1965, when purchased by my father for the College; he also privately purchased from the scrapmen the signal box nameplate Crumlin High Level Station, but this was stolen from Pontypool College many years ago, and its current whereabouts are unknown. One piece of the railings now survives in my ownership, as do the signal box plates from Pontypool Road East Junction, Panteg and Coedygric Junction and a few Ponty cabside number plates!

Acknowledgements

In 2012 there was relatively little published information about this depot, apart from John Drayton's books and the odd magazine article. I must thank my father John Williams for his help in providing footplate staff contacts, and Harry Rawlins for shed fitting staff information and contacts. This book has been produced to record the surviving railwaymen's memories, primarily due to my lack of knowledge on this subject.

I would like to thank the following people for their assistance with providing information for this book, with great enthusiasm: my father John Williams, Harry Rawlins, Charlie Reynolds, Derek Saunders, Henry Williams, Gwyn Hewlett, Colin Polsom, Andy Atkins, Terry Target, David Williams, Robert Morgan. John Pring, the late Graham Merryfield, Arthur Edwards, Terry Warwood, the late Terry Jones, Terry Biggs, the late Bob Garrett, and the late Ted Hounslow.

I would also like to thank railway enthusiast Keith Jones of Mountain Ash for his memoirs and for introducing me to ex-Aberdare firemen Terry Wilkins and Phil Marks, so that the western end of the Vale of Neath line and Aberdare loco shed can be remembered. Finally, thanks to Ken Davies's widow Sheila Davies, for giving me Tom Davies's memoirs so they can be recorded for posterity.

Special thanks are due to Harry Rawlins, Derek Saunders, Charlie Reynolds, John Williams and Terry Target.

Harry Rawlins is a former locomotive fitter who worked at Pontypool Road from 18 August 1952 to November 1964. He undertook the majority of his apprenticeship at Pontypool Road, and spent one year at Swindon. He has since continued his interest in railways by joining the Dean Forest Steam Railway in 1995, undertaking some of the restoration of pannier tank No 9681 after 1995, when he was the loco's Chief Engineer for a few years. I first met him around 2001, and this friendship was renewed in 2012. He has collated a mass of information on Pontypool Road, and thus the idea for a book was suggested. Without Harry's friendship and enthusiasm this book would not exist and the information in it would not have been recorded.

Derek Saunders, a former Pontypool Road driver, began his railway career at Pontypool Road in 1944, and has recalled the war years up to closure; he has also provided footplate logs and pre-closure job roster information used by him in his efforts to prevent closure in April 1967. He undertook a personal attempt to save the depot when he was on the LDC, in his own time as homework, and his efforts in doing this must be recognised and applauded.

I met **Charlie Reynolds** in 2012. He fired the last tender engine to cross Crumlin Viaduct, thus beginning a four-year period of research.

My father **John Williams** provided me with numerous footplate friend contacts and allowed me to use his extensive Eastern Valley archive of photographs taken between 1965 and 1982.

Finally, **Terry Target** first met my father in December 1982 while photographing a rail recovery train at Varteg station on the former GWR Top Line branch to Blaenavon. Having made a selection of Terry's photographs of the

Acknowledgements

Blaenavon Top Line railway after closure, I am reminded of what a remarkable piece of civil engineering this branch was, from Trevethin Junction at Pontypool to Blaenavon Furnace Sidings. It is a tragedy that it was not preserved from at least Pontypool Crane Street to Blaenavon, as it would have made the finest preserved standard gauge line in the UK, with its fierce gradients, numerous curves, S-bends and incredible civil engineering, such as the 180-degree horseshoe curve, the Big Arch at Talywain, overlooking the British Ironworks, and the outstanding Garndiffaith Viaduct.

The illustrations

I would like to thank the following for their help in writing the captions: the late Phil Williams (driver), Harry Rawlins, Derek Saunders, Gwyn Hewlett, Colin Polsom, Henry Williams, John Williams, Terry Target and D. K. Jones of Mountain Ash.

I would like to place on record the kindness of my old friend David Moores in making available old Ordnance Survey maps.

I would like to thank the following people for the use of photographs: Dick Whittington of Pro-Rail and Barry Hoper from the Transport Treasury; Harry Rawlins; Terry Target (Vol 2); my father John Williams, and other photos from the John Williams collection; Edgar Harvey, a latcher for PJ & JP Ltd at Blaenserchan Colliery in the 1920s and 1930; and the late railway employees Dave Fry, Rollei Kinnersley (Vol 2), Dick Bassett (Vol 2) and Herbie Harrington (Vol 2); the late Desmond Coakham (Vol 2); David Postle from Kidderminster Railway Museum; Paul Chancellor from Colour-Rail; Mark Vrettos; Alastair Grieve; Lawrence Waters of the Great Western Trust for use of photographs from the Michael Hale collection; Tony from Rail-Online; and Rodney Lissenden for the R. C. Riley photographs in Christine Riley's ownership (I would like to thank Neil Parkhouse of Lightmoor Publications for kindly scanning this on my behalf).

A special thank you is given to Ken Gibb, who supplied a copy of the Pontypool Road Loco Depot Plan (Vol 1), and Bob Marrows for use of his photos at Pontypool Road and on the Vale of Neath. Keith Jones of Mountain Ash is thanked for extensive access to photographs from the Stan Brown and Sid Rickard collections and other photographers within his collection. John Bird of Southern Images, Colin Stacey of Initial Photographics, Graham Vincent, John Chalcraft (Railphotoprints) (Vol 2) and Robert Hall of Griffithstown all allowed use of photographs from their collections.

Finally, I would like to thank The Signalling Record Society, The Manchester Locomotive Society, R. K. Blencowe, R. S. Carpenter, Ralph Charles (Vol 2), Terry Walsh (Vol 2), Steve Davis (www.britishrailwayphotographs.com) (Vol 2), Barry Foster (Vol 2) and Terry Target (Vol 2) for making available photographs from their collections.

Chapter 1: The Eastern Valley

1. Driver Tom Davis

Talywain, 1963

I was on snowplough duty in 1947 and 1963. Generally, the engine with fittings for the snowplough would be an 0-6-0 tank engine, which would be used quickly to run over the sections with the first light fall of snow. This could be done fairly easily providing the signals and points were in working order, but with a sustained and heavy snowfall different arrangements had to be made, as in 1963.

On booking on duty with nearly everything at a standstill owing to a 4-foot covering of snow, I was told that a ship was waiting in the docks at Newport for two trains of coal that were snowed in at Talywain, which was some 6 miles up in the mountains. As the snowplough was unavailable for this work, the Loco Inspector had decided that the line could be cleared by using a 2-8-0 tank engine and just running it at the snow with a certain amount of speed and power. With a full head of steam, regulator three-quarters open and a 45 per cent cut-off, we entered the section with a ruling gradient of 1 in 100, and for approximately 4 miles met with some success. But as we were driving our way forward we were proceeding higher up into the mountain, and into deeper snow and, in spite of setting back each time, we became stuck. Having made another run at it we finally gave up and had to remain where we were.

However, our Inspector, who had risen from the ranks and had once been an engine driver, had other ideas. He sent a message to our loco department for two more engines of the same class with presumably selected (mad) engine drivers, for now I look back and think about this episode I am sure it was a little wild, and surely not within the code of safety practices of British Railways.

The other two engines arrived, both 2-8-0 tanks, and coupled up. At a given signal we pressed forward with a concerted effort and, at great risk of becoming derailed, arrived at the Talywain coal sidings. Great difficulties were being experienced by platelayers in digging out a track to enable us to get at our train, for the wagons were embedded in quite a lot of snow, and furthermore the down line over which the trains were supposed to travel was completely blocked by the snow, which had been pushed over from the up line in our crazy, but successful, attempt to get up there.

It was therefore decided to use the two spare engines to take both trains of coal over the up line, with due regard to the numerous catch points that had to be secured. Altogether it was a pretty successful episode, for to release two trains of coal in such inclement weather conditions was a valuable effort in supplying a commodity that was then in short supply.

2. Driver Derek Saunders

The old Monmouthshire line to Newport

You were sent this way by the signalman if the main line was busy. At Mill Street, Newport,

The Eastern Valley

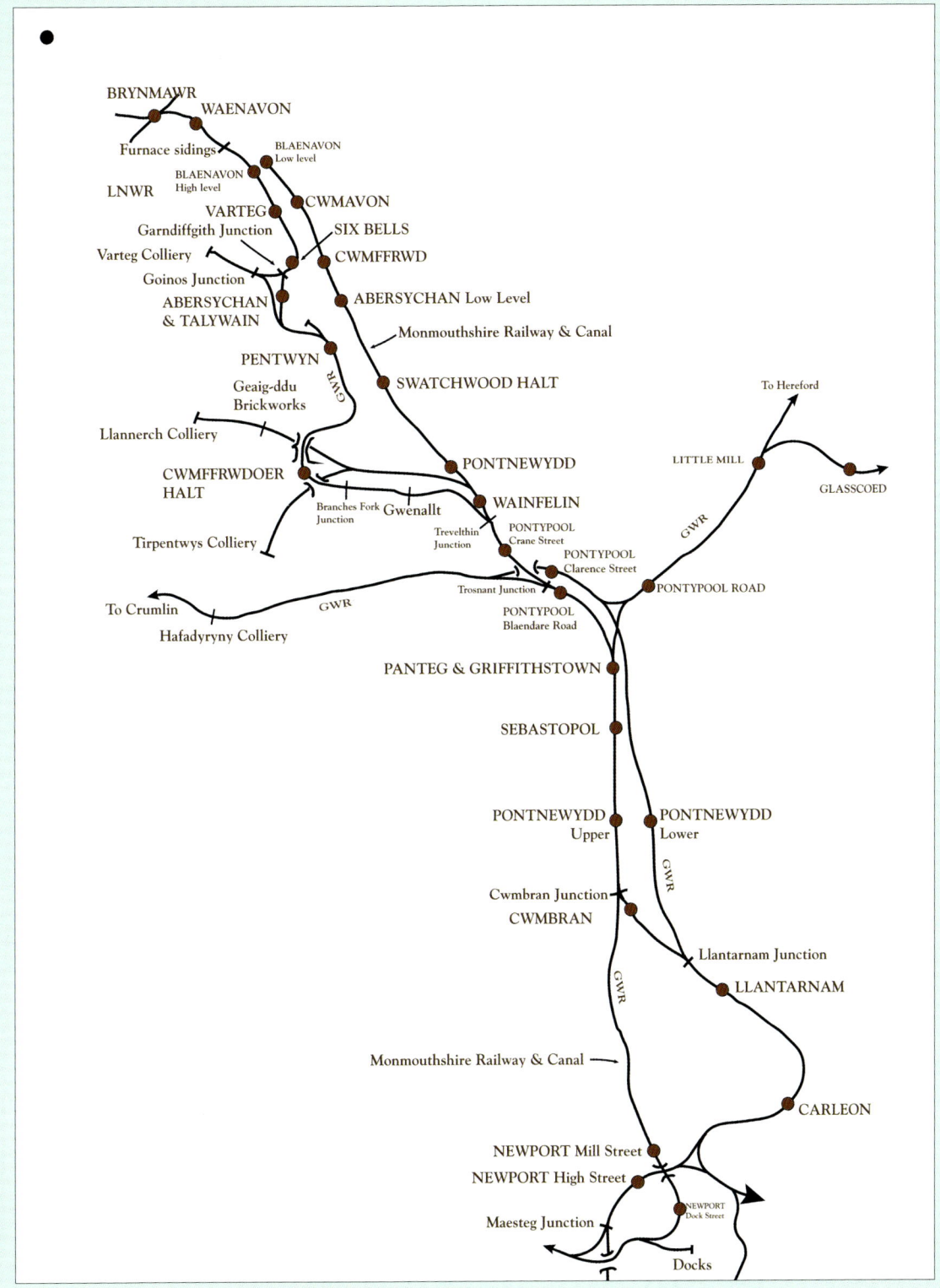

A simplified sketch map of the Eastern Valley line and its connections (not to scale).

Panteg station looking south on 3 June 1963, with Panteg Steelworks dominating the background. On the left is the single line to Panteg sidings (from the Old Yard or the High Level Goods line, used for light engine movements from the loco shed to Panteg sidings), and the access line from Panteg sidings to the Eastern Valley line. The shed at the north end of the up building was used by the porters. The coal yard is seen behind the station, and the goods shed is south of the up platform. *M. Hale, Great Western Trust*

there were sidings on both sides of the railway, and this was the only place I saw a starting signal coming out of a siding with a distant beneath it; this was because of the sharp dip under the main line by Newport Castle.

After you went under the main line and past the castle, heading south, on the left-hand side was Canal Wharf and Moderator Wharfs; traffic only went in or out when a ship was berthed there. Further down was Cashmore's scrapyard, then we passed the old Dock Street loco shed, crossed the road and made our way to Courtybella Junction (alongside Cardiff Road) and onto the main line.

Llantarnam banker

I have worked this job on my own as a cleaner. Of the drivers at Ponty, some were from Newport and Cardiff. I was working with driver Fred Stanley, a Newport man. In the war drivers were pushed through for promotion, and Fred was one of them. He said to me, 'I don't know much about this job, but I've got the garden under hand.' When not on afternoons, Fred would catch the 8.30am train to Newport and go home, but didn't book off till 10.05 or 10.10am.

I went to Llantarnam as a cleaner to bank the 261 up from the Llantarnam loop – the Bristol to Manchester freight – on my own.

Panteg

You pushed the train into Panteg Steelworks at both the bottom and top ends. The steelworks used Panteg Sidings for trains going in; scrap and materials for the works such as spare rollers would go in at these sidings. Coal

The Eastern Valley

Ex-GWR 0-6-0PT No 3717 shunts Panteg station coal yard during the 1950s. *Ralph Charles collection*

for the works must also have gone in this way. Products came out by road. Mr Simmonds, the coal merchant, had a contract to deliver steel coils by lorry to Birmingham. The bottom end was near the old Panteg station, on the main line, and the train would go up through the tunnels and into the yard.

Panteg station coal yard was shunted by the Panteg Pilot. There were three or four coal merchants there, and at one time perishable goods were offloaded in the goods shed, which was used for wagons of fruit and vegetables, as well as coal for the coal merchants.

Around Pontypool Road

I recall Skew Bridge loop points as a ground frame, before the war, but it was out of use when I started working on the railway.

All passenger trains stopped at Blaendare Road Halt, but I don't recall Trosnant Siding being used. [Author's note: the Trosnant Junction map states this it was used for ashes.]

Crane Street goods yard dealt with mixed traffic and there was a coal yard at the back of the box for coal merchants.

The 'Rodney'

This was the last train out of Newport at 10.35pm on a Saturday. It had an engine at each end, with about six coaches.

At Caerleon in the late 1940s a couple went across the crossing and the lady caught her shoe between the rail and the platform. Both were killed.

Blaenavon Low Level

I didn't work this turn very often. One week I worked with George Grave, on the 'auto' push-pull train with a '64xx' pannier tank. I was supposed to be a passed fireman, which I wasn't. On one occasion Jack Kersley, the Loco Inspector, wanted to get on the

Ex-GWR 0-6-0PT No 5752 is ready to leave Blaenavon Low Level with the 2.40pm train to Newport. The line closed completely, north of Pontnewynydd Junction, from 30 April 1962. *M. Hale, Great Western Trust*

footplate, and I told him to ask the driver first. Jack would check to make sure that the auto gear was connected correctly on the footplate, and not uncoupled. Auto gear couplings were not always coupled up, as they were heavy and awkward, but I always coupled them up.

Looking south at Blaenavon Low Level, '94xx' Class 0-6-0PT No 9488 awaits departure with the return 8.20am Newport-Blaenavon train on 13 January 1962. *L. Fullwood, Transport Treasury*

The Blaenavon Low Level station sign as seen on the SLS rail tour of 7 May 1962. *Barry Foster*

The 4.35am newspaper train to Blaenavon from Newport was an auto-train working, as was the 4.05pm evening train, which also had papers on, and would call at Sebastopol station with the *Argus*. The auto-train was kept in the up carriage siding, and there were a couple of sets. A diesel was used to Monmouth.

Classes '43xx', '41xx' and '66xx' were used to Blaenavon Low Level for Barry excursions and to Porthcawl.

Diesel memories

Training for driving diesels at Ponty was done at Cardiff.

Class 37 diesels were used at Furnace Sidings, Blaenavon. You would pin down 37 wagon brakes out of 40 all the way to Panteg. The Inspector said you couldn't do it, but the station master at Talywain, Les Birch, would report anyone who didn't stop at the stop board there, both in steam as well as in diesel days. The diesel would stick and slip before enough brakes were pinned down. You didn't stop at Crane Street either, but continued to Panteg & Griffithstown station, where the brakes were picked up. You would then push the train into the South Sidings at Pontypool Road. This was a work of art with 40 wagons, as you had to push hard from Griffithstown; you had to open up the diesel and wait for the rebound to get the train moving. The Class 37s arrived first at Ponty, followed by Class 47s.

Eric Telfer was with me at Furnace Sidings on the Class 37s; he was on the Pilots for a long time.

You would change diesel out of Skew Bridge loop from Coedygric, relieving someone from Hafodyrynys. You would be in reverse going up against the train in the dark, then drift down from there to Caerleon. On one occasion I was about to open up the loco at Caerleon and found that it was still in reverse!

3. Fireman Charlie Reynolds

Eastern Valley sidings, Pontypool to Newport

Blaendare (Trosnant) siding was possibly used for storing wagons for Mynydd Maen Colliery, and from memory there were four sidings.

A train of coal heads south from Pontypool Crane Street, with the Trosnant area of Pontypool in the immediate background. This photo was taken from the quarry at the side of West Monmouth Grammar School. Trosnant Sidings are seen in the foreground, with the Vale of Neath line in a cutting behind them. The tender engine at the rear of the coal train was added to provide additional braking. *Phil Williams collection*

Ex-GWR '64xx' Class 0-6-0PT No 6403 takes water at Panteg station while working a Stephenson Locomotive Society special on 11 July 1953. It will proceed to Trevethin Junction and take the former GWR line to Talywain, and from there the former LNWR line to Brynmawr and on to Ebbw Vale. The auto-coach behind the engine survives in preservation, though unrestored. *P. J. Garland, R. Carpenter collection*

The siding at Blaendare was for runaway wagons, and originally had no connection to the Vale of Neath. When Hafodyrynys New Mine opened, the single track was doubled at Trosnant, and a connection made to the Vale of Neath line.

Trosnant box controlled the signals at Pontypool Clarence Street, on the Eastern Valley line, and the siding to Mynydd Maen, later the running road to the Vale.

Coal for Panteg Hospital was one job undertaken in the evening while on the way to Pontnewynydd yard with a train of empties. At Pontypool Road yard a few wagons of loaded coal were attached to the front of the train, next to the engine, for dropping off at the hospital.

At Pontnewynydd yard a train of loaded coal would be collected and worked from there to Uskmouth and East Usk yards; you might go to the yard just as an engine and van – you rarely took anything up to the yard, maybe empties on occasion.

At Panteg Hospital you could put four wagons in the siding. A tram road from the hospital boiler house came across the canal bridge and alongside the wagons of coal. The drams – iron tram-road wagons – were pushed by hand on the tram road, a wagon of coal was dropped into them and loaded drams were pushed back into the hospital. Someone had to be there to meet you, and access was via a ground frame. A wagon of coal would last a few weeks. Wagons would be pulled off going up with, for example, the Blaendare Pilot or other working.

At Pontnewydd, just north of Cwmbran, a lot of coal would be shunted in, sorted out, the empties loaded up, back on the van, then down the loop to get to the main line by Cwmbran Sidings box. When at Cwmbran you would put empties in other sidings to go back down. Passing underneath the road bridge near Cwmbran station you accessed the line towards Newport Dock Street to shunt the Cwmbran coal delivery sidings; there was also a goods shed there. A nearby works was shunted on the opposite side of the line.

Both Cwmbran and Panteg had water columns, and also Llantarnam Junction, between the main and the relief (loop) lines.

At Lower Pontnewydd there was a siding

On Friday 20 August 1971 a short freight train, which was initially photographed at Pontypool Road New Sidings, has travelled down the Eastern Valley line and has reached the main line at Llantarnam Junction, where the crew surrender the single-like token and continue southwards. *All J. S. Williams*

for a pipeworks. This was served by a branch tripper, and I worked it occasionally.

Near Llantarnam Junction were sidings for Weston's Biscuits as well as a toy factory. Weston's Biscuits had coal sidings between the station and the biscuit factory, and a third line coming down alongside. To access the works you went down a bank onto the flat, then you would pull a wagon out, shunt and return to Llantarnam station. Someone from the works would state which wagon went where. The wagons were pushed under a

Two views of the interior of Llantarnam Junction signal box, looking south and north (with the single-line token machine) on the same day. *Both J. S. Williams*

The Eastern Valley

Above: Cwmbran station was accessed from Cwmbran Junction, on a line that joined the main line at Llantarnam Junction. This route was used by Eastern Valley passenger trains to gain main-line access to Newport. *Phil Williams collection*

canopy, and you would block access for staff on tea breaks.

A line ran off to the left past Llantarnam box on the way up the Eastern Valley towards Cwmbran station to a dead end for the toy factory. Before the dead end there was a turntable where the wagons were turned, then the men

Above and left: At Cwmbran station on 13 January 1962, '94xx' Class 0-6-0PT No 9488 is seen awaiting departure northwards with the 8.20am Newport-Blaenavon train. Cwmbran Junction signal box is seen, with the 'Old Mon' line behind it.
L. Fullwood, Transport Treasury

would push them into sidings leading off the turntable. The Alfa Laval works was on the other side.

To reach Newport Dock Street you went down past Cwmbran on the old Monmouthshire line, and ran to the canal terminus past the cold storage on the main road, under the railway bridge by Newport Castle, down to Newport Dock Street, past the Royal Gwent, over the road crossing, alongside Bell Vue Park, and past the water tower to Alexandra Dock Junction or to Rogerstone Yard.

'42xx' failure at Panteg station

I recall a loco failure shortly before steam finished. A Newport '42xx' failed while working a train of empties for the Blaenavon line at Panteg station. The loco was taking water there and was about to leave when a washout plug in the front tubeplate blew out. The train was made safe, and the engine dragged out of Panteg station and left on the siding above the level crossing, on the right-hand side. I was the fireman on a loco from the shed that took the loco back to Pontypool Road for examination. It was put on the ash pit. I had a look in the smokebox – all the paint was stripped off and it had started to rust. The top of the engine was covered in ashes from the smokebox. The Newport crew wondered what would have happened if a backplate washout plug had failed! Another engine, driven by Stan Parsons, was sent to Panteg to replace the failed one.

Branches Fork Junction and the branch lines to Tirpentwys Colliery and to Blaenserchan and Llanerch Collieries are seen in this 1920 Ordnance Survey map. The horseshoe curve of the GWR branch to Talywain dominates the landscape. *Crown copyright*

The Eastern Valley

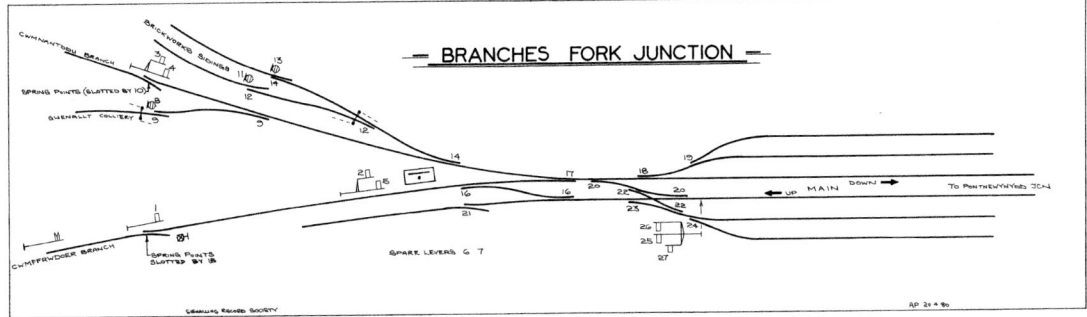

Branches Fork Junction signalling diagram. *Signalling Record Society*

Branches Fork loco depot, Pontnewynydd

Branches Fork engine shed is seen after closure on 15 April 1963, with tracks removed. It opened in 1892 and closed in January 1952, and was a sub-depot of Pontypool Road. *M. Hale, Great Western Trust*

This was a sub depot of Pontypool Road. Situated in Pontnewynydd, it had six drivers and firemen and one shed labourer. It had a water tank, and engines were coaled by hand from a wagon situated behind the shed – the shed labourer did this. Drivers who worked at Branches Fork were officially based at Pontypool Road. Coal went from there to Newport Docks.

The Branches Fork drivers and firemen would book on and off there. The shed's drivers didn't like the main-line work, as it involved extra speed, work and knowledge. There were three turns for Branches Fork, and if I had started on the railway earlier I would have liked to have been based there.

There were no spare men at Branches Fork, and these were supplied as required by Pontypool Road. You were sent to work at Branches Fork when someone was sick or on holiday.

When booking on at Pontypool Road to work at Branches Fork, an hour was allocated to walk there from Pontypool Road shed, and three-quarters of an hour to walk to Pontnewynydd yard.

Driver Bill Dale was killed by his own engine by the shed at Branches Fork on 12 December 1946. To do some work on an engine they would drop it down to the points and drive it into the back road at the side of the shed. It would be run out of the shed towards the points and the steam brake slammed on; the driver would jump off and change the points as the loco slid past to a halt, although this was unofficial practice. On this occasion Bill slipped as he got off the engine near the point lever, fell under it and was killed – he had slipped on the sleepers. I heard what happened from several men who worked there.

No 6742 was the resident engine. It

Branches Fork sidings, looking towards Pontnewynydd, on 4 September 1951. A Severn Tunnel Junction '42xx' has shunted its brake van into the loco yard, while a pannier takes water. Top right is Gwenallt signal box on the Talywain branch. *Desmond Coakham*

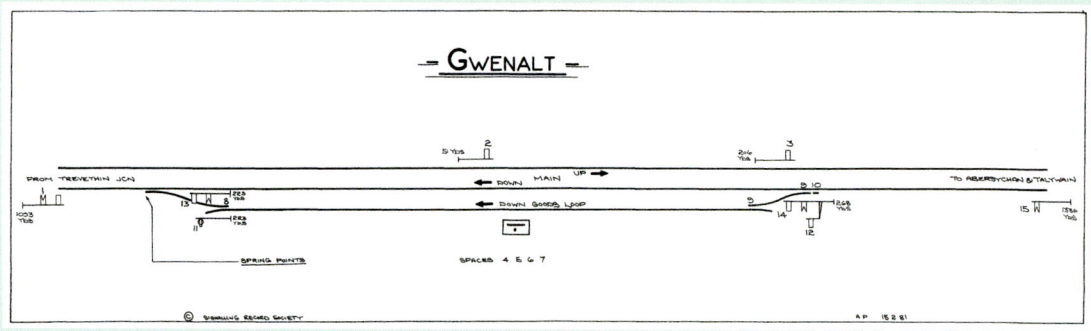

Gwenallt signalling diagram. *Signalling Record Society*

disappeared during the collier's fortnight in 1951 – the last week of July and the first week of August. It was a strong engine, and was transferred to Abercynon or Llantrisant.

There were coal sidings at Branches Fork, and a big back entrance to Pontnewynydd Works, with a lot of traffic in and out. It took in empty wagons and sent steel products out, in tarpaulin-covered wagons. The works made steel sheets – during the war Anderson Shelters were made there.

Branches Fork loco shed would hold three or four engines, but at closure only two were present. After the shed closed, Pontypool Road supplied engines and footplate crews to work the two branches, but the engines had to go back to Pontypool Road at night to have their fires dropped. Fresh engines were sent each day.

The two colliery branches from

The Eastern Valley

Above: Branches Fork Junction and signal box on 4 September 1951. Gwenallt Colliery, known as the Jack Pit, is seen in the background, and wagons on Viaduct Colliery siding on the right. The Tirpentwys branch is on the left, and the Blaenserchan branch, by now truncated at Graig-ddu, on the right. *Desmond Coakham*

Right: Pontnewynydd Works is seen in 1930. *Edgar Harvey, J. S. Williams collection*

Pontnewynydd had different gradients – to Tirpentwys was 1 in 22, and to Blaenserchan and Llanerch was 1 in 19. On the latter branch, the mountain slipped below Llanerch, burying the track immediately above Graig-ddu brickworks; prior to this the Great Western had worked up into Target End at the top of the valley.

Branches Fork signal box was located in between the two lines near Gwenallt Colliery, which was called the Jack Pit as men used to take their water down in water jacks. The signal box was the second at this junction. The original box had been located by the road bridge by the river, but was demolished by a runaway train from Blaenserchan Colliery during the First World War. No one was hurt, but the signalman suffered a broken leg – he was a First World War veteran and had a wooden leg, so the joke was that no one was hurt!

Branches Fork took water from the stream by the Jack Pit. The Tirpentwys water was black. There were also water columns at Pontypool Crane Street and Pontnewynydd

In this view looking across the valley from Cwmffrwdoer, the Jack Pit is seen on the left, and the brickworks on the right, with the railway to Graig-ddu in the foreground. The Top Line to Talywain and Blaenavon is in the immediate foreground. *J. S. Williams collection*

Yard, and two in the sidings at Branches Fork (one at the shed and one at the side) to cover the Pontnewynydd Pilot roster. You filled up from the shed, then from a column in the yard.

Branches Fork covered the following turns:

1. Middle turn on the PR2, 10.30am to 6.30pm: book on, go to Blaenavon High Level and wait to relieve Ponty men, then shunt Pontnewynydd yard, etc.
2. Trippers: days and afternoons to Graig-ddu and Tirpentwys. There were two turns to Tirpentwys, and two to Graig-ddu.

The Pontnewynydd Sidings Pilot engine shunted the works one way and the Branches Fork engine shunted the other end of the works. Branches Fork shunted wagons for Pontypool forges into a siding on days and afternoons.

The Middle turn had the Blaenavon PR2. This pilot engine worked the yard, Pontnewynydd Forge and Elled Colliery. There was also traffic from a level above Elled Colliery.

I worked the afternoon shift on the last week. I arrived at Ponty shed at 1.20pm to book on, and caught the 1.40pm train from Panteg to Crane Street or Pontnewynydd.

Staff would book on at different times. The early turn was 5.00am – there were two early and middle turns and an afternoon shift.

Blaenserchan Colliery is seen in 1930 viewed from the quarry alongside the No 2 shaft. The Llanerch bank is seen in the background. *E. Harvey, J. S. Williams collection*

The Eastern Valley

Blaenserchan washery and the Llanerch bank, also seen in 1930. This is one of a series of photos taken by latcher Edgar Harvey to illustrate the severe gradients and dangerous working conditions as part of a trade union dispute by locomen employed by Partridge Jones and John Paton Ltd, at the Big Arch, Abersychan.
E. Harvey, J. S. Williams collection

Tirpentwys branch

The branch to Tirpentwys was worked by regular men from Branches Fork. If you were spare, and Pontypool Road needed a fireman for the Tirpentwys branch, you would get the job. You would leave the engine on the shed at Branches Fork, except for Saturdays when you had to take it to Pontypool Road. The driver would walk to Pontnewynydd station to catch a train to Griffithstown, then walk to the shed to book off. When the driver knew I was from Pontnewynydd he would sign me off, and I would

Two GWR pannier tank locomotives from Branches Fork shed, one with an open cab, have propelled a train of empties to Blaenserchan washery in 1930.
E. Harvey, J. S. Williams collection

Tirpentwys Colliery, Pontypool. *Phil Williams collection*

have a short day!

Tirpentwys worked two shifts, and one engine would be continuously working, requiring two drivers to work a 16-hour shift. All-day working was required, with empties up and loaded coal back down. Trains would be taken up to one of the empty roads at Gellydeg Sidings, then the colliery engine would collect them. There would be 15 to 20 wagons on a train.

Graig-ddu branch

The line to Graig-ddu and on to Llanerch Colliery was used to remove coal waste from the tips. The first sidings along the branch were four on the left, for coal for the boilers at the Jack Pit. This colliery was used

The pit bottom of the down cast shaft, 440 yards deep, at Tirpentwys Colliery. Behind the cage on the left was a 'bowk' giving access to the 'Wee Pit', to the sump at the bottom of the shaft. The pump house is behind the photographer. Hafodyrynys is to the left, and Blaenserchan Colliery to the right in this view. *Phil Williams collection*

during the war as a pumping station for those at Llanerch and Blaenserchan. Water from the pit was pumped to a pond, and used by the steelworks – the waste water then went into ponds for the town forges. The Town Forge had a little engine to take materials into the Town and Lower forges.

On the opposite side the first set of points was for the pipeworks, which had a tall chimney and kilns. Next on the right was the siding for Viaduct Colliery, producing fire clay for the brickworks. There was a ramp with a high wall where the fire clay was loaded into railway wagons running beneath. The level had six horses, and the drams were on a continuous rope. Fire clay from Bucks level went to Cwmbran for the brickworks.

Graig-ddu brickworks, served by the branch, made fire bricks, and they had a good reputation. On the left-hand side of the branch above the brickworks was a self-acting incline up the side of the mountain. Quarry stones were brought down from Monks Quarry to Graig-ddu and used for pavements. The incline was visible from near Llanerch Colliery, and the quarry was on top of the mountain on the right. There was a passing loop halfway up the incline. Stone was loaded into drams to come down, and would pass the Robin Hood pub, come under the viaduct carrying the Top Line to Blaenavon, and pass the Jack Pit on the left to Branches Fork Junction.

In March 1955 Driver Alf Batley had loco

Ex-GWR 0-6-0 pannier tank No 3628 is seen at Gellydeg Sidings at Tirpentwys Colliery on 19 August 1954. *J. Drayton, M. Vrettos collection*

In 1922 Llanerch Colliery was modernised, and a steam crane was delivered to install new boilers. Here a brand-new engine, fresh from Swindon and believed to be GWR 2-8-0T No 5203, has run away from Blaenserchan washery and has been diverted into the dummy. The following persons are present: one of the people on the bank is Billy Yates, while on the ground are Fireman Bill Canning (left) and Driver Bill Dale (right). The driver had a reprimand for removing the sheeting from the locomotive to have this photo taken! The engine was built in February 1923, which dates the photo to that period. *J. S. Williams collection*

No 8716 at Graig-ddu brickworks, and ran away. The loco ran almost to the Jack Pit, then came off the road and jumped across a deep ditch and through a bank about 4 feet high with a fence on the top. It landed up in the siding at the Jack Pit, like a bird sitting on its nest with the bank spoil pushed

A view looking north at Graig-ddu brickworks on the Branches Fork-Blaenserchan Colliery branch in 1930. *E. Harvey, J. S. Williams collection*

forward. Luckily no one was hurt. Alf had opened the regulator when they were picking up the brakes, but he couldn't go forward and started to roll backwards. The fireman was Eric Fry, who jumped off at Graig-ddu, but Alf stayed on the engine, and lay on the floor when the engine came to a halt.

There would be four or six wagons behind the engine. Graig-ddu brickworks had no road access; coal would be taken up by rail and bricks and stone brought down. Muck was also brought down from the Llanerch tip. Llanerch Colliery had been tipping waste down the side of the mountain for years, causing the slip of December 1935. The slip had been on the move for years. The owner of Graig-ddu brickworks had men on overtime digging the bank clear of the line, and filling wagons with the rubbish. This was before the war, and the colliery paid for the men to do this. The line to Blaenserchan was covered by rubbish above the points to Graig-ddu brickworks. After the war concrete blocks from former sea defences were installed to prevent further movement; they were taken by rail and unloaded with a steam crane. After a few months they began to move due to the pressure from the slip.

Fire clay was extracted from an old level above Graig-ddu brickworks, and there was

A derailed train of coal from Blaenserchan Colliery is seen at Branches Fork Junction during the First World War. *Charlie Reynolds*

another clay level on the right-hand side going up, called Bucks; this was below the viaduct on the horseshoe curve. This was also known as Viaduct Colliery, and the men would fetch coal out and take it home, but the level was used to extracted fire clay. Trams were pulled up on a cable. A works below Viaduct Colliery made clay pipes; it

The Eastern Valley

On Tuesday 8 March 1955 ex-GWR 0-6-0PT No 8716 is seen derailed at the Jack Pit, Pontnewynydd, with a train of bricks from Graig-ddu brickworks. The pipeworks is on the left, and the Pontypool Road breakdown train is seen in the background.

was served by a line on the right before the points to the Jack Pit. Coal for the boiler would be pushed into this siding by the Pontnewynydd Pilot. Clay was also taken to Cwmbran to be made into fire bricks.

Wagons were propelled up the line, with a little brake van next to the engine. At Graig-ddu the train stopped short and the guard put all the brakes on. The driver then opened the regulator wide to go forward, and the brakes would be eased off. There were four sidings inside Graig-ddu brickworks. Wagons were dropped into the siding and pulled back up on a rope that passed around a pulley on the side of the track going off the points at Graig-ddu.

The Graig-ddu branch was regarded a public walk. Two little girls were killed in the sidings there while playing 'house' under the wagons. This had been going on for a little while.

Graig-ddu had one or two trains a day. You went up once in the morning with anything they wanted, such as coal for the brickworks, and bring back a train of loaded wagons from the day before, then go back up at the end of the afternoon to sort things out for the end of their day shift. Graig-ddu had its own horses.

Just below Graig-ddu on the left was an old mine shaft, with a fence around it. It was left open and you could throw stones down it and hear the water splash. At Greenland there were five shafts; all are now filled, including an old air shaft on the side of the road past the gate, about 50 yards on the left, on the steep part below the level crossing. It is fenced off and filled with solid earth. Another one, also fenced off and filled, was on a flat piece on land where I used to play cricket. Where the bank started to rise on the right-hand side another shaft was found – it was covered over and filled in.

At Gypsy Lane, towards Graig-ddu at the far end, there is a drop to the old Robin Hood pub, then the rise to the railway bridge. On the right-hand side, about 80 yards from the end of the lane, there was an old wall tight against the lane. As kids we would sit on this patch of grass and make a safe by cutting clods of earth. I went there one day, after the Coal Board had taken over, and was told I couldn't go up there – it was the top of a mine shaft covered with soil. A man with a crowbar had it slip through his hand when he prodded the surface. So be careful when you go in the Robin Hood – there were five collieries there! There was a level there as well.

On the loco we would go as far as Graig-ddu with the regulator wide open to push the wagons over the top and drop down over the points; they would then run around the layout at Graig-ddu, round a sharp road to the furnaces.

Pontypool Crane Street station and goods yard, with a southbound freight in the down platform.
Phil Williams collection

Pontnewynydd Pilot Duties

Pilot work was undertaken to Crane Street goods and coal yard. Coal went into the goods yard for Pontypool, being delivered nearly every day. The footbridge was extended over the line to the goods yard, where there was a large siding that handled town goods such as potatoes. Coal merchants' lorries would line up alongside the siding to load their coal. Beyond the signal box on the left coaches were stored, as well as parcels vans and corn for the corn merchants.

The Pontnewynydd Pilot is seen at Pontypool Crane Street, date unknown.
J. S. Williams collection

In GWR days with the GWR lorry are, from left to right, Dick Evans, Jim Sullivan (back), Derek Nutt, Alec Horton, Ray Hurn (back), Stan Hales and George Powell. *Rollei Kinnersley, J. S. Williams collection*

Crane Street had a goods shed for deliveries of parcels, picked up by four or five lorries. There was a long goods siding full of house coal for coal merchants to unload; Bevistock and Bakers would collect coal from there.

From left to right, Jim Sullivan, Ray Hurn, Alec Horton, Derek Nutt (front), Billy Baker and Dick Evans. *Rollei Kinnersley, J. S. Williams collection*

Right: On Pontypool Crane Street up platform are Bob Harris (left) and George Taylor (centre); the other man is unknown. The Pontnewynydd Pilot takes water in the background. *Terry Target collection*

Below: On the down platform at Crane Street, looking north, are Mrs Margaret Attwood (left) and Mrs Griffin. Mrs Griffin would go down to Blaendare Road Halt and book tickets, using a little ticket machine. Mrs Attwood worked in the goods shed as a secretary/typist. *Terry Target collection*

Below: Ex-GWR '5205' Class 2-8-0T No 5231 enters Pontypool Crane Street with a short northbound freight on 13 January 1962. *L. Fullwood, Transport Treasury*

The Eastern Valley

Over the bridge at Crane Street, on the right on the down side, was the Pontypool fish bay, a yard with two or three sidings for Turners Fishmongers. A wagon of fish was stabled halfway up the siding. Coming up on the first train of the morning, the 5 o'clock from Newport, it was put away by the Pontnewynydd Pilot; others would come up afterwards.

The Corn Stores were on the opposite side by the signal box, with three or four roads. Empties from Crane Street goods yard were stored here, and wagons dropped off a train if there were too many for the goods yard. The Pontnewynydd Pilot would pull them over.

There was a siding at St Luke's Church, Pontnewynydd, for coal merchants, and one below the station at Abersychan Low Level. After Abersychan there was nothing until Blaenavon, where there was a coal merchant. Coal to Blaenavon Low Level was handled by the Pontnewynydd Middle turn. The signal box was at the top end of the platform to operate the gates, and the sidings were beyond the gates.

The last week of Branches Fork shed working

Pontypool Road had two '77xx' panniers tanks, Nos 7724 and 7740. No 7724 was out-based at Branches Fork shed for weeks, returning to Pontypool Road shed for repairs and boiler washouts. It was the last engine to use the shed when it closed on 31 October 1951. It was brought off Branches Fork shed on that last Saturday morning by Driver Harry Young and Fireman John Bigham for the day's work, and that night was taken back to Pontypool Road. Rollei Jones from Charles Street, Griffithstown, was the driver, and I was the fireman.

I worked there with Rollei Jones for the shed's last week, having been sent there to cover for another driver and fireman. We worked the afternoon shift, booking on at Pontypool Road at 1.20pm and walking to Panteg station to catch the 1.40pm train from there to Branches Fork. If you were lucky, as you arrived at Pontnewynydd station you might see the engine waiting, just over the wall by the pub at the old Elled Colliery. You would get off the train, walk up alongside Pontnewynydd Forge, around the corner and up to the engine. If there was no engine in sight when the train arrived at Pontnewynydd, you walked up the platform, up to the Forge Hammer pub, then down to the bottom of the siding there, by the end of the long pond.

When the shed had finished at night, officially you were supposed to walk up by the Bridgend pub and go down Hanbury Road to Pontnewynydd station to get back to

Ex-GWR '66xx' Class 0-6-2T No 6656 leaves Pontnewynydd station and passes Pontnewynydd Forge on the journey south to Newport on 7 May 1962. This was the last steam-hauled train to use the Bottom Line, and was organised by the Stephenson Locomotive Society. *R. K. Blencowe collection*

Pontypool Road shed to sign off. However, a lot of footplate crew would walk down through the sidings to get to the station. The engine was left on shed, where there was a shed labourer on nights, and he could move the engine within the shed limits. He would drop the fire, and re-coal ready for the engine to work in the morning.

Six men finished when Branches Fork shed closed. One had the Middle turn on the Pontnewynydd Pilot, three men were sent to Pontypool Road, and two men finished altogether. Bill Oakley was transferred to Pontypool Road, and another driver remained to work as a transfer pilot at Pontnewynydd yard, as he had a few years to go to retirement. One or two drivers stopped to work the Pontnewynydd Pilot. Fireman Bigham then transferred to Pontypool Road and married his landlady; he later finished working on the railway.

Blaenavon 'Top Line'

My first trip to Blaenavon and Brynmawr was on a '72xx' tank engine from Pontypool Road, with Driver Norman Hunt from Newport, in 1953. I was in the Banking Link, and available for spare jobs. Five or six '72xx' tank engines were based at Pontypool Road for use on this job. A '72xx' couldn't go over Crumlin Viaduct, but would go down the 'muck hole' line to Llanilleth and Ebbw Vale. A design fault on these engines was access to the bunker to get coal down. The route from Blaenavon to Brynmawr closed in October 1954.

I remember taking '20xx' and '21xx' locos for the Big Arch up to Talywain sidings and being left on the curve at the top of the sidings by the pub on the main road. On one occasion one engine was changed by going towards the Big Arch by Pentwyn Junction. Engines were taken up on a Monday morning.

A raft of empties is seen during shunting operations at Panteg sidings. *Ralph Charles collection*

Coal was for the north road from Pontypool Road. You would take it to Panteg sidings, and it was sorted from there.

The 'horseshoe curve' on the Blaenavon line was the only place in Britain where you could see the four sides of a chimney without leaving your seat. I would be asked by my driver to watch the chimney stack at the brickworks below when working a train along the line.

There were three turns a day on the PR2, each being an 8-hour shift. The first turn was from 5.00am to 1.00pm – this was the Morning shift. To start you would go to the lamp room under the coal stage at Pontypool Road and collect lamps, tools and a shovel to take to the engine. If you were lucky the engine might be at the top of the round shed – if unlucky, at the bottom end of the long shed. Preparation time was 45 minutes for a tank engine, or an hour for a '72xx' or tender engine. The loco might have steam, or not.

To get your engine ready, you checked the tools and stowed away your food box. There would often be no tools apart from the fire irons, so you would go to the stores, and to the lamp room to pick up the lamps required. These were quite heavy. A pilot engine would carry four lamps, while most trains used two lamps. The pilot engine had a red and white lamp at each end, and red shades to drop in the front of the white. The lamp men were good. You lit the lamp and put it on the engine. You then checked the fire to see if it needed attention. Then you would pull the sand handles to release sand, get off the engine and check the sand boxes and for sand on the rail. If there was insufficient sand, the four sand boxes would need to be filled from the sand house. Here there was a steel chest with a wire mesh, above which was a steel container on legs, heated by a fire to dry the sand in the hopper above. Sand buckets were oval with a spout. You would take one in each hand, put them under the hopper and open the flap. The sand was red hot (the sand was red). You then carried the bucket of sand to the engine. To fill the sand boxes could require two to three trips. Some engines needed two buckets, most needed four. Never touch anything without cotton waste in your hand – if it burns, drop the waste!

Next you climbed on the front of the loco and checked the smokebox. Ash was shovelled out into a separate place from the fire ash, and was loaded into wagons and made into breeze blocks.

You then cleaned the engine, put the tools in their right place and waited for driver to finish oiling. Upon filling the tank with water, you were ready to go – the engine would have been coaled up the day before when it arrived on the ash pit at the station end of the engine shed.

There was a string of coal wagons on the coal stage. When coal was wanted a wagon would be dropped down; empty wagons stood on the end of the coal stage road. At the coal stage you got on the bunker to break the coal. Sometimes you would have coal on the roof, which the coal man would knock off. Different drivers would drive differently. Some were rough, some were excellent.

You left the shed at 6.00am. To get to Coedygric Sidings depended on where you were on shed. At the north end you went to the Station South box and over the crossover on the Relief line to the East box, then through the yard to Panteg sidings. The south end was easier. You would leave Panteg for Furnace Sidings before the dump train arrived at Panteg.

I worked the morning shift. I had been firing two years and had swapped with someone who wanted to do the night shift, which paid more money. I worked this job for a week in October 1952.

Trains for Hafodyrynys started from the Loop sidings or Little Mill Sidings, while Panteg sidings were used for trains to Blaenavon. You followed the 6.10am passenger train from Panteg with a train of empties for Blaenavon. The guard or shunter would get you on the train, and a brake van would be near the train in the sidings. You took water at the shed, Talywain and Furnace Sidings – you would never go past a water column. There were none at Cwmffrwdoer

Pontypool Road's '72xx' Class 2-8-2T No 7210 takes water at Talywain station with a train of empties from Panteg sidings to Blaenavon Big Pit on 14 January 1961. *Trevor Owen, ColourRail*

and Pentrepiod on the Blaenavon line – you would go straight through to Talywain, where you would stop for water, and sometimes put off certain wagons. Then you went over the viaduct at Garndiffaith, through Varteg station and past Cemetery Sidings at Blaenavon; these were the old sidings for Varteg Hill Colliery, and were there for years after the Vipond branch closed in 1941. I recall maybe going into Cemetery Sidings only once.

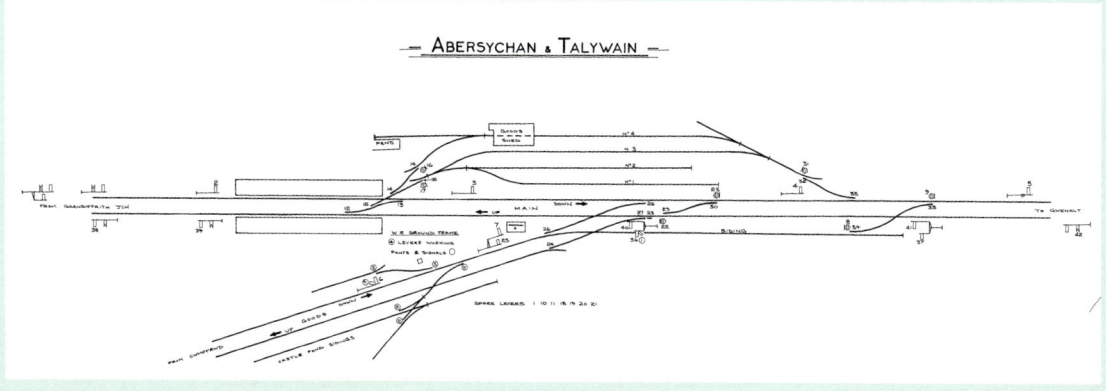

Abersychan & Talywain signalling diagram. *Signalling Record Society*

Garndiffaith Viaduct is seen with a train heading north to Blaenavon High Level. The original signal box at the south end of the cutting on the right can be seen; it was later moved to the south end of the viaduct.
J. S. Williams collection

Varteg station buildings looking north in December 1969. *J. S. Williams*

Above: A southbound coal train approaches Varteg station with Big Pit coal for Llanwern Steelworks in August 1971. *J. S. Williams*

Below and top right: Empties for Blaenavon Furnace Sidings pass northwards through Varteg station in August 1971, approaching the former Vipond's Colliery Incline bridge. *Both J. S. Williams*

The Eastern Valley

Empties were taken to Furnace Sidings, where a train of loaded coal would be assembled and taken back to Panteg sidings. It would be assembled in three parts, with eight or more loaded wagons in the first section. The engine would pull the rear third of the train out of the sidings on the left, and leave them on the section of double track, then stop an engine's length from the catch point. The brakes would be pinned down and you would go back to the siding and collect the brake van, and 10 or 12 wagons to form the front section. This front section, with the brake van attached at the front, would then be pulled further up, leaving a gap in the middle of the train. The middle section would then be pulled from the sidings and left between the front and rear sections. The loco would run around the train and attach to the rear. Herbie Harrington was the shunter and he would brake the middle section down to the rear of the train by hand. The rear portion would be braked down to the middle of the train in a similar way.

Herbie Harrington, the Blaenavon Furnace Sidings shunter, walks the track at Cemetery Sidings.
H. Harrington, J. S. Williams collection

Herbie Harrington is seen again on the footplate of a Pontypool Road 2-8-2T '72xx' at Blaenavon High Level station, with a southbound train of coal. *Herbie Harrington, J. S. Williams collection*

We would therefore have so many brakes pinned down before leaving. There would be 35 to 40 wagons in the train. The loco would be an engine length away from the catch point at the top of the cutting on the left-hand portion of the double track. The driver would then pull away; if he had to pull the train, he would whistle twice, and the shunters would know he had sufficient brakes pinned down. If he didn't blow two, the train would roll too easily, and the shunters would put more brakes down.

We would run to Tyre Mill signal box and stop to have about 15 brakes picked up. Experienced drivers wouldn't do this, but would continue past Tyre Mill signal box, under the road bridge at Forge Side to a signal before the High Level station, which would save time. This signal could hold a long train between Tyre Mill and above High Level. Between High Level station and Tyre Mill the track was double (the only other section of double track was a quarter-mile section at Furnace Sidings). You would wait here for the train to come up from Talywain. The guard would walk down, pick up half the brakes and get up on the engine. After the train from Talywain had passed, you would roll down to High Level station, over Varteg Road bridge to the stop board about 30 yards south of the bridge. The brakesman and the guard then put brakes down again, and the guard returned to his van. The driver would blow two and run to Talywain. Drivers knew the road and the loco; if you had a runaway from here, the only refuge was the loop at Gwenallt.

I was the fireman on a near miss from Furnace Sidings. We had a new guard from the West of England learning the ropes, but he was too confident. On this occasion he signalled to the driver that all was well and we left Furnace Sidings. But all was not well

On 8 June 1957 ex-GWR 2-8-0T No 4258 waits for the road at Abersychan & Talywain station. From here to Brynmawr had been LNWR property, the section from Blaenavon to Brynmawr closing on 24 June 1954.
M. Hale, Great Western Trust

– we free-wheeled at speed to Tyre Mill where the track was level, and the signalman and brakesman pulled down as many wagon brakes as possible. I had wound the handbrake on full when leaving Furnace Sidings, but to no avail. Normally at least a third of the train would be braked, but there were no brakes down! Below Tyre Mill there was a gradient to High Level station, to the stop board on the other side of Varteg Road bridge. We stopped short of this board, but I had already grabbed my coat and had told my driver that I was about to jump off. My driver was Jack Nicholls, from Charles Street, Griffithstown, and the loco was a '72xx' tank.

Empties were taken to Furnace Sidings, and dropped back into the empty wagon sidings. Loaded coal from Furnace Sidings was pulled out, and taken over the top to Brynmawr, where it was left in the yard.

Loaded coal wagons brought coal back to Furnace Sidings from Brynmawr, together with the occasional feed van. Sometimes you brought back empties. You would then perhaps take loaded coal to Tyre Mill, and take the engine back to Blaenavon High Level. You would get relief there at about midday, then walk to Low Level station and catch a train to Panteg and sign off at the shed – but I would be told by my driver to disappear at Pontnewynydd.

The Middle turn booked on from Pontnewynydd yard at 10.30-11.00am and went to Blaenavon Low Level, with relief at the High Level station. They would then go to Tyre Mill and do a shunt, or shunt Cemetery Sidings, returning as engine and van. They were Branches Fork men, in the days before the shed closed, and even after the shed closed they still did this turn.

Ex-GWR '72xx' Class 2-8-2T No 7210 stands at Blaenavon Furnace Sidings with a train of empty wagons for Big Pit Colliery on 14 January 1961. *Trevor Owen, ColourRail*

No 7210 is seen again on the same day with a guard's van during shunting operations to assemble a train of coal from Furnace Sidings. *Trevor Owen, ColourRail*

The Eastern Valley

Above: Ex-GWR 0-6-0PT No 3717 acts as the Old Yard Pilot and is seen at Panteg & Coedygric Junction in the 1950s during shunting operations. *Ralph Charles*

Left: Empties for Panteg sidings are seen during shunting operations in the 1950s. Panteg station is on the right and Richard Thomas & Baldwin's Steelworks is on the left in the background. *Ralph Charles collection*

Below: The Old Yard Pilot awaits instructions to propel back; behind the engine is the site of the former Coedygric engine shed. *Ralph Charles collection*

When Brynmawr closed, the PR2 was reduced to mornings and afternoons. The Brynmawr branch was used to store empty wagons.

The Afternoon turn men would book on at 2.00pm and go to Blaenavon Low Level by passenger train, then walk to the High Level station to relieve the Branches Fork footplate staff. They would prepare trains at Furnace Sidings for the Newport men and go to Brynmawr, then come back, do shunting at Furnace Sidings and work a train to Talywain and Panteg sidings. The loop adjacent to the Masons pub was used by trains putting off at Pontypool Road, and by trains of coal from Mill took you to Brynmawr. After the war, as a boy I can remember seeing the occasional train of scrap going to Blaenavon for Tyre Mill furnaces, passing Waunddu in Pontnewynydd. These were trains of ex-Army guns.

At Pentwyn Junction there was a distant signal to tell you that you had the road for Talywain, rather than for Castle Pond sidings. These sidings were a Newport turn and were never visited by the PR2 as it was for Blaenavon only.

The signal box was by the station. There were four sidings for ballast from the Big Arch crusher. The ballast trains were worked by Newport men, carrying crushed slag from the

Pentwyn Junction, looking north on 17 August 1950. *Desmond Coakham*

Blaenavon or Hafodyrynys. Loaded coal was split in the loop for you to put it back in the siding to Coedygric or the Old Yard. This loop was also used to allow passenger trains to pass. Coal to Newport went down to Cwmbran and the Dock Street line to Mill Street in Newport. It was a busy job over three sections.

Trains from Cemetery Sidings were taken to Tyre Mill sidings, then dispatched. This was a Newport job. The train staff at Tyre slag tips of the British Ironworks, extracted from tips within the Big Arch yard. In earlier years there was a crusher and sidings where Talywain Rugby Club now resides; Great Western '28xx' Class locomotives worked these trains in the 1920s, together with '43xxs'. The only remains now are the gate posts that used to hold the wooden gates for the two railway lines to the Big Arch.

At Talywain the sidings into the goods

The Eastern Valley

shed were shunted by the Newport morning goods. Here there were two roads between the running road and the goods shed, and three roads behind the goods shed. On the return trip we stopped for water, having previously taken water here on the way up, and at Furnace Sidings before coming back down. At Talywain you would wait for a Newport man to take his train to Newport Docks – you might have to wait an hour or so. The brakes were put on at Talywain, where wagons would be dropped off for the coal merchants, or a shunt performed for the Newport man – coal for Newport Docks would be dropped off at Talywain. Pontypool Road men would take coal to Panteg. The Newport men would be relieved at Talywain by footplate crew travelling on the passenger train to Abersychan Low Level station.

If there was a blockage at Pontnewynydd, you might have one train in the loop and one on the line at Gwenallt. Pontypool men would work the train to Panteg, where it would be stopped in the loop, split, and propelled into the Old Yard at Coedygric. Newport men then worked the train to Dock Street, via the old Monmouthshire line below Cwmbran station.

4. Railway enthusiast Rob Morgan

Rob is a local railway enthusiast whose father was a lengthman on the horseshoe curve at Pontnewynydd on the Top Line. In the 1950s his father won an award for the best-kept section of track in the local area. He can remember Mrs Griffiths and Mrs Tuck working in Gwenallt signal box.

At Pontnewynydd a pannier tank would take a goods train to Talywain early in the morning. Rob can remember Nos 7201 and 7210 working the PR2 turn, while Newport men would drive the '42xx' or '52xx' locos to Blaenavon. Engines would slip to a standstill at Pentrepiod Halt if the rail was wet.

Looking towards Pentrepiod Halt in 1982. *Phil Williams*

Pontypool Road '72xx' Class 2-8-2T No 7210 approaches the Big Arch with a train of empties from Panteg sidings to Blaenavon Big Pit on 14 January 1961. *Trevor Owen, ColourRail*

The Top Line: signals from Panteg Junction to Blaenavon

There was a signal on the end of the platform at Panteg station – you could go up the valley or to the right and into the yard at Coedygric. There was a starting signal right at the Pontypool Road side of the Masons pub bridge for Panteg Hospital siding, where coal was put off for the hospital; this siding was controlled by a ground frame. The next signals were for Blaendare, then you went under the road bridge at Crane Street, and there was a signal at the Newport end of the station.

Above and top right: Cutting up an old signal in the New Sidings, circa December 1970. *Both J. S. Williams*

The Eastern Valley

There was a signal at the end of the platform by the signal box at Crane Street, and around the corner at George Street you had a signal before the bridge to direct you either to Talywain or through Pontnewynydd yard.

At the bottom of Wainfelin there was a distant signal for Gwenallt, then there was only one signal on the up line at Gwenallt, up past the box. The next one was at Pentwyn, one for Talywain, then one for the Big Arch. There was nothing at this junction. The next signal was on the down road, almost over the Big Arch, and one almost alongside this signal on the up track. You could go into the station or the sidings at the back of the box.

You would pull up to the far end of Talywain station to take water. There was a signal before the tunnel at the top end of the station. You went under the long bridge, and on the left-hand side was a siding leading into three roads, but I never went in there.

There was a signal box at the Talywain end of the viaduct, on the up road. You could wait there for a down train to pass, either when in the platform or by the signal box at the bottom end of the viaduct.

The next signal was near Cemetery Sidings, below the Varteg Road bridge at Blaenavon. You could drop back into the LNWR shed at Blaenavon High Level. There were two tracks from High Level to Tyre Mill, where there were signals to stop you. It was then single track to Furnace Sidings, then beyond the rail overbridge at Big Pit it became double track through Furnace Sidings. Furnace Sidings had a signal box on the left-hand side to control the crossover and sidings. There was another signal box at Waenavon. The present-day roundabout at Brynmawr in beneath where the road bridge used to cross the railway lines.

LMS Beames 0-8-4T No 7947 of Blaenavon shed stands on the up line at Blaenavon High Level station on an unknown date. *Dick Bassett, J. S. Williams collection*

Left: An LMS fireman stands on the up platform in front of Blaenavon High Level signal box before May 1941, when the LMS closed its engine shed at Blaenavon.
Dick Bassett, J. S. Williams collection

Below: A shunter poses with an engine and van at Blaenavon High Level outside the goods shed. *Dick Bassett, J. S. Williams collection*

The Eastern Valley

An early view of Abersychan station showing a former Monmouthshire Railway locomotive.
Mrs Wheeler, J. S. Williams collection

Blaenavon Low Level

An auto-train went from Griffithstown to Blaenavon, starting from Newport at 5.10am, carrying parcels on the upward journey. It went up the line at 5.30am, calling at Llantarnam, Cwmbran, Pontnewydd, Panteg (for Sebastopol and Griffithstown), Crane Street, Pontnewynydd, Abersychan and finally Blaenavon.

A diesel multiple unit (DMU) started from Pontypool Road and arrived at Blaenavon at 5.05am; this was the first train up the valley, timed to meet the 6.00am factory starts. DMUs replaced steam locomotives on the Blaenavon passenger services, although there were occasional steam workings for excursions. The DMU sets were kept in the carriage sidings at Pontypool Road station, except for excursions to Barry, etc.

A DMU calls at the down platform at Cwmffrwd Junction on the last day of passenger trains to Blaenavon Low Level, 28 April 1962. J. S. Williams

Also on 28 April 1962, farmer Bill Davis crosses the level crossing at Cwmffrwd Junction. *J. S. Williams*

Blaenavon carriage sidings were located at the top end of the level crossing at the Low Level station. On weekdays the last train of the night would be pushed into the carriage sidings, and the steam engine then ran light to the shed. At weekends the carriages were not kept overnight in these sidings, but were returned to Pontypool Road carriage sidings.

The day's last passenger train to Low Level was the 10.00pm from Panteg. It worked through to Blaenavon, then went back down the valley to Panteg, where it terminated. It was then worked as an engine and coaches to Pontypool Road station sidings.

The Glascoed and Girling train

On Mondays the first train to Blaenavon Low Level in the morning was worked as an empty train, being two trains in one, with an engine at either end, to minimise train movements. Two '66xxs', a '66xx' and a '41xx', or two '41xxs' were used. One train was for Glascoed Ordnance Depot, the other for the Girling factory in Cwmbran. It was worked to Blaenavon as a 12-coach train, six for Glascoed train and six for Girling. As the first train up in the morning, you would slip and slide, with the engine at the front end pulling.

The coaches were coupled up at Pontypool Road station, then to Panteg sidings and up to Blaenavon from there. At Blaenavon there were three dead-end sidings above the level crossing at the top end of the station, each holding about eight coaches.

From Tuesday onwards the front engine would go over the level crossing and into the carriage sidings to couple onto the carriages left overnight in the sidings. Coaches wouldn't be left in the siding at Blaenavon over a weekend, in case they were damaged;

instead they were stored at Pontypool Road station carriage sidings. The rear engine would push its coaches into sidings alongside, and stable them.

You would be in the siding for 20 to 30 minutes on the first engine. Bucketsful of water from the steam heat connection at the back of the train would be observed pouring out when this valve was opened to heat the carriages. The coaches would be lovely and warm. While in the sidings an auto-train would arrive in the station from Newport.

The Glascoed train left Blaenavon first, using the front engine. The second engine would run round its train and couple onto the back of it. The Glascoed train left Blaenavon at about 5.45am. The second train was known locally as the Girling's train, as it dropped off passengers at Cwmbran on the way to Newport.

The Glascoed train worked to Panteg, where it entered the down platform. The Newport train would then arrive with four coaches and would pass over the crossover and couple onto the front. It was now a train of 10 or 12 coaches, and the rear engine would be disconnected. This engine would now be used to bank the train as far as Coedygric box, where the train passed through the yard and out to Glascoed Ordnance Depot. My engine would then work as the Station Pilot, or might go back to shed. The Station Pilot would form trains, and shunt parcels back for unloading and put them away.

On the way back, the Glascoed train came as one train to Panteg station. One engine would wait by Coedygric box or the Old Yard siding, and would follow the train to Panteg. The Newport half of the train would then go to Newport and the Blaenavon half to Blaenavon, and work a trip to Newport and back up.

Firing Blaenavon auto-trains to Newport

The auto-trains ran every hour. One auto-train ran to Blaenavon before the Glascoed and Girling trains went up. On its return it passed through Pontnewynydd at about 5.30am to go to Newport, and I caught this for work. Going up to Blaenavon the driver and fireman would be on the engine together, but on the return you would be on the engine on your own, as fireman. I did it a lot. I wasn't qualified to work autos – the drivers were picky unless they trusted you, and so were the roster clerks.

The driver would go to the cab at the rear of the auto-train at Blaenavon for the trip to Newport; it might have two coaches, but that wasn't done a lot. A train with coaches at each end wasn't used on this job. You would give the coal a good soaking before leaving Blaenavon Low Level station.

The driver could put the brake on and open and shut the regulator from his driving compartment. You had to watch the regulator – if the linkage through the two coaches was slack, as you shut the regulator it would stay open. As a fireman you could open the regulator due to little movement in the linkage; the driver would get it partly open, and a soon as you saw it close you would shut off. You had to be a passed man to work the autos as a fireman, as you did a certain amount of the driver's work. You would be on the engine on your own all the way to Newport. You did the firing, opened the ejector to blow the brakes off, and notched up. All the driver could do was open and close the regulator and apply the brake – he operated the brake, but couldn't recreate the vacuum. You had to watch the brake if you were going too slowly to recreate the vacuum – if the driver slammed it shut straight away you knew you had made a mistake. Firing wasn't hard as you weren't burning much coal going down the valley. Running into Newport you would watch the signals; if stopping at Panteg you might stop short. I wasn't a passed fireman – it was done on trust.

Going up the valley there was a signal at the top end of Pontnewynydd yard to take you round into the station. There was a platform at Snatchwood, but no signals. The next signal was by the signal box at Abersychan,

The Great Western Railway Eastern Valley 1925 auto-train timetable for the Top and Bottom Lines. *Terry Target*

then one by the Rising Sun pub at Cwmffrwd and a signal onto the single line all the way to Blaenavon Low Level, where there was a signal taking you onto two roads. On non-auto trains, the gates at the top end of the station were opened to allow the engine to run forward, and drop down past the train to run round for the return journey. If the one platform was busy, the train would use the back road. There was a short platform against the wall on the up road.

To relieve the Usk Pilot at Newport, the fireman would drive the engine and I would fire it, with the driver sitting in the coach. With a rough engine, a dirty fire or bad coal you would get a telling off from the driver.

To Porthcawl and Barry

You would sometimes work trains to Porthcawl from Blaenavon or Pontypool Road with a '63xx' tender loco, via the Vale of Neath. These trains were worked from Pontypool Road every Saturday dinnertime in the summer, with two trains on a Sunday for Pontllanfraith Working Men's Club, twice each summer.

Going to Barry, you dropped off the passengers, put the train in a siding and took the engine to the shed for a wait of 4 or 5 hours. The shed staff looked after the engine while you had a few hours there before getting back to the engine about an hour before departure. We walked around in overalls, although some men carried a spare shirt or slacks. It was an all-day job; you were at Barry till 6 or 7 o'clock at night before returning. The shift would last for 12 hours.

When you arrived at Barry Island station, the engine from the previous train would be waiting in a spur outside the platform to pull your train to the carriage sidings. The train engine would then drop back into this spur to pull the carriages from the next incoming train to the carriage sidings, before being serviced at Barry shed.

Travelling from Pontypool Road to Barry could be achieved by using three or four different routes: over the Vale and down through Hengoed, to the top of Caerphilly via Penhros Junction, through Taff's Well to Cardiff and Barry, or over Taff's Well Viaduct and on to Cadoxton. Another way was to Penarth and Barry and out by Cadoxton. If there was maintenance work on the track between Cadoxton you would be routed to bypass it.

5. Fireman Gwyn Hewlett

My father was Charlie Hewlett. He started as a cleaner at Ponty, then became a fireman, then a driver (pre-war, around 1932). He fired the passengers on the Top Line to Blaenavon and Brynmawr and instructed the Improvement Class in the 1930s. He then sought further promotion by working as an outside runner to the Foreman. He did that for the war period, then worked at Barry as a foreman, then to Canton as an outside foreman. He was then made an inspector, and came back to Ponty as shed master. His saying was 'Never better'.

John Hodge took photos at Cardiff Canton on a Sunday with Charlie's permission, and John presented my father with a photo of him taken at the shed beside a newly cleaned engine. He was the same age as driver Tom Davis, and was in that era of men.

I myself started at Pontypool Road in 1948. I did my cleaning, then did my National Service, during which I was stationed in Hong Kong for a couple of years. On my return I went through all the links as a fireman. I got interested in the Improvement Class – I was later the secretary – and taught it for the last five years. In 1964 I went to Hereford as a driver. I was there for 18 months to two years, then returned to Pontypool Road. When Ponty closed, I transferred to Radyr for four months, then Newport Ebbw, Severn Tunnel and finally Newport High Street. I retired in 1992.

Pontypool Road shed

Two men were employed on fire-dropping – one on ash pans, one on smokeboxes. Around

40 or 50 engines were dealt with each shift. If there were a lot of engines on the fire pit, out as far as the signal, they might be put in the Birkenhead Sidings or on the adjacent ash road behind the rows of ash wagons, to await their turn. The row of wagons was filled with ashes and clinker within two days, and was sent to Maesycwmmer and dumped on the side of the track for use as ballast. It would be burning on the ground when it was thrown out of the wagons.

Once you finished cleaning you went on the coal stage. '29xx' and '26xx' locos were still in vogue, but I never worked on them. The driver would drive these engines off the coal stage, down to the shed for the shed man to put away, if they had plenty of steam. The driver would drive one engine off the coal stage, and let you drive the next one.

All coaching stock was kept at Pontypool Road station. The non-corridor stock for ROF Glascoed was kept there; it worked one trip in the morning and one in the evening.

We were allocated five 9F 2-10-0s, and we used to go to Hereford or Shrewsbury with them on freights. The morning 4.15am Chester was a Class D freight, the fastest we used to go. We would relieve a Class C freight (vacuum-braked throughout) coming back.

I was working with Driver Bill Stone when we had No 7206, straight out of Swindon after repair. It was a nice engine, and we took a train of 30-odd empties for Furnace Sidings, Blaenavon, then to Brynmawr with Big Pit coal.

At Furnace Sidings we picked up the coal for Brynmawr – three lots of wagons. We pulled the brake van and ten wagons of coal up to Waenavon and pushed them into the loop there. We then went back down and picked up another ten, then returned for the third lot, backing onto the train at Waenavon. We then worked the train to Brynmawr, and usually came back engine and van, as Brynmawr rarely had any wagons, although sometimes you would bring empties back.

On this occasion we came back as engine and van. Coming over the top at Waenavon, in those days the fireman would control the train by using the hand brake. I said to my driver, 'I'll put the brake on,' but it wouldn't go any further. I shouted to the guard, so he applied his brake and we stopped. What had happened was that the brake pin for the block was in the wrong way; the pin was touching the loco frame when applied, preventing braking. It was OK when new brakes were fitted, but as they wore the pin made contact with the frame. We used the brake van for braking back to Pontypool Road, where we took the engine to the shed; the brake pin was knocked out and fitted the other way around, which cured the problem. The engine was having new blocks each trip. No one spotted that. It could have been nasty coming down with a full train of coal.

I used to swap regularly for the early-morning auto-train, as some men didn't like getting up at 3.00am. I would swap a top goods job for this.

We picked up two trailers with a '64xx' from the South Bay at Ponty, left from the last turn at night. We went to Panteg, then to Crane Street, as the first train down. The driver with me on the early turn never bothered to connect up the regulator, but you had to be careful that there wasn't an inspector around – they'd have you straight away. I would drive the engine.

We went down to Newport, took water and crossed over to Platform 8. Then we went to Blaenavon, stopping all the way up, and back to Newport. On the way up we had relief at Panteg. All our own '64xxs' were good engines and would steam; they weren't used anywhere else.

Coedygric Loop could hold two coal trains, and the signal for it was operated from Coedygric signal box.

Furnace Sidings, Blaenavon

We worked the Furnace morning and afternoon turns – Newport men worked the rest.

Coming down from Furnace Sidings, you would stop at Tyre Mill if not going too fast.

The Eastern Valley

A number of times I have been with new drivers on this turn. As you came to Tyre Mill you thought you were going to stop and didn't. You had your arms out to hand over the single-line staff and pick up the next, and you'd miss it, and the driver had to stop. The guard didn't like this as he had to pick up all the brakes and re-brake the train. Otherwise you went down to Blaenavon High Level where you had to stop and adjust the brakes to come down to Talywain.

You had 35 wagons with 35 brakes on. You would work the train with the hand brake, bunker-first; if you started to slow, you eased off the brake. You were working, and the driver just sat there, unless you were going too fast, when the driver used the engine brake.

At Talywain we shunted the goods shed for the Newport men the next morning. You then went back on the train. Shunting at Talywain in the winter was terrible.

You had brakes down all the way from Blaenavon to Griffithstown. You would ease them at Gwenallt, and again below Crane Street. The train was worked as far as Coedygric Junction, and pushed back into the Old Yard.

You would get relief at Blaenavon High Level and would walk down to the Low Level station, catch the passenger train to Panteg and book off. The relief crew would take the train to Coedygric, and push it back in to the Old Yard. A '72xx' was booked for this job. We had eight or nine – Nos 7233, 7234 and 7235 are recalled. A '42xx' or '52xx' would be used if a '72xx' wasn't available. A driver in the Western Valley or Eastern Valley working these trains was far more competent than drivers in England. You always had brakes down. A lot of skill was involved.

Ex-Great Western '52xx' 2-8-0 tank loco No 5200 enters Blaenavon High Level station with empties for Big Pit on the last day of steam, 31 May 1965. This was a Newport Pill depot working.
Herbie Harrington, J. S. Williams collection

This is Pontnewynydd Junction on 15 April 1963. Branches Fork was accessed by the line on the left, while the lines to the right continued to Pontnewynydd, Abersychan and Blaenavon Low Level. M. Hale, *Great Western Trust*

6. Fireman Henry Williams

Tirpentwys and Graig-ddu brickworks

A Severn Tunnel engine would call into Pontypool Road and bring empties to Branches Fork yard and Pontnewynydd yard in the morning, and take full wagons back to Severn Tunnel Junction. Branches Fork yard covered the pipeworks and the brickworks on the Graig-ddu and Tirpentwys branches.

I worked up both these branches after Branches Fork shed closed, being based at Pontypool Road. You had to propel the train on these turns, with a shunter and a guard. Originally they would ride on the engine with the driver and fireman, then reduced-height brake vans were introduced. The wagons were propelled with the van between the train and the engine; there was no van at the front of the train.

At Pontnewynydd sheetworks and Pontypool Town Forge (by Pontnewynydd Junction) the works engine pushed wagons out so far, then the Pontnewynydd Pilot would pick them up. Whatever came off the upper Blaenavon line would go to Pontnewynydd yard.

The PR2 trip always went into Skew Bridge down loop on the way back, especially if you were a bit late, and they'd have a relief crew there to take you off.

The Top Line

I've known Pill men come from the Top Line with brakes down, stop at the bank at Pontnewynydd Junction to have brakes picked up to run down into the end of Crane Street station, where more brakes were put back down. I've seen this train go through Coedygric Junction like an express! You ought to see the sparks coming off the wagon brake blocks! The cab would be blacked out with the shutters up and paraffin headlamps on.

The Eastern Valley

The railway bridge leading to the Town Forge is seen in this Whitsun 1931 view, when parts of the Eastern Valley were flooded after heavy rainfall. *J. S. Williams collection*

I worked the Brynmawr route with Tom Pearce, who lived in a farm by St Mary's Church at Panteg. You could only bring back two trucks of coal and a brake van due to the gradient on the bank coming back out of Brynmawr to Waenavon. As soon as you started out of Brynmawr there were big notices, 'Don't look outside the cab', as there were restricted clearances.

The first train up in the morning, from Newport to Blaenavon, the 5.30am at Blaendare Halt, would have a parcel van on the back for all the parcels for Pontypool (the Co-op, Home & Colonial, Maypole, F. W. Woolworth, Fowlers, Briggs the shoe people, etc). The train would proceed to Pontypool Crane Street, go past the signal box, over the points and back into Ford's siding on the left-hand side. It was an auto-train, having two trailing coaches as well as the parcel van. A shunter from Pontnewynydd would be there to hook the van off, and the train continued to Blaenavon. The Pontnewynydd Pilot would then arrive and put the van in the platform for the parcels to be unloaded onto trolleys. The Pilot would take the van from there, and wait for the next train down, which was the return auto working, and shunt the van behind the engine. The formation to Newport would be two auto-coaches, engine and parcel van on the back. At Newport's Platform 8, the station pilot would take the parcel van off the back of the engine.

Fish and Chip Siding at Pontypool

This was installed during the war as a private siding, but when the operator shut up and went away it was used for storing extra coaches. When Barry trains were run on a Sunday there were two coaches stored here on the down road. The Barry train would come from Pontnewynydd through Trevethin Junction, then near Crane Street signal box it would go over the points and the Crane Street signalman would change them and off would come the 'dummy' (ground signal) and the train would reverse. A shunter from Pontnewynydd yard would be there to hook you on. That train would be full of passengers. In Great Western days all passengers would be asked to leave the train and this manoeuvre was carried out as an empty stock movement.

7. Fireman Terry Warwood

Newport Pill dock work

Dock work was really interesting. You would see all different ships, and also the mail boats from New Zealand with names like *Orangutangi*; I never thought I would go there in future years. You would also see the Newport ships. A yellow funnel on a ship meant you would be on the go all night. Austin Metropolitans, two-seat sports cars, were exported to America, and Austin Healey Sprites would go out by the thousand. Equipment for Rhodesian Railways was exported in wagons, and export of coal was colossal.

Coal was stored at Maesglas, moved to East Maen sidings, then to the coal hoists on the dock. Coal hoists 1 to 10 were straight down, while Nos 12 and 13 were the furthest away, nearest the dock entrance. You would pull the train down to the hoist and hook the engine off, pick up the empties and bring them back to East Maen sidings.

General cargo was also moved, and we would watch the cranes in operation.

Iron ore boats arrived – the *Afghanistan* is recalled, which was very modern. We would go alongside for the iron ore hoppers to be filled up; these were new 33½-ton wagons, and when leaving the dockside their bearings were tight. We would work 15 wagons out of the dock, and would be struggling. A swing bridge separated the north dock from the south dock, which we would go across and around the corner to a weighbridge on a slope, struggling to get there. We had to pull the train up here to be weighed, then pull up a bit further to back into a siding to pick up another five wagons, to make a train of 20 wagons. This train was then worked to West Maen, where two BR 9Fs would work it to Ebbw Vale steelworks.

The first train worked from here stripped all the threads from the couplings; they were subsequently changed to Instanter-type couplings, as screw couplings weren't strong enough.

I worked on one 9F, light engine, and all you did was fire the back corners of the firebox. A colleague was an Ebbw fireman, and at Aberbeeg a 9F cut itself through the rails, as there was a problem with the regulator when these engines first came out.

Newport Pill to Furnace Sidings, Blaenavon

Pill had EV1, EV2, EV3, etc, jobs in the Eastern Valley Link. The shed had no '72xxs', as they were banned from going across the bridge at East Mendalgief, as it had a weight restriction. Known as East Sidings, it is a retail park now, and the bridge is a single-span structure.

It could be 2 or 3 o'clock in the afternoon to book on. The engine was always prepped for you and would be ready for you to take off shed. You would go to Maesglas light engine, collect the train, work along the old Monmouthshire line, down Mon bank, through the town and past Mill Street to Cwmbran Junction. You then proceeded on to Pontypool Crane Street and turned off at Trevethin Junction to travel round the horseshoe curve above Pontnewynydd. I never thought trains could get up this section the first time I went around it as it was so steep! You worked through to Talywain station, through the tunnel, and picked up the single-line staff at Garndiffaith signal box for the single-line section to Blaenavon High Level. You had the road at Garndiffaith, as Talywain was the passing place.

You changed staffs again at Blaenavon High Level, Tyre Mill and Furnace Sidings. You held out both hands for the new staff, exchanging it with the one from the current section of track – catching the new one would

The Eastern Valley

Trevethin Junction, Pontypool, looking north. The railway to the left is the GWR 'Top Line' branch to Talywain, the line in the centre leads to Pontnewynydd yard and Branches Fork Junction, and the line on the right is the GWR branch to Blaenavon Low Level. *J. S. Williams collection*

hurt your hand.

At Furnace Sidings you pulled up and pushed the van off. Then you pushed the train round into Big Pit sidings on the left. Next you would go back up the line, cross over, and back onto your train, which you took as far as Talywain, where Newport Pill men would be waiting to relieve you. Sometimes relief was at Blaenavon. You then walked from Talywain to Abersychan Low Level to catch the train to Newport High Street, where you would walk back to Pill shed.

Another job at Pill was to relieve a crew at Mill Street, who had gone to Blaenavon and back, and bring the train back.

The signalman at Trevethin Junction Box poses for a photograph, date unknown. *J. S. Williams collection*

No 9484 calls at Abersychan Low Level with the 3.49pm train to Newport on 8 June 1957.
M. Hale, *Great Western Trust*

Working to Talywain

The first time I ever went there I booked on at 2 o'clock one Saturday afternoon. It was engine and van from Maesglas to Griffithstown, where we picked up the empties, then up to Talywain, where we shunted them off.

It wasn't my regular job, as I was a dock fireman at Newport, but when you came off the dock you were spare and would work any odd job that was going. The shed master was known as 'Bungalow Bill'. Eastern Valley jobs were Top Link jobs at Newport Pill. Sometimes the senior fireman would want to see Newport County playing, so he asked to swap jobs. The day shift worked 6.00am to 2.00pm, but you got relieved at midday and away home; the afternoon shift would come in early to finish off the jobs, and be away early in the evening at 5.00pm.

I said yes to a job on the Eastern Valley link to work to Talywain. The engine was No 5200 and the driver was Ted White; this was the first '42xx' I had been on. We went light engine to Maesglas, but the pressure had dropped and the water was down to half a glass. I thought I had dropped myself in it. We backed onto the brake van, then it was light engine to Griffithstown via the old Monmouthshire line. Water was taken at Cwmbran Junction going up. The driver

At Cwmbran Junction the 'Old Mon' line continued south to Oakfield and Newport. Here is a train of Vipond Colliery coal wagons, once a very common sight. *Phil Williams collection*

never worked trains back down; that was the fireman's job, working to wind the hand brake on and off.

I was firing all the time, trying to keep steam – on a light engine you usually don't fire all the time. I thought it was lack of experience, and the driver was looking at me a bit funny. As soon as we stopped at Griffithstown the pressure rose, and I filled the boiler right up after we had backed onto 15 wagons at Panteg sidings. As soon as we started the pressure dropped back again. I was shovelling like mad. At Crane Street station my driver opened her right up round the corner to Trevethin Junction and half way up the horseshoe bend, where we came to a stop. We had run out of steam, and the driver was doing his nut.

'I wish you young firemen wouldn't swap turns! I'll have a word with him next time I see him!'

My driver grabbed the shovel, opened the firebox doors and said, 'Oh, there's a good fire in there.' When we stopped the pressure went straight back up. So we filled up the boiler and managed to get to Talywain, dropping back down to the signal on top of the Big Arch.

My driver said, 'Put the reversing lever in mid-gear and when I tell you open the regulator.'

He got off the engine, walked to the front and opened the smokebox door. He said, 'Open her up.' I opened the regulator and there was just a cloud of steam, as the superheaters had blown.

My driver closed the smokebox door, returned to the footplate and apologised to me. 'No fireman would have kept steam in this thing.'

The loco was a cripple, and it was dropped off at Pontypool Road loco shed. We were relieved at Talywain.

On return journeys on the Top Line the brakes were pinned down at Blaenavon High

Level, with more brakes down at Talywain at the Big Arch, then the train worked to Crane Street. There the brakes were adjusted and kept down until Coedygric, where they were picked up in the down loop at Station Road, Griffithstown. Diesels working from Hafodyrynys would stop in this loop with fitted wagons to pick up brakes.

Back in Newport we pulled up in Maesglas sidings, where the Maesglas Pilot would pick up the loaded train and take it to East Maen. The dock engines would then work from East Maen to the coal hoists in the docks. There was a little signal box there, where the shunter would control the train. The loco was a '67xx' pannier tank. '15xxs' were used as the Alexandra Dock Pilot and working the goods shed at Newport High Street. The AD Pilot worked the dockyard all day and all night. I was 17 when I worked on these engines as the Transfer Pilot at Newport High Street.

You walked up to Mill Street station and relieved the Eastern Valley train there to work it to Maesglas, or relieve the train at the iron gates, where Dock Street shed was, and a ground frame there.

8. Fireman Colin Polsom

Working Pontnewynydd yard was an odd turn as it was coming to its end. I used to nip home for breakfast as I lived in Wainfelin, then nip back down, go to Branches Fork to do a bit of shunting, and come back down.

We came off the road there one day, me and Bob Thomas. We were doing some shunting, and this particular day Bob was having a night out. I was always up for an early finish, but when we came out on the line adjacent to the Blaenavon Top Line we ran through the dummy signal and our pannier tank came off, all six wheels. That was a funny experience!

Myself and Bill Symes had No 6634, the front engine double-heading the last steam-hauled rugby excursion that went up to Blaenavon. We should have gone down to Llantarnam to pick up the train, but only went as far as Panteg.

The snows of 1963

This was on the PO5 working. It snowed on Boxing Day 1962 to a depth of 4 feet. We were the first back at work on the Monday after Christmas, when the colliers were back. We failed to get to Blaenavon, but managed to get to Talywain as the Newport man had got there with the snowplough and a '42xx'. Newport Pill worked one turn to Golynos Junction and one to Furnace Sidings at Blaenavon.

When the snowplough got through to Blaenavon on the Tuesday, it had knocked a check rail out at Tyre Mill. To clear the line to Blaenavon we coupled our '72xx' to the back of the '42xx' and plough from Newport. We got our train through to Blaenavon on the Wednesday – we were first up there with a train. At High Level the snow was 4 feet deep, up to the top step of the loco.

We opened up the engine as soon we got through High Level station to run through under the bridge at Forge Side and on to Furnace Sidings. Graeme Evans was my mate on this job, in the Branch Link. We heard a bang going through Tyre Mill – what happened then? At Furnace Sidings we pulled up past the signal box, ready to drop back in. Larry Newcombe was the guard, and he came running. 'Graeme, is your engine all right?'

We discovered a cracked spring behind the cab steps. We dropped the train off and returned light engine via the old Monmouthshire line to the East Junction and back to the shed from there.

The next day, a Thursday, we went up lovely, and coming back down with a train of coal, by Jackdaw Quarry above Varteg station, everything was fine. We ran under the road bridge into Talywain station to see a red-faced ganger running towards us, waving his hands frantically. They were trying to stop us after leaving Blaenavon High Level, as a check rail has been dislodged or hit out on the single line on Garn Viaduct.

On the Thursday or Friday we had to assist the Newport man who couldn't get his '42xx' up to Golynos Junction. An Inspector

The Eastern Valley

Cwmavon Reservoir, as viewed from a train of empties heading for Big Pit, Blaenavon, circa 1973 – a view now blocked out by trees! *J. S. Williams*

asked us to bank him, so we left our train in Talywain station. We went down to the Big Arch to start banking and tried four times. We took water before the fourth attempt, but the Inspector come down and stopped us half way. The '42xx'/'52xx' in front had cracked the levelling pipe between the tanks, and we had to take that engine back to Pontypool Road shed.

Later on I had a trip with a '72xx' to Furnace Sidings with my driver and a trainee driver. On the return trip we put down extra brakes at Blaenavon High Level. The trainee driver was in the guard's van writing up his route notes and I was on the engine with the driver. Passing Cwmavon Reservoir the driver was leaning out watching the scenery, and I was eating an apple. As we passed Jackdaw Quarry the speed of the train began to increase, and my driver applied the vacuum brake, but to no effect. At Varteg station the track begins to flatten out, and by now the guard had applied the brake in the guard's van, slowing the engine and the first few wagons next to it. The driver applied the vacuum brake again, and the train was now under control.

9. Terry Target

The Monmouthshire Canal at Pontypool and Pontnewynydd

This canal was built between Pontnewynydd and Newport, and transported coal and all sorts of other goods. It opened in February 1796, and plans were made to extend it down to Newport Docks; it terminated just past Newport Castle between where Friar's Walk shopping centre is today and Newport Market.

Its northern end was at St Luke's Church, Pontnewynydd, north of which was a tram road leading to Abersychan and a junction at the Rising Sun pub, where it connected to a tram road from the Balance Pit at the Balance on the Varteg. Iron from Varteg Ironworks, Golynos Ironworks and the British Ironworks

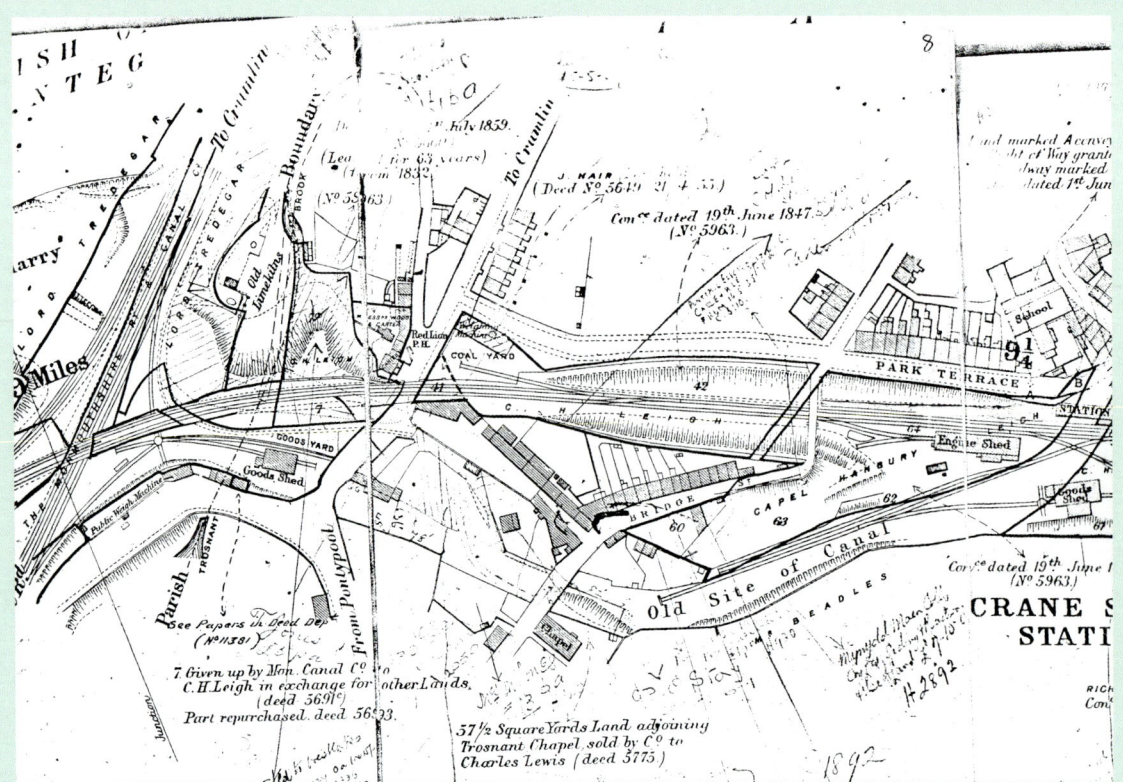

This map of Pontypool Crane Street shows the original Monmouthshire Railway & Canal Company engine shed (right), and the route of the Newport to Pontnewynydd canal. *Terry Target*

was transported. At the head of the canal at St Luke's Church the feeder tunnel is still there, fed from the Afon Llywdd. The river curves at the bottom of Snatchwood Hospital, and there was a weir and sluice gate there (marked on old maps but no longer present); they'd lower the sluice gate to divert water into the tunnel. The southern end of the tunnel is no longer visible, but the northern end, although overgrown, can be seen by walking up the river; you can see it from the bottom end of the houses opposite the Victoria pub.

At one time there were huge stones at St Luke's Church, which must have come out of the canal. The canal terminus had a broad head in which to turn the barges. On old maps the place is surrounded by tram roads, which came down what is now St Luke's Road to Abersychan, and went on either side of the canal head. Another poor-quality map I have seen shows small warehouses at the terminus.

It closed as a working canal a few years before 1854, and even before that the tram roads were extended down so that goods could be taken straight down to Pontymoile, just south of Pontypool. The canal was extended to Brecon in 1812. For 18 months after the railway opened at Crane Street there was both a railway and a canal in Pontypool town centre.

The canal went down over Trosnant Locks, through Robert Price's builder's yard and the goods shed there, curved around through Clarence Street station and cut down through the Settlement. It then continued at the back of Stan Tough's fish and chip shop (opposite Pontymoile Foundry), under the bottom of Maesderwyn, towards Fountain Road and into what is now the basin at Pontymoile.

The Eastern Valley

The canal was drained in January 1854 from St Luke's Church down through Trosnant to Pontymoile. They had navvies up there and lowered the bed so that they could get steam power up there and lay rails. The new railway line was opened to Blaenavon in November 1854, having taken nine months.

My railway career

I started at Abersychan Low Level station on Monday 30 August 1954. I was 15 years old – three months under my 16th birthday. I was there until the early part of 1957, when I was transferred to Pontypool Crane Street booking office. I had the best part of a year at Crane Street, when British Railways loaned me to the RAF for two years to do National Service. I finished that in January 1960, and came back to Crane Street, into the Goods Section for a few months, then back into the booking office. I was in the booking office until the early part of 1961, when I took a job on relief, relieving sickness, vacancies or holidays. I spent time in Abergavenny, Blaina, Nantyglo, Cwmbran and Llantarnam stations.

In the summer of 1961 I got promotion to Newport High Street booking office. It was quite fortunate really, because not long after I got the job closure of the valley stations was announced as part of the Beeching cuts. I had seven years in the booking office at Newport, then I went to Cardiff Divisional Office for 14 years, and to Newport Civil Engineers in 1982. I finished in 1995 with 40 years service. In 1995 it was still British Rail and they were practising for privatisation.

While I was working in Newport station the only cheque we accepted was from a surgeon from the Royal Gwent Hospital in Newport, who would travel by train to London to give talks, using a 1st Class return to Paddington that cost £5 0s 6d – all other payments were cash. Then suddenly we went over to the general public using cheques, with the proviso that you looked at the person paying by cheque, and if they had some form of identification to back it up, fair enough. But if not, as long as they looked genuine, you accepted the cheque. You would think, what con man would turn up scruffy? You would act the part, wouldn't you? There must have been a number of cheques that bounced when they came in, and they must still bounce now.

Abersychan Low Level

The station master was Danny Pope. One of the porters was George Wilcox, from Blaenavon, and the porter/signalman was Ken Benfield, who did a lot of work in the signal box when the pilot came up with the odd wagon for the goods yard. He also spent time in Cwmffrwd signal box. The other porter was Ivor Sylvester, who lived in the station house. Porters would get there early to open the station. I started at 8.00am and regularly worked Saturdays as part of the turn. A lot of people travelled to Cwmbran. Normally the train was run using a pannier tank and two coaches, and on a Sunday excursions were run.

Two incidents are recalled. Abersychan had staggered platforms, and the main building was on the up side, serving Blaenavon. In the summer people would send pigeons away for training, and one day a gentleman came in with pigeons to send to Hereford. We weighed the pigeons and charged him and away he went. He knew that the pigeons would be sent to Panteg via the down platform, and loaded onto a Hereford train that had come up the Eastern Valley from Llantarnam. He knew the arrival time in Hereford.

But the porter made a mistake. He placed the pigeons on the up train to Blaenavon, assuming that the train would then take them back to Panteg. At Blaenavon the porter thought that the pigeons were for them, and set them free, to fly back to Pentwyn. The gentleman arrived home to find the pigeons had already arrived and he had to resend them the following day. He wasn't very pleased!

The auto-coach was used on the Blaenavon service, where the driver would sit in the front coach while the fireman stayed on the loco. Sometimes the auto-coach wasn't available and the engine would be at the front. The right of way to leave was given off the up platform to the guard on the down platform. Normally he jumped into his compartment, but other times he jumped onto the middle part of the train. On this occasion he jumped onto the middle part, but two ladies were inside talking; they realised that they had missed their stop, pushed the guard out and jumped off. The guard was left on the floor and the train had gone. We had to stop the train at Pontnewynydd while the guard caught a bus!

The goods yard later became the location of a doctor's surgery. It wasn't very busy; an odd wagon went in. Mr Pope dealt with the goods. Before my time Les Birch had been the station master, and he was later in charge of the Enquiries Office at Newport.

At the southern end of Abersychan Low Level station, on the up side, was the station house (which is still there); this was occupied by one of the porters, Ivor Sylvester. Then there was the Parcels Office (a tin building), and next to this was a large area for lorries to deliver parcels. The station building was next; at the southern end was the Waiting Room and Booking Hall, then the Booking Office, attached to which were the toilets.

The booking clerk, station master and porter worked in the Booking Office, and it was very cramped. Finally, there was a small cabin, in which was kept the water meter and gas meter. I have a key for this.

The down side, accessed by a footbridge, had a small Waiting Room. After I left in 1957 the station master had a separate office installed on this platform.

Neighbouring stations

Cwmffrwd, the next station north, was an unstaffed halt. Station master Danny Pope at Abersychan Low Level was responsible for it, as well as Cwmavon. Its main purpose was to control the change from double line to single line towards Blaenavon. The signal box was always manned because of single-line working. There were two signalmen: the older man was George Gollop, who lived in Waterworks Lane, and the other was Bert Badham, who lived in Cwmavon. During the Second World War Bert was in the Parachute Regiment and was dropped at Arnhem.

On a Sunday the staff went to Cwmffrwd and Cwmavon stations with a supply of tickets.

Andrew Muldoway was the station master

No 9484 calls at Cwmffrwd Halt with the 2.54pm service to Blaenavon on 8 June 1957.
 M. Hale, Great Western Trust

The Eastern Valley

On the same day 0-6-0PT No 5752 is ready to leave Cwmavon Halt with the 2.40pm train to Newport. M. Hale, *Great Western Trust*

at Blaenavon Low Level. The booking clerk was Owen Leek; he left the railway to work at Daniel Doncaster's in Blaenavon, and was Secretary of Blaenavon Male Voice Choir for many years until his death. Mike Davis also worked there.

South of Abersychan, Snatchwood Halt was closed during my time. It had staggered platforms, the up-side one at the north, the down-side one to the south. The latter was a wooden platform and hung over a retaining wall, with steps to Rosemary Lane. The up-side platform was accessed from St Luke's Road. Both platforms had 'pagoda'-type huts. It closed in 1953.

Pontnewynydd station had one morning turn and one afternoon turn. Vince Charles worked there. Access was via the road bridge, which was replaced in the late 1950s. You walked by a sloping path (now a set of steps) to the station building on the up side. At the path end of the building was the gents toilet, accessed from the platform. Then came the up-side Waiting Room. Inside on the left was the Booking Office window, and on the right the ladies toilet. It was quite a large, dark Waiting Room, as it backed onto a bank that led to the Forge.

To get to the down platform you turned right to go over the footbridge, or you could go right past the Waiting Room, under the footbridge, and use the crossing over the line. There was another nice little Waiting Room on the down side. I recall a signal on the curve north of the road bridge on the down line, adjacent to a fence made of railway sleepers. It was located in a semi-circular brick indentation that is still there. It was located near the Mason's Arms pub (later the Pegasus), towards the flats in Pontnewynydd (originally Railway Parade) behind the fence.

George Street sidings were on the right-hand side looking up the valley, and were not used in my time.

South of Pontnewynydd was Wainfelin Halt, south of Merchant's Hill railway bridge. There was a gate on the road, next to the gas lamp, leading to the halt, but I never knew it as it had closed in 1941.

Pontypool Crane Street

I started in the Booking Office and the Chief Clerk was Arthur Attwood. His wife Margaret worked in the goods as a typist. Among the porters were Walter Harris, and Walter Godsall from Pontnewynydd. George Taylor was one of the supervisors, and Mr Hughes was the station master before I did National Service; he was later the station master at Pontypool Road.

The chief clerk in the goods in 1960 was Ken Probert, and the station master was Mr Corley. Clerical staff in the goods were Tony Waters and Hazel Waters, Alan Fletcher, Arthur Eyeball from New Inn, and Bryn Ford, who emigrated to Canada.

At the southern end of the up platform at Crane Street was a black tin-sheet shed, which was the Parcels Office. The station building, from the southern end, contained a Porter's Room and the Booking Office, which was part of the up Waiting Room. Tickets were kept in a small box in the main Booking Office on the down side for security; it was a small box as there were only five stations on the up line. The box would be brought across to the up platform, tickets issued for the day and the box returned to the down platform.

After the Waiting Room was the Goods Office, which was an offshoot of the Goods Office in the goods yard. The toilets were

Pontypool Crane Street station and goods shed staff pose for a photograph on the up platform in 1914.
J. S. Williams collection

The Eastern Valley

Left: Looking north at Crane Street on the same day, '94xx' Class 0-6-0PT No 9488 is seen awaiting departure with the return 8.20am Newport-Blaenavon train. *L. Fullwood, Transport Treasury*

Below: A Pontypool Crane Street goods department memorandum dated August 1918 detailing a wagon of pit wood for Blaenserchan Colliery. *Phil Williams collection*

outside the north end of the building.

The down side was accessed by a footbridge at the top end of the down platform; walking to the left took you to the up side, or right down into the goods yard and pedestrian exit to the station approach. At the north end of the down platform building was the station master's office, where his clerk also resided. There was a large Waiting Room with the entrance doors to the outside and platform in the middle. Then followed the main Booking Office and toilets, then a gap followed by a cabin for the station supervisor and station staff.

There was always provision for a coal fire in the Waiting Room in winter, even at Pontypool Road station just before it was closed.

I recall the first DMU arriving at Crane Street for driver training. British Railways published pamphlets detailing the new service, which contained a list of the stations

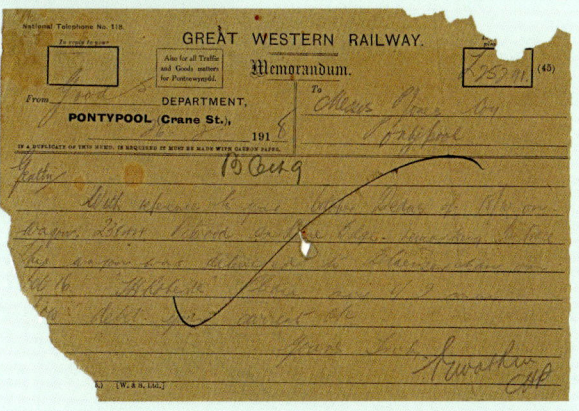

from Caerleon to Blaenavon Low Level, with the names of the station masters.

On a Thursday I went from Crane Street to pay wages at Trevethin Junction, Pontnewynydd yard (wagon repairers) and Branches Fork. The Yard Master from Pontnewynydd came to the station for the wages. If the weather was bad he would arrive on the Pontnewynydd Pilot, and we would all jump on the engine, go to the yard and get off there; we would also go to Branches Fork,

LIST OF STATION MASTERS and TELEPHONE NUMBERS

Station	Telephone Exchange	Number	Station Master
Aberbeeg	Aberbeeg	241	Mr. S. Counsell
Abercarn	Abercarn	220	Mr. H. C. West
Abersychan (L.L.)	Talywain	244	Mr. H. L. Birch
Abertillery	Abertillery	235	Mr. P. E. Tong
Bassaleg Junction	Rhiwderin	263	Mr. W. G. Glover
Blaenavon	Blaenavon	231	Mr. T. A. Davies
Blaina	Blaina	245	Mr. A. R. Sutton
Bournville (Mon.) Halt	Blaina	245	Mr. A. R. Sutton
Brynmawr	Brynmawr	215	Mr. H. S. Townsend
Caerleon	Caerleon	232	Mr. T. Forster
Cross Keys	Cross Keys	245	Mr. N. C. Edmunds
Crumlin (L.L.)	Crumlin	217	Mr. W. Jones
Cwm	Cwm	234	Mr. C. Morris
Cwmavon (Mon.)	Talywain	244	Mr. H. L. Birch
Cwmffrwd Halt	Talywain	244	Mr. H. L. Birch
Cwmbran	Cwmbran	2115	Mr. H. J. Holmes
Cwmcarn	Cross Keys	263	Mr. H. C. West
Ebbw Vale	Ebbw Vale	2235	Mr. J. H. Rees
Llanhilleth	Aberbeeg	222	Mr. I. Gibbs
Llantarnam	Newport	58461 (Ext. 349)	Mr. H. J. Holmes
Nantyglo	Brynmawr	450	Mr. A. R. Sutton
Newbridge	Newbridge	449	Mr. W. Jones
Newport	Newport	58461	Mr. R. D. Hitchens
Panteg & G.	Griffithstown	16	Mr. O. J. Lewarne
Ponthir	Caerleon	232	Mr. T. Forster
Pontnewynydd	Pontypool	715	Mr. B. F. Corley
Pontrhydyrun Halt	Cwmbran	2107	Mr. H. J. Holmes
Pontypool (Blaendare Road) Halt	Pontypool	715	Mr. B. F. Corley
Pontypool (Crane St.)	Pontypool	715	Mr. B. F. Corley
Pontypool Road	Pontypool	222	Mr. H. J. Hughes
Risca	Risca	330	Mr. S. G. Richards
Rogerstone	Rhiwderin	277	Mr. S. Gwenlan
Sebastopol	Griffithstown	16	Mr. O. J. Lewarne
Six Bells Halt	Abertillery	235	Mr. P. E. Tong
Tyllwyn Halt	Ebbw Vale	2235	Mr. J. H. Rees
Tynycwm Halt	Risca	330	Mr. S. G. Richards
Upper Pontnewydd	Cwmbran	2107	Mr. H. J. Holmes
Victoria	Cwm	238	Mr. J. H. Rees

SEASON TICKETS

Season tickets, allowing unlimited travel during the period of validity, are issued between two or more stations for any period from one month to twelve months, including odd days, e.g. one month and four days, four months and twenty-seven days, etc.

Weekly season tickets are issued for distances not exceeding 75 miles and are available for an unlimited number of journeys from Sunday to Saturday, inclusive.

Ordinary season tickets at half the adult rate are issued to juveniles under 14 years of age.

Reduced Rate season tickets are issued for residential purposes only to juveniles of 14 and under 18 years of age as set out hereunder:—

ENGLAND AND WALES

(a) **At half rate**
  (i) To all juveniles of 14 and under 16 years of age.
  (ii) To all juveniles of 16 and under 18 years of age who are not in receipt of salary, wages, remuneration or any other monetary payment (otherwise than by grant for educational purposes) amounting in the aggregate to more than 25s. 0d. per week.

(b) **At two-thirds rate**
  To all juveniles of 16 and under 18 years of age who are in receipt of salary or other monetary allowance exceeding 25s. 0d. per week.

Where issued, weekly season tickets are also obtainable at the appropriate half or two thirds rates.

See also page 3

CIRCULAR TOUR TICKETS

are issued at reduced fares for business or pleasure journeys.

NOTICE.—The train services, fares and other facilities shewn in this booklet are subject to alteration or cancellation at short notice and do not necessarily apply at Bank or Public Holidays or on Race days.

Station master contact details for the Eastern and Western Valleys, as printed in the September 1960-June 1961 DMU timetable for the area. *Terry Target collection*

where Hector Fry was the supervisor. In good weather you would walk up the line.

At this time Gwenallt signal box was controlled by two ladies, who worked alternate morning and afternoon shifts. The signal lady would be in the cabin at Pontnewynydd with a chitty to collect her colleague's pay. On a Thursday, whichever lady was on duty at Gwenallt would have a 'pay bearer' slip, which she'd sign, so instead of the lady having to get to the station to pick up her wages when she came on shift, the other lady would collect them for her. We made them come down into the top of Pontnewynydd yard, where the cabin was situated (later the site of a Royal Mail Sorting Office).

Ken Williams was killed in the Pontrhydyrun railway bridge bus crash of 1982; his father worked at Pontnewynydd yard, and I used to pay his wages.

When I finished, I walked to Pontnewynydd station and caught a train to Crane Street. I never went back to Crane Street on the engine.

The goods yard at Crane Street was shunted as required. There was a Corn Stores behind the signal box, but didn't have much traffic. A passenger train would come up from Newport with a wagon on the back on a regular basis. There was a tight curve behind the signal box, and the wagon had to be fly shunted back into this siding by the passenger train; however, if it wasn't done quickly enough the wagon buffer would lock on to the coach buffer, blocking all traffic, and a fitter from Pontypool Road would arrive to sort it all out. Very often on a Thursday, when I'd paid everyone at Pontnewynydd, the porter would be saying, 'The passenger hasn't gone up yet – it has buffer lock.' It hadn't gone up to Blaenavon to come back down.

One of my duties on a Monday was to read the water meter for the water tower between the station building and the signal box. Water was supplied from the water main. The next water column was at Blaenavon Low Level.

Mrs Griffin would take an old bus conductor ticket machine and clips daily to Blaendare Halt to issue tickets.

Access to Trevethin signal box, just north of Crane Street, was via Malthouse Lane, off Osbourne Road, where there was a gap in the retaining wall.

Coal trains stopped at Crane Street for brakes to be picked up; they would stop at the bottom end of the down platform, or maybe overrun, to have the brakes adjusted for the journey on to Panteg. The guard would pick up the brakes, and pin some down at the front of the train until the driver felt comfortable. He would then blow the whistle and leave; the back of the coal train would still be in the down platform. Someone once said that 'a good driver can come into one end of Pontypool Crane Street coming down at a fair old lick and stop by the end, at the stop board, but others are stopping well before you come to the platform to make sure they do stop. You have drivers and drivers…'

I don't remember a lot about goods trains; all I remember is that the Pontnewynydd Pilot took the odd wagon up the line. I never saw it, but it delivered wagons to Bailey's siding at the back of St Luke's Church at Pontnewynydd; W. L. Bailey, a coal merchant, had a single siding on the up side, at the site of the old canal head. When the canal opened it was taking coal down the valley, then at the very end it was bringing coal up to Pontnewynydd for Bailey to deliver. Eventually Bailey moved to Pontymoile, to a yard between Robert Price's builder's merchant and the garage.

There were catch points for the up line on the Crane Street side of Albion Road bridge. There had been a motor siding, which I don't remember, on the down side opposite the up-line catch points.

For handling parcels traffic a four-wheel trolley was used to take parcels to and from the train. It was a 'universal' trolley, and didn't work until you pulled the handle down, which was the brake. A Crane Street station trolley was transferred to Pontypool Road in the 1960s. The parcels were destined for businesses, houses or individual customers. For quite a long time Crane Street had the parcels contract for British Nylon Spinners (BNS) at Mamhilad. In the evening the Waiting Room on the station would be very busy receiving parcels from BNS lorries to go all over the country. This contract ceased after the 1955 ASLEF strike, when BNS created its own delivery service and parcels were taken by road. You had to weigh each parcel, work out the charge and put it on the train. Normally, there was a parcels van on the service train.

I did relief turns at Cwmbran and Llantarnam for maybe a fortnight. Mr Sutton was the station master at Blaina, and also covered Nantyglo. I would get there by train, travelling from Pontypool Clarence Street to Crumlin High Level, then Crumlin Low Level up the Western Valley.

Closure

In 1961 the *Argus* announced the withdrawal of the Eastern and Western Valley passenger services. The *Free Press* on the same day announced the closure of Pontnewynydd Forge instead of the railway. A week before closure, railway services were still being advertised in the *Free Press*!

Mr A. E. Jones was celebrating his 90th birthday in 1962, and he was big in the temperance movement. He came in to see Danny Pope and suggested that the Top Line be reopened to passenger trains. That line served a bigger population, up through Wainfelin and Cwmffrwdoer to Pentrepiod, Pentwyn, into Talywain, around to the Garn (Garndiffaith) and up to High Level. Between Abersychan and Blaenavon there was only Cwmffrwd Halt and Cwmavon Halt, serving fewer people in comparison to the Top Line. When I first saw Mr Jones, when I was going

Pentrepiod Halt looking north on 15 April 1963. *M. Hale, Great Western Trust*

to work, he was in his early 80s. He worked for James & Emanuel in Newport, and wore what I called Lloyd George collars. He was always coming in, and there was a photograph of him on the front of the *Free Press*. We used to call him Temperance Jones.

The Blaenavon Low Level line closed on 30 April 1962 (a Monday). The last timetable for the Eastern Valley covered September 1961 to 17 June 1962, and in small print 'until further notice'. Further notice kicked in later. On 28 April 1962 I bought a special cheap ticket, to travel on the day of issue and only on certain trains, between Newport High Street and Cwmffrwdoer Halt or Pontnewynydd direct, 3rd Class. The ticket cost 4s 2d. I was working on that Saturday. After the 30th, all tickets were sent back to be burned.

Cycle and walking paths were established on the old Bottom Line; the first one was from Snatchwood Halt down to St Luke's Church, then another from Snatchwood Halt to the Doctor's surgery at Abersychan,

the site of the old Abersychan goods shed. Abersychan signal box was opposite, slightly further north on the right, and was supported on girders overhanging the retaining wall. In making these paths, at Snatchwood they widened the line on the down side where the halt building had been located. The wooden platform and wooden building were outside the retaining wall, supported by girders through the wall and under the track; these girders protruded through the wall and were left in situ after the line closed. When the line was lifted you could see where the girders had gone under the track; they were enclosed in a semicircular metal surround filled with concrete. Snatchwood Halt had been opened long after the line was built, in 1912, when railmotors were introduced. To built it, the track was removed, the girders laid, covered with concrete and the track relaid. You can see where the girders came through the wall.

At the site of Snatchwood Halt there is an information board detailing what has happened in the area, and an early photo of

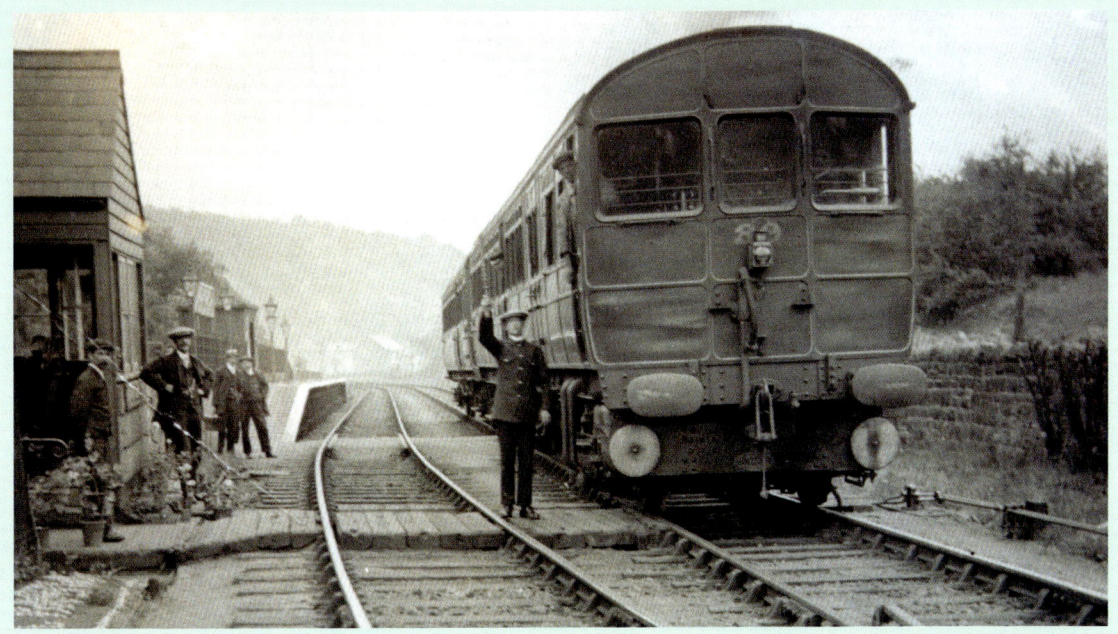

The steam railmotors to Blaenavon Low Level first ran in 1912. One of them is seen at Cwmffrwd Halt.
J. S. Williams collection

Below and overleaf: The Great Western railmotor timetable for July 1912, covering the Eastern Valley Top and Bottom Lines. *Terry Target*

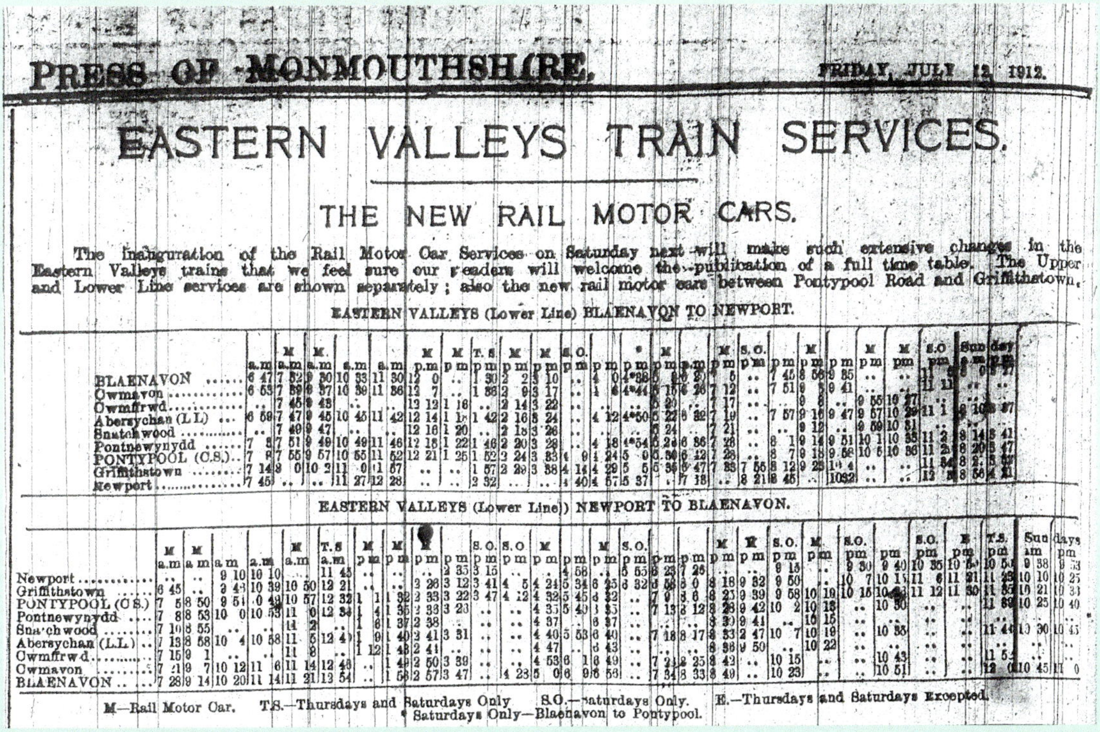

PRESS OF MONMOUTHSHIRE. FRIDAY, JULY 12, 1912.

EASTERN VALLEYS TRAIN SERVICES.

THE NEW RAIL MOTOR CARS.

The inauguration of the Rail Motor Car Services on Saturday next will make such extensive changes in the Eastern Valleys trains that we feel sure our readers will welcome the publication of a full time table. The Upper and Lower Line services are shown separately; also the new rail motor cars between Pontypool Road and Griffithstown.

EASTERN VALLEYS (Lower Line) BLAENAVON TO NEWPORT.

	a.m	M a.m	M. a.m	a.m	a.m	M p.m	M p m	T.S p m	M p m	M p m	S.O. p m	p m	* p m	M p m	p m	M p m	S.O. p m	p m	M p m	p m	M p m	M pm	S.O pm	Sunday a.m	Sunday p.m
BLAENAVON	6 47	7 52	9 30	10 33	11 30	12 0	..	1 30	2 2	3 10	..	4 0	4*38	[illegible]	[illegible]	7 5	..	7 45	8 56	9 35	..	..	[illegible]	[illegible]	[illegible]
Cwmavon	6 53	7 59	9 37	10 39	11 36	12 7	..	1 36	2 9	3 17	..	4 6	4*44	5 16	6 26	7 12	..	7 51	9 5	9 41	..	..	11 11	..	..
Cwmffrwd	..	7 45	9 43	..	..	12 12	1 16	..	2 14	3 22	..	..	..	5 20	..	7 17	..	..	9 8	..	9 55	10 27	..	..	..
Abersychan (LL)	6 59	7 47	9 45	10 45	11 42	12 14	1 18	1 42	2 16	3 24	..	4 12	4*50	5 22	6 32	7 19	..	7 57	9 10	9 47	9 57	10 29	11 1	[illegible]	[illegible]
Snatchwood	..	7 49	9 47	..	..	12 16	1 20	..	2 18	3 26	..	..	..	5 24	..	7 21	..	..	9 12	..	9 59	10 31	..	..	..
Pontnewynydd	7 3	7 51	9 49	10 49	11 46	12 18	1 22	1 46	2 20	3 28	..	4 18	4*54	5 26	6 36	7 23	..	8 1	9 14	9 51	10 1	10 33	11 3	8 14	5 41
PONTYPOOL (C.S.)	7 8	7 55	9 57	10 55	11 52	12 21	1 25	1 52	2 24	3 33	4 9	4 24	5 0	5 30	6 42	7 28	..	8 7	9 18	9 58	10 5	10 36	[illegible]	8 20	5 47
Griffithstown	7 14	8 0	10 2	11 0	11 57	..	..	1 57	2 28	3 38	4 14	4 29	5 5	5 36	6 47	7 33	7 55	8 12	9 25	10 4	..	..	11 34	[illegible]	[illegible]
Newport	7 45	..	..	11 27	12 28	..	..	2 32	..	..	4 40	4 57	5 37	..	7 18	..	8 21	8 45	..	10 32	..	..	[illegible]	8 56	[illegible]

EASTERN VALLEYS (Lower Line) NEWPORT TO BLAENAVON.

	M a.m	M a m	a m	a.m	M a.m	T.S a.m	M p m	M p m	M p m	p m	S.O. p m	S.O p m	M p m	p m	M p m	S.O. p m	p m	p m	M p m	E p m	S.O. p m	M p m	S.O. pm	pm	S.O. pm	E pm	T.S. pm	Sundays am	Sundays pm
Newport	..	..	9 10	10 10	..	11 45	..	..	..	2 35	3 15	..	.	4 58	..	5 55	6 23	7 26	..	..	9 15	..	9 30	9 40	10 35	[illegible]	[illegible]	9 38	9 53
Griffithstown	6 45	..	9 43	10 39	10 50	12 21	..	..	2 26	3 12	3 41	4 5	4 24	5 34	6 25	6 32	6 58	8 0	8 18	9 32	9 50	..	10 7	10 15	11 6	11 21	[illegible]	10 10	10 25
PONTYPOOL (C.S.)	7 5	8 50	9 51	10 49	10 57	12 32	1 1	1 32	2 33	3 22	3 47	4 12	4 32	5 45	6 32	..	7 9	8 6	8 23	9 39	9 58	10 10	10 16	[illegible]	11 12	11 30	[illegible]	10 21	10 33
Pontnewynydd	7 8	8 53	10 0	10 53	11 0	12 34	1 4	1 35	2 33	3 23	..	..	4 35	5 40	6 35	..	7 13	8 12	8 28	9 42	10 2	10 13	..	10 30	..	..	[illegible]	10 25	10 40
Snatchwood	7 10	8 55	..	..	11 2	..	1 6	1 37	2 38	..	..	..	4 37	..	6 37	..	..	..	8 30	9 44	..	10 15	..	..	..	..	..	..	..
Abersychan (L.L.)	7 13	8 58	10 4	10 58	11 5	12 40	1 9	1 40	2 41	3 31	..	..	4 40	5 53	6 40	..	7 18	8 17	8 33	9 47	10 7	10 19	..	10 35	..	..	11 44	10 30	10 45
Cwmffrwd	7 15	9 1	..	..	11 8	..	1 12	1 43	2 44	..	..	..	4 47	..	6 43	..	..	..	8 36	9 50	..	10 22	..	..	..	..	..	..	..
Cwmavon	7 21	9 7	10 12	11 6	11 14	12 48	..	1 49	2 50	3 39	..	..	4 53	6 1	6 49	..	7 21	8 25	8 42	..	10 15	..	..	10 43	..	..	[illegible]	..	..
BLAENAVON	7 28	9 14	10 20	11 14	11 21	12 54	..	1 56	2 57	3 47	..	4 23	5 0	6 9	6 56	..	7 34	8 33	8 49	..	10 23	..	..	10 51	..	..	12 0	10 45	11 0

M—Rail Motor Car. T.S.—Thursdays and Saturdays Only. S.O.—Saturdays Only. E.—Thursdays and Saturdays Excepted.
* Saturdays Only—Blaenavon to Pontypool.

```
EASTERN VALLEYS (Upper Line)—BLAENAVON TO GRIFFITHSTOWN & NEWPORT.
          WEEK DAYS ONLY.    M—Motor Service    S.O.—Saturdays Only
                              M       M               M       M       M        M   SO  M
                              a.m.  a.m. a.m.  p.m. p.m. p.m.  p.m.  p.m. p.m. p.m. p.m.
Brynmawr ............. depart  7 52  8 45 10 55 12 55 2 40 4 55 6 20 .... 8 0  ....  10 20 ....
Waenavon .....................  7 59  8 52 11 2  1 2  2 47 5 2  6 27 .... 8 7  ....  10 27 ....
BLAENAVON .................   8  8   9  2 11 11  1 11 2 56 5 13 6 36 .... 8 16 ....  10 36 ....
Varteg ........................   8 15  9  9 11 18  1 18 3  3 5 20 6 44 .... 8 23 ....  10 43 ....
Six Bells .....................   8 20  ....  11 23  ....  5 24  ....  ....  ....  8 28 ....  10 48 ....
Abersychan & Talywain ......   8 24  9 16 11 27  1 27 3  9 5 28 6 50 .... 8 32 10 40 10 52 ....
Pentwyn .......................   8 27  ....  11 30  1 30  ....  5 31  ....  ....  8 35 ....  10 55 ....
Pentrepiod ....................   8 30  ....  11 33  1 33  ....  5 34  ....  ....  8 38 ....  10 58 ....
Cwmffrwdoer ..................   8 34  ....  11 37  1 37  ....  5 38  ....  ....  8 42 ....  11 2  ....
Wainfelin ......................   8 38  ....  11 41  1 41  ....  5 42  ....  ....  8 46 ....  11 6  ....
PONTYPOOL (Crane Street) ..   8 41  9 30 11 44  1 45  3 24 5 46  7  5 ....  8 49 10 55 11 10 ....
Panteg & Griffithstown ........  ....  9 35  ....  1 50  3 29 5 51  7 10 ....  ....  11 0 11 15 ....
Newport ................. arrive  ....  10 0  ....  ....  4  0  ....  7 41 ....  ....  ....  11 27 ....

EASTERN VALLEYS (Upper Line) GRIFFITHSTOWN TO BLAENAVON.
        WEEK DAYS ONLY.    M—Motor Service    S.O.—Saturdays Only.
                              M              A            M                   SO   M
                              a.m. a.m. a.m. a.m. p.m. p.m. p.m. p.m. p.m. p.m. p.m.
Newport ............. depart  ....  6 55 ....  ....  12 28 ....  ....  4 2  ....  6 45 ....
Panteg & Griffithstown .....  6 45  7 29  8 56 ....  1  2  ....  3 50  4 36 6 43 ....  9 17
PONTYPOOL (Crane Street) .  6 55  7 40  9  3 11 58 1 13  ....  3 57  4 47 6 50 8 55 9 23 11 2
Wainfelin ...................... 6 58  ....  9  6 11 58  ....  ....  4  0  ....  6 53 8 58 ....  11 5
Cwmffrwdoer ................. 7  1  ....  9  9 12  1  ....  ....  4  3  ....  6 56 9  1 ....  11 8
Pentrepiod ..................... 7  5  ....  9 12 12  5  ....  ....  4  7  ....  7  0 9  5 ....  11 12
P ntwyn ........................ 7  8  ....  9 16 12  8  ....  ....  4 10  ....  7  3 9  8 ....  11 15
Abersychan & Talywain ...... 7 12  7 55  9 20 12 12 1 27  ....  4 14  5  1 7  7 9 12 9 40 11 19
Six Bells ........................ 7 16  ....  9 24 12 16  ....  ....  4 18  ....  7 11 9 16 ....  ....
Varteg .......................... 7 20  8  1 9 28 12 20 1 33  ....  4 22  5  7 7 15 9 20 ....  ....
BLAENAVON ................ 7 26  8 10  9 34 12 26 1 40  ....  4 28  5 14 7 21 9 26 ....  ....
Waenavon ..................... 7 36  8 21  9 44 12 36 1 51  ....  4 38  5 25 7 31 9 36 ....  ....
Brynmawr ............. arrive 7 43  8 28  9 51 12 43 1 58  ....  4 45  5 32 7 38 9 43 ....  ....

PONTYPOOL RD. TO GRIFFITHSTOWN.
G'Town   P'Road   P'Road   G'Town
 dep.     arr.     dep.     arr.
 8  6    8  6     8 10     8 15
 8 28    8 32     8 50     8 53
10  5   10 10    10 50    10 53
 1 53    1 56    12 52    12 56
 2 32    2 35     2  7     2 12
 5 54    5 57     2 20     2 23
 7 36    7 40     4 18     4 21
 8 53    8 56     4 49     4 52
11 18   11 21     6 17     6 23
         Sundays.          6 37    6 40
         a.m.              8 12    8 15
 8 38    8 43    Sundays:
                  p.m.
                  9 26     9 30

PONTYPOOL ROAD TO NEWPORT.
        (Direct Trains).
P'Road    Newp't   Newp't   P'Road
 dep.      arr.     dep.     arr.
                             a.m.
 8 10     8 45     7 57     8 32
                    p.m.
12 52     1 20     8 20     8 56
 2  7     2 45    Sundays.
 6 17     6 55     a.m.
         Sundays.  8  5     8 43
          p.m.    For rail motor car
 9 26    10  0    connections between
Trains leave Grif- Griffithstown and
fithstown 4 mins.  P'Road, see separate
after P'Road.      table.
```

Pontnewynydd station is shown, but printed in reverse! Snatchwood Halt had closed in 1953, and the late Michael Mensing, the well-known railway photographer, gave me a copy of the Closure Notice.

At Abersychan, at the car park where the station was located, you can see the line of the track, with the retaining wall on the left looking south, behind the houses on Station Road. At the former White Hart pub you could get onto the railway, and the bottom end of the up platform was still there, but you can no longer see where the signal box was.

If you walk down the path from Snatchwood, you come out at the site of Pontnewynydd station. Before you get to the road bridge, on the left-hand side coming down, the signal post retaining wall is still there.

The bypass roundabout leading to Tesco in Pontypool is just north of the site of the old Crane Street station, and is higher than the top of the up platform roof apex. George Street bridge is now the site of the traffic light junction further along the bypass, built up to road bridge height.

Top Line closure

Big Pit Colliery, Blaenavon, closed in January 1980, and the last enthusiasts' passenger train ran on Sunday 13 April, organised by the Oxford Publishing Company (see Chapter 5). The last coal train had passed through Pontypool Crane Street during the Christmas holidays of 1979, as seen by Phil Williams. The two last trains to use the line were used to recover the all-welded rail. The first was run on Wednesday 8 December 1982 to recover rail at Varteg. It was snowing heavy, and Alastair Warrington, who worked for the British Rail Civil Engineering Department at Newport, was in the engine at the back. Ten days later, on the 18th, another recovery train took the second set of rail out from the horseshoe curve at Cwmffrwdoer. It was up there at 8.00am, but the crew to operate the recovery wagons were late, as they couldn't find the location. Both these trains accessed the main line at Llantarnam Junction, but travelled north to Panteg Junction to cross over onto the down line, as the down connection at Llantarnam Junction had been removed.

Track removal began at Llantarnam

The Eastern Valley

Merchant's Hill railway bridge is seen in January 1986 prior to demolition by scrap merchant Brian Harris. *Phil Williams*

Junction, and it was lifted up to the end of the all-welded rail section at Jackdaw Quarry, Varteg. The section between there and Cemetery Sidings, Blaenavon, has now been removed to make way for a cycle track.

The steelwork of Merchant's Hill railway bridge at Pontnewynydd was removed on Saturday 18 January 1986 by local scrap merchant Brian Harris. On Saturday 25th the south retaining wall was removed; earth was removed from behind it, and it was drilled through with a pneumatic spike and demolished. The street gas lamp and side gate leading to Wainfelin station remained in situ. The north abutment of the bridge remained in situ for a short while before being subsequently removed.

10. Barry Foster

My maternal grandfather lived at the Lowlands in Pontnewydd and was a miner at Henllys Colliery; he would walk to work. The mine was at Upper Cwmbran next to a reservoir, and the seams were full of water. He would walk underground for a mile or two until he got to the coal face. My paternal grandmother lived opposite Panteg station in Griffithstown. I have lived in Sebastopol all my life.

Trainspotting

When I was small a group of us gathered on a set of sleepers, which we used a bench by the Black Ash Path near the East signal box, where we had a good view of the shed. You could see everything, and around the Vale of Neath line to the West Junction. The subway beneath the main line used to flood, so you would have to walk across the railway lines to continue your journey.

The main event of the day was the 1.35pm Manchester train, when a 'Royal Scot' or

'Patriot' went up to the West Junction on the Vale of Neath, down to the South box, and back into the station, but not to the shed as it wasn't allowed (although in earlier times it had been), as it had to keep time. It worked the 3.19pm to Manchester, and the train was always on time using a Manchester Longsight (9A) loco. *Bahamas* and *Scots Guardsman* are recalled. I would watch the train in my school break; it was the highlight of the week and everyone would come to have a look. You'd see a different 9A engine each time. The 1.39pm Manchester to Cardiff was worked by a tank engine to Cardiff.

When Bristol 'Jubilees' were transferred to Shrewsbury, you'd see one or a 'Black Five' on the Eastern Valley. The train was always on time, and stopped at Caerleon, Ponthir and Llantarnam on the way up.

Other ex-LMS engines seen were the 'Super D' 0-8-0s. These were common, and Crewe South engines are recalled leaving the New Sidings by the gasworks. You would see them leave at 1.00pm while waiting to watch the Manchester train from Crewe South. Ponty 'Super Ds' were those from Abergavenny Junction, and would arrive in the afternoon. They would wheeze!

I can recall seeing Webb 'Coal Tank' No 1054 at the back of the shed for a long while.

Canton-based 'Kings' appeared on the Manchester trains – one a day would go up on the 2.00pm Manchester, and come back down from Shrewsbury. *King George V* worked from Bristol to Shrewsbury in the evening for many years, but I never saw it; my father, who worked in Panteg Steelworks, saw it regularly.

The 9.05am Liverpool to Plymouth came through Pontypool at 1.25pm and was an out and back working. Shrewsbury men would lodge at Newton Abbot and go back the next day. Occasionally a 'Castle' worked this train, but 'Counties' are recalled working the roster. They were immaculate – I remember *County of Berks*, *County of Bucks* and *County of Hants*. Other Shrewsbury engines working the Plymouth train were *County of Wilts* and *County of Monmouth*.

At one time a decrepit 'County' would regularly work the 5.10pm Cardiff to Crewe, using the Eastern Valley route from Llantarnam Junction to Panteg & Coedygric, through the yard past Coedygric signal box, then the East Junction to Pontypool Road station. It would wait for an hour at Hereford, then on to Crewe.

The Manchester to Plymouth train was diverted from Llantarnam Junction for quite a few Sundays in the summer, and a Newton Abbot 'Castle' was always used.

The 'Castle' Class engines that I recorded were, in the '50xx' series, *The Gloucestershire Regiment*, *Nunney Castle*, *Morlais Castle*, *Earl of St Germans*, *Earl of Ducie*, *Sir Felix Pole*, *Spitfire*, *Hurricane*, *Blenheim*, *Hampden*, *Wellington*, *Gladiator*, *Fairey Battle*, *Beaufort*, *Lysander*, *Defiant*, *Lockheed Hudson*, *Swordfish*, *Tintern Abbey*, *Neath Abbey*, *Cleeve Abbey*, *Tresco Abbey* and *Sarum Castle*.

In the '70xx' series I remember *Viscount Portal*, *Sir James Milne*, *Eastnor Castle*, *Bristol Castle*, *Carn Brea Castle*, *Drysllywyn Castle*, *Penrice Castle*, *Cromwell's Castle*, *Denbigh Castle* and *Ogmore Castle*.

Of the 'Manor' Class, *Broome Manor* was a Hereford engine, and used to work up the Eastern Valley via Llantarnam.

'Britannias' were also seen, including *Western Star*, *Polar Star*, *Lightning*, *Morning Star* and engines from Crewe. They would work the Plymouth to Glasgow, joining up with the Plymouth to Liverpool coaches at Pontypool Road.

I was in the yard master's office (at the main office at the base of the steps at Coedygric Viaduct) when the Margam diesels started to run. These would run to time all the time. They started in the yard, and would come back and run through the yard via the South Junction. In later years they were routed via Trosnant Junction.

Sunday excursions to Barry Island were always double-headed, using two '56xxs'. One train came out from Pontypool Road station, then down the Eastern Valley calling at all stations, starting at Panteg. The Blaenavon train would call at all stations to Blaendare Road, then go non-stop to Barry Island.

The Eastern Valley

The Blackpool excursion on a Saturday was also double-headed. Starting at Newport, it came up the Eastern Valley. I once saw a 'Saint', *Clevedon Court*, on this train.

Finally, bankers would be seen being attached on the Relief line at Pontypool Road station, and they would race around the West box up to Cwm Glyn.

Goods traffic

Panteg Junction was used by freights out of the yard, but not very often. Ponty 'RODs' would use this route. I can recall, when little, being shown a derailed oil tanker train by my father.

Panteg Junction remembered

All photos J. S. Williams

Above and right: A southbound passenger/car train passes Panteg Junction in August 1971 hauled by a Type 4 diesel-electric locomotive.

Two views of Panteg Steelworks sidings looking south, as 'Baby Sulzer' No 7677 waits to propel its train of steel coils back to the New Sidings, having departed from those sidings as an engine and van to collect the train.

The Eastern Valley

The Panteg Steelworks diesel shunter is seen in action.

The footplate crew pose for a photo: Severn Tunnel Junction Driver Dennis W. Collett and Secondman Mostyn Richards. *J. S. Williams*

Panteg Junction to New Sidings

All photos J. S. Williams

Another journey from Panteg Junction to New Sidings is recorded, on 19 July 1972. In the first 'Baby Sulzers' Nos D7510 and D7677 head south for Panteg Sidings with a train of empty flat wagons.

An unidentified Type 4 diesel-electric locomotive heads north with a freight train, past the north end of Panteg Steelworks.

The Eastern Valley

Nos D7510 and D7677 are seen again passing through the New Sidings.

On an unrecorded date a steam breakdown crane is seen on the main line adjacent to the New Sidings waiting to lift a new overbridge, south of Coedygric Road Viaduct.

New Sidings

All photos J. S. Williams

Below and top right: On 19 July 1972 a guard's van is propelled towards and coupled to a loaded train of coils.

The Eastern Valley

Relaying work is in progress, viewed from the New Sidings Reception Road on Sunday 9 August 1970.

Above: On Sunday 19 July 1970 a DMU heads south through Pontypool Road South Junction.

Right and below: On that same Sunday an unidentified Type 3 diesel-electric locomotive passes the East Junction with a ballast train to relay ballast on the main line at the New Sidings.

The Eastern Valley

At Panteg & Coedygric Junction I've seen three coal trains in the down loop opposite the Mason's pub, waiting for a passenger train to clear. It was continuous traffic with coal from the Eastern Valley, and trains of pit props.

There was a lot of Eastern Valley line freight. It came up from Dock Street, Newport, past Mill Street over the motorway at Newport up to Oakfield, into Cwmbran, then to Panteg. Some would go up into the yard, the rest to the Eastern Valley.

On the up platform at Panteg, from north to south, there was a small building (a tin shed) used by the porters, then the Booking Office and the Waiting Room. There was another Waiting Room on the down platform.

One day a train of oil tank wagons, heading south via the tunnels on the Low Level Down Goods line became derailed at the main-line junction behind Panteg Steelworks.

Shed bashes

On a Sunday there was a train from Pontypool Road at 8.40am to Droitwich Spa, then the Bristol to York used to arrive there via Worcester. I used to catch the steamer going up to visit Derby shed and works; it went up the Lickey one day without a banker, behind an ex-LMS 4-6-0 'Jubilee' Class loco. We used to be up at Derby by 12.00 or 12.30pm, and there was time to go round the works and the shed.

We used to go up to Birmingham by a through train to Snow Hill; you could get there and do quite a few Midlands sheds on a Sunday – Aston, Saltley and Tyseley. If you went up overnight there was the 1.10am Bristol to Sheffield, a mail train. There also used to be an 11.24pm or 11.30pm train to London via Gloucester, which we used to catch at Gloucester.

Railway career

I started work aged 15 in 1957 in the Pontypool Crane Street goods shed. The DMUs had started but there were several steam workings – the auto-trains with a '64xx' pannier were still working. The 9.00am from Newport would arrive with a fish van attached at the rear. The van would be shunted into the siding at the side of the signal box – it did stink!

I worked in the goods shed for six months. A train would arrive in the morning and afternoon; it would shunt wagons into the goods shed in the morning, and pull wagons out in the afternoon. Wagons would have to be moved to get others out. Sugar, parcels, carpets and all sorts of things went into the goods shed in railway vans. The shed could hold three wagons and, once empty, each wagon would be shunted up a bit.

There were also containers present in the goods yard, as well as coal wagons and box vans. There were seven lorries in the coal yard, and a fuel tank by the railings by the road bridge. It had a hand-operated petrol pump, which I operated to fill the lorries with fuel.

I then replaced Terry Target in the Booking Office; he had left to undertake National Service. Jack Hughes was the station master, and Arthur Attwood the clerk, having previously been a porter. He later went to Pontypool Road. Bob Harris was one of the porters, and his claim to fame was to record, using 16mm film, Arthur Attwood as a parcels porter pushing barrels on the platform. Arthur was later a member of the clerical staff.

Fares weren't high, and we were busy with tickets. They were sold mostly for Newport, Cardiff, Cwmbran and Llantarnam. A lot of penny fares were sold for Blaendare Halt, as well as for Panteg & Griffithstown and Caerleon. In the summer, tickets to Barry Island and Porthcawl were sold.

I knew a Ponty driver who would shunt the goods yard at Crane Street, and I would have a ride in and out, up to the gate and back, but couldn't stay too long as I had work to do in the Booking Office. This happened once or twice.

On a Thursday I would travel with the station master to Branches Fork with pay. I

A 'Noah's Ark' brake van is seen stored in sidings at Trevethin Junction.

would walk up the line to Trevethin Junction and have a ride to Branches Fork in a 'Noah's Ark' brake van, which were comfortable to ride in. I would spend an hour at Branches Fork, then return to Trevethin Junction and walk down the line to Crane Street. After Branches Fork closed I went to Talywain to distribute pay.

I worked at Abersychan Low Level for maybe two years before being transferred to Pontypool Road. The station master was Les Birch, who had previously worked at Hagley station. Les later went to Pontypool Road as a supervisor, then to Newport.

I have always lived in Sebastopol and wouldn't live anywhere else. When I was at Crane Street the trains weren't very convenient from Sebastopol; it was all right in the morning for connections, but after work I would catch the bus or walk home. The Booking Office at Sebastopol was manned, and it was quite a busy station, with a porter on each turn. I went there once or twice to have a look at it – it was always spotlessly clean. A few of us would wait in the bus stop on the corner, and if the bus was full, as soon as the signal went up, north of the road bridge, we would catch the train. On a freezing cold day I would wait in the Booking Office by the road bridge to get warm; you'd see the train coming northwards out of the fog, and I would run down the platform to catch it to Abersychan.

I started in the Booking Office at Pontypool Road in 1960. Mr Peppin was the Area Assistant and was located at the middle of the platform; his boss was in the main office at Pontypool Road yard. There were two ticket collectors working early and late shifts. Miss Mount worked in the refreshment room. A preacher from Griffithstown did the station announcements from the Middle signal box on the station platform, and could be heard everywhere! The Divisional Office was above

Sebastopol Halt booking office, looking south on an unknown date. *Robert Hall*

Sebastopol Halt looking north on 8 August 1961. *M. Hale, Great Western Trust*

the Booking Office and used as flats; a driver from Pontypool Road and his family lived there. Underneath was the Booking Office, Coal Office and Engineer's Office. There was also an office where uniforms were kept.

The platform buildings consisted of the Ticket Collector's Office, Supervisors, Parcels Office, Area Manager's Office and Refreshment Rooms.

There were three of us in the Booking Office. One man did the parcels, while myself and the other man did the early and late shift and the Booking Office window.

There were four ticket cases, with stock tickets; they were sold for Scotland, Ireland, the Cambrian Coast, North Wales, and Newcastle (via Manchester). A lot of Cardiff passengers would book trains to Ireland.

A lift was used to carry parcels and luggage to and from the platform. It was costly to operate, using water, and was always breaking down. Passengers who couldn't use the steps to the platform would use it. One day there was a flood in the Booking Office, and passengers couldn't walk through the subway; they were brought in on a trolley, through the subway to the lift and on to the platform.

The working day, Monday to Friday, was 7.00am to 1.30pm, and 1.30pm to 9.00pm I would sometimes work all day on a Saturday to get a day off. On Sunday you would work from 8.40am to 11.30am to cover Barry excursions and Birmingham trains; the regular turn on a Sunday was 1.00pm to 9.00pm.

The North Bay at Pontypool Road was not used in my time, but the South Bay was used for the Vale of Neath trains.

The carriage sidings were shunted all day. Coaches for the Vale of Neath were stored here, while carriages were cleaned in the sidings opposite the South box. A lot of shunting was done in the evening for the Liverpool train, which continued on to Glasgow. When the Cardiff portion arrived at night there were two coaches for Glasgow, which were full of sailors from the West of England; they would book 2nd Class and travel 1st Class!

Some trains were split for different destinations upon arrival at Ponty. The morning Manchester would be split, and the afternoon Bristol to Plymouth train would have one part that travelled to Cardiff.

Trains came down overnight until 6.00am from places such as Bolton. Between 12.30pm and 1.00pm four trains went through Ponty – two Paigntons, one Penzance and one Plymouth.

Two extra trains at Pontypool Road on a summer Saturday were the Llandudno and Blackpool trains. Another train was the Birkenhead 'Flyer', which included a buffet coach. It was the 4.40pm express non-stop to Shrewsbury and Birkenhead.

Two trains combined at Crewe, to travel south to Plymouth. Two coaches from Glasgow for Penzance were shunted onto the Manchester to Penzance train at Crewe, then they were then removed at Plymouth or Penzance. In January 1963 the Manchester train went forward about 3 hours before the Glasgow coaches come in at Crewe, as the Glasgow train was stuck in the snow on the West Coast. The Manchester train came down at about 4 in the morning, and the two Glasgow coaches missed it at Crewe, and were a few hours late when they arrived at Pontypool Road at about 7.20am.

The reason why I remember this is that I was distributing the cash to the Booking Office. I used to wait until about 7.30am until the rush had gone, and that particular morning I heard the sound of an engine that I thought sounded like a 'Duchess'. It was No 46222 *Queen Mary*, which came down from Crewe and worked the train to Bristol. I have since been told by Peter Day, a former Pontypool Road fireman, that it worked back from Bristol and was on Pontypool Road shed for three days, and worked the parcels back up to Crewe. When he got there to have a look at it, it had just gone out on the parcels!

Abergavenny was a minor station, but was added as an additional stop for the Manchester train. Sometimes the train wouldn't stop, and run straight through to Pontypool Road.

The Vale of Neath line was always quiet

The Eastern Valley

for passengers, but busy on bank holidays. Not many tickets were sold for this route, but there was a lot of transfer of passengers from other trains. I used to do the books at Pontypool Clarence Street and would travel there by train. I could do the proofs in 20 minutes. Mrs Haddigate worked there for some years and did the tickets, and it was covered by the Pontypool Road station master. I remember Swansea tank No 80133 working the 1.05pm Neath train to Swansea; I went on this train with that engine a few times. Normally it was a '41xx' or a pannier tank. I was on the last train from Swansea, with pannier tank No 4639. When the Vale of Neath closed, Pontypool Road station was dead quiet. That's when parcel trains became important.

In 1963 I was on the last train from Brecon, and nearly got snowed up! From the following day the cutting at Pontypool Road was snowed up for a few weeks. Porters on the platform played football; one lost his slip-on shoe and it landed on the glass roof.

Pensions and pay were sorted at the Booking Office for the staff at Pontypool Road shed and yard, and the Vale of Neath and Eastern Valley stations at Clarence Street, Hafodyrynys, Crane Street, Pontnewynydd yard and Branches Fork, and the signal boxes on the Eastern Valley line from Trosnant Junction to Blaenavon Furnace Sidings. Trosnant signal box was the dirtiest, as it was manned by relief signalmen who didn't care; all the other signal boxes were kept spotless. Chris Deakin worked in Coedygric box by Coedygric Viaduct when I was doing the pay at Pontypool Road.

Six of us did the pay in the Booking Office on a Thursday. I worked from 8.00am to 10.00pm, making it up at the station then

At Trosnant Junction on 3 June 1963, Trosnant sidings are on the left, serving the Third Line for traffic from the Blaendare Trading Company, for shunting Mynydd Maen Colliery, and the Gwent Wagon Works. Following closure of the Third Line in 1959 a connection at Trosnant was made with the Vale of Neath line.
M. Hale, Great Western Trust

going to Pontypool Road yard main office. You had to take bookings at the window at the same time.

I took the pay to Clarence Street station, which covered the station and signal box. From there I took a taxi to Glascoed where the permanent way people resided, and also Little Mill signal box. In later years I would also go to Hafodyrynys Colliery Halt with the pay – you'd sink in coal dust!

After visiting Glascoed I would travel to Little Mill station to pay the permanent way staff based in the Waiting Room there. At 1.25pm the 'County' came down from Shrewsbury, followed by the Midland loco on the Manchester train. The whole Waiting Room would shake when this went past!

After work I would on occasions walk home through the shed with the Inspector from Pontypool Road station. When the shed had diesels, the roof was removed to save paying rates!

The Pontypool Road offices at Coedygric Viaduct were, from the south, the signing-on point, Inspector's Office and General Office. In my time the canteen had gone, and was used as a rest room; in diesel days the enginemen would go there if they weren't wanted urgently. At the north end was a store room accessed by steps, where lamps were oiled. It was a short room, and quite big; it went over the yard master's office (located in the General Office) and General Office. We used to store the paper here for recording such things as wagon numbers; most of the invoices were also stored here and gathered dust! During my time there were all these engine books, all mint, and no one wanted them, so we burned them on the fire!

Three members of the Slade family worked at Pontypool Road. Graham's father was a Signal Inspector in the offices there, Graham was a shunter, and his younger brother was a signalman at Llantarnam Junction. Graham later moved to Newport station as an Inspector until he suffered from ill health.

I finished at Pontypool Road station in 1964 or 1965 and transferred to the Area Manager's Office at the Main Office at the base of the steps by Coedygric Viaduct. I was doing bonuses and didn't like it, and later went to Cardiff.

11. Railway enthusiast John Williams

Thomas Williams, colliery engineer

My paternal grandfather was Thomas Williams, who was born in 1849 at the Old Furnace on the old Hafodyrynys Road, and died on 26 January 1925, aged 76. He was buried in Panteg Cemetery in a three-depth double grave. He had a brother Harry, and 12 children: daughters Lil, Doll, Florence, Rose and Ethel, and sons Tom, Jim, Will, Cliff, Enoch, Stan (who was killed in First World War) and Horace.

Thomas Williams began his working career at Tirpentwys Colliery as a blacksmith, and his brother Harry was the engineer at

John Williams's great-grandparents, Thomas Williams and his wife Sarah-Anne. *J. S. Williams*

The Eastern Valley

the colliery at the time it was sunk. Harry later got a job in the Rhondda Valley as the engineer for a group of collieries at Llynipia, for the Cambrian Colliery Company. This was in the early 1900s, and Thomas Williams succeeded him as the engineer at Tirpentwys.

Thomas was the engineer when an accident occurred at the upcast pit on 1 October 1902. A piece of wood near the boxed-in surround of the head gear became dislodged, and got caught between the pit wheel and rope, prising the rope off the wheel and causing it to snap. Eight men were killed as the cage was nearing the surface, and descended back down the shaft. A piece of rope was kept at home for years afterwards. The inquest stated that the plank of wood had been left nearby after recent maintenance work on the pit wheels.

Thomas was responsible for installing the new pit frame and winding engine house at the pit, which were at 90 degrees to the old ones. A German-built vertical winding engine was installed, while the pit frame was unique to South Wales at it had two wheels, one above the other. The old winding engine house was still present in 1978 in a ruined condition.

In 1912, during a strike, Thomas worked with his son Tom to operate pumps on the pit bottom to prevent the pit from flooding. While working at Tirpentwys he had a house built at 8 Bryn, St Luke's Road, Pontnewynydd.

Some time later the Company Secretary, Ben Nicholas, gave Thomas the sack so that he could give the job to his own son Norman. Norman was later gassed to death while working on his car in a garage on Leigh Road – he had left the engine running with the garage doors shut.

Thomas took odd jobs until John Paton, who owned several collieries, lived in Blaenavon and knew he was looking for a job, offered him the post of engineer at Hafodyrynys Colliery (Crumlin Valley Colliery), which was being sunk in 1912. Bricks to line the shaft are said to have come from the old Park Terrace School, Pontypool, when it was being demolished. The first coal was up the pit in 1915. Glyn Colliery also came under his responsibility, and he would walk there every day as part of his daily duties. He moved to a large house adjacent to Hafodyrynys Colliery, and lived in the side nearest the wood; the other part was occupied by Mr Silcox, the under-manager.

Thomas's sons all worked in the coal industry. Cliff worked in the power house at Tirpentwys, and was the last person to drive the steam winder at the Glyn Pit, Pontypool. He used to keep the Bridgend pub in Cwmfrwddoer, as well as working at Tirpentwys. He died at 54 years of age. Will worked at Tirpentwys in the engineering shop but emigrated to Australia; upon his return for a visit to the UK in 1963, he went to Tirpentwys and saw marks in the lathe that he had put there as a boy. Jim also worked in the engineering shop and lost a finger. He was sent to Preston for training at an engineering company and never came back – he met a headmistress while staying in lodgings, they married, and he lived in Southport. Enoch worked underground driving haulage engines. Stan also worked at Tirpentwys, but was killed in the First World War. Tom, too, worked at Tirpentwys and married a widow who had a son from a previous marriage; he kept the Bush pub at the top of High Street, Pontypool.

Horace worked at Tirpentwys as a mechanical fitter and a rope splicer. He was a lieutenant in the First World War, and upon returning home he worked at Hafodyrynys Colliery. On 29 November 1918 it was reported that 'Mr Horace Williams, The Villas, Crumlin Valley Colliery, Pontypool, has received a commission in Royal Navy Service. He joined up in April 1915, saw much active service, and was attached to the King's Liverpool Regiment at Oswestry. Sub-Lt Williams is the son of Mr T. Williams, chief mechanic at the Crumlin Valley Colliery. Previous to joining the army, he was employed at Tirpentwys Colliery. A brother, Armourer-Staff Sgt Stanley Williams, AOC, was killed in March this year.'

Memories of Abersychan

Great Western '42xxs' stopped outside Garndiffaith Junction signal box, at the south end of the viaduct, with empties for Blaenavon, awaiting a coal train heading south. Once this had passed, the '42xx' would proceed the full length of the viaduct before crossing onto the single-line section to Blaenavon High Level. Sometimes I would climb the stones on top of the cutting at the north end of the viaduct and watch this. On the left, behind Garndiffaith signal box, was the triangle connecting Golynos Junction to Talywain Junction. Hired '2021' Class pannier tanks for Blaenserchan Colliery would be turned on this triangle if they had arrived the wrong way round.

There were three roads at the south end of the viaduct. The left-hand road was a siding, used by Vipond's engine for pushing full wagons of coal for storage. When I was playing near Albert George's farm at Penyrheol (Waterworks Lane), returning trains could be seen passing Varteg station with the engine pulling against pinned-down wagon brakes.

Also observed from the top of the cutting at the north end of Garndiffaith Viaduct was a '14xx' tank engine with an auto-coach

John Williams's great-uncle, Stanley Williams, is seen in his army uniform during the First World War. He was killed in action in March 1918. *J. S. Williams*

Garndiffaith Junction, looking south, on 2 June 1963. *M. Hale, Great Western Trust*

travelling northwards. Little Webb 'Coal Tanks' would pull trains of coal northwards from Abersychan & Talywain station, and return with trainloads of coal, or wagons full of railway wheel tyres for the 'Big Four' railway companies, as well as solid wheels and axles from the solid wheel and axle plant at Blaenavon – this was before 1941.

I lived at Melrose Cottage, Abersychan, as a young child and the cutting was accessed by a path at the side of the embankment. There was a path along the side of the railway from Blaenavon, and at the cutting it went up and over to the Abersychan side. Behind the left-hand wall on the Garndiffaith side of the cutting was a coal seam (on the left going towards Blaenavon). North of the cutting was Six Bells, where there was a halt and a pub. From the pub, on the Garndiffaith side of the railway, '42xxs' could be heard coming down from Varteg station, identified by the tick of the vacuum pump and the clank of the side rods.

My Sunday School teacher was Arthur Jones, who lived on Stoney Road, Abersychan, and worked at Lower Varteg Colliery. He was called up in the early part of the Second World War, but there was later a coal shortage and coal mining became a reserved occupation. He returned to work at Lower Varteg and was killed on the afternoon shift.

Above: Ganger Brian Toddle walks the line between the snail creep bridge and Six Bells Halt in December 1969. *J. S. Williams*

Right: Looking south towards Six Bells Halt on the same day, empties for Blaenserchan Colliery are seen in the distance being hauled by an unidentified NCB steam locomotive. *J. S. Williams*

When the railway bridge at Six Bells was built, around 1878, several fossils were found, and these were displayed in a cabinet, with a model coal train on top, in Victoria village Junior School. On the Blaenavon side of this bridge there was a rail flange lubricator, on the left-hand side looking towards Blaenavon; as wheels passed over it, oil was released on to the rail.

Great Western '42xxs' and '72xxs' would be watched from the road outside the Big Arch; they would shunt in the evenings and the loco would pull a train of 20-ton loco coal wagons onto the Big Arch and propel it forwards; the engine would slip when doing this.

David Morgan from Blaenavon was the Permanent Way Inspector on the Top Line, and lived in Blaenavon. He had worked for the LNWR, and later the LMS.

Jack Timms lived next door but one to me, and was the guard on the first runaway train from Blaenavon High Level, with driver Edgar Charles and fireman Ted Ashman, with engine No 4264 from Pontypool Road shed. Uncle Jack Smith was walking up Viaduct Road when the first runaway came over the viaduct. The other runaway train came down in daylight, and John Gollop, who worked in the goods office at Talywain, saw it come through, and stated that it could have been stopped if enough people with brake sticks had been around, as it had started to run away above Talywain.

In the 1930s and '40s a GWR 3,500-gallon tender was stored just off the side of the large wooden goods yard at Abersychan, later the location of the doctor's surgery.

Bottom Line memories

During the war there was a landslip near Cwmavon, past the Den bridge. One Saturday night a man was walking down Cwmavon Road and heard a rumble – the river had washed away part of the embankment. He notified the signalman at Cwmffrwd, and there weren't any trains to Blaenavon Low Level for a while. A steam crane was used to lift massive blocks into the river.

A pannier tank with two coaches, one being an auto-coach, could then go only as far as Cwmffrwd Halt and onto the single-track section as far as the Rising Sun pub, then reverse into the down platform. If there were more than two coaches, a '41xx' or '51xx' would be on it.

As kids we would collect on the platform at Cwmffrwd, and the footplate crews were quite friendly. The driver would show us the lubricator on the driver's side, and show us the gobbet of oil going up the glass. If they had more than three coaches, the engine would uncouple, travel to Abersychan and come back up on the wrong road. If we were lucky we would have a ride on the engine, over the points at Cwmffrwd and back down the other side at Cwmffrwd Halt.

A bus service was provided working to Blaenavon due to the line being blocked. Joe Paul worked for the Western Welsh bus company, and is remembered by the police for driving his bus too slowly on the straight mile by Pimlico garage in New Inn!

'Notching up' would occur just outside Abersychan station coming up, where the road now goes through onto the old railway line. Sometimes, when doing this you would see circles of steam going up, like smoke rings! As the crew pulled out of Cwmffrwd Junction to go from the double to the single line, they would also notch up there.

Cwmffrwd Incline was used to transfer the products of the British Ironworks to the tram road that ran from Pontnewynydd Canal Wharf to Cwmffrwdd. Wilfred Carter, an electrician at Blaenserchan Colliery, said that his father could remember rails on the incline. He lived in the house right up in the garden, next door to Rollei Kinnersley.

Talywain old yard sidings were always full up with wagons. From Golynos Junction the railway crossed over the road and into four sidings, which continued down to the back of Talywain Church to the edge of the road. Beyond the sidings you could walk down the Cwmffrwd Incline and could just about see the remains where it swung around on to

The Eastern Valley

the Bottom Line at Cwmffrwd Junction. There were Great Western signs, one near the road on Manor Road and one near the bottom of the incline, supported on pieces of broad-gauge rail.

You could hear the clanking of the side rods and big ends on the connecting rods of '72xxs' at Varteg, when steam was shut off. They would pull through Varteg, where there was a swamp in the track; if the wagon brake levers weren't pinned down properly they would bounce up and down. When I was working at Hafodgwelog Farm opposite Varteg as a teenager, you could hear the noise from there.

My parents said, 'Get yourself a job at the Big Arch.' I went to see my Uncle Will Harper who was the Foreman of the Wagon Shop, and a week later I was told to start. I joined the staff of the Wagon Shop at the end of 1947; the mines had just been nationalised. I had a hard time initially as I was Will Harper's nephew. Uncle Will Williams also worked there.

I can remember '56xxs' shunting at the back of Talywain goods shed, where there were three sidings. Twenty-ton loco coal wagons containing lump coal were stored there; this was coal from Blaenserchan and Llanerch Collieries (until September 1947, when it closed). This would be shunted during the day, and I used to watch this when I was an apprentice in the Wagon Shop.

In the early 1900s a Mr Parry was an engine driver at

Staff pose for a photograph alongside Cwmffrwd Junction Signal Box ground frame, date unknown. *J. S. Williams collection*

Cwmffrwd Junction looking north, after closure in April 1962. *J. S. Williams*

North of Varteg station was the Vipond Colliery Incline, opened in 1860. The remains of the incline bridge are seen in December 1969; it survived until at least mid-1983, when it was dismantled for scrap, once the Top Line had been lifted to the end of the all-welded rail north of the Jackdaw Quarry. *J. S. Williams*

the Big Arch. His widow lived on the lower part of Pisgah Road, in a red-brick house; this was in 1943 or 1945, and I used to deliver milk there. Opposite Pisgah Chapel there was a row of houses where German bombers dropped a string of time-bombs in the war; the Army defused and removed them.

Top Line memories

Before the war, when we were kids on Viaduct Road, I can remember seeing Blaenavon Top Line iron ore trains running up over the viaduct. I recall LMS engines working them, and they were banked. The front engine would be in the Garn Wood, above the cutting at the north end of the viaduct, and the banker would be still on the Garn Viaduct; I watched them at lunch times, when I was taking shopping messages to Aunty Doll, who lived in No 6 Manor Road.

My father-in-law, Frank (Ernest John) Oates, worked as a collier at Garn Drift, Big Pit, Blaenavon, as well as at Vipond's Top Pits. He could recall Vipond's wagons crossing the Ash Tree bridge at Varteg on the LNWR Top Line to Blaenavon. He recalled the weekly Blaenavon coal output for the Top Line was 21,000 tons per week, while Garn Drift produced 1,000 tons a day during the day and afternoon shifts.

Trains of locomotive tyres came down from Blaenavon, for the major locomotive construction companies. They were used on Great Western 'Kings'; those for No 6000 *King George V* were made at Blaenavon (as recorded in Great Western literature in the possession of my old friend and fellow railway enthusiast Mark Vrettos).

The *Free Press* of Friday 29 October 1943 recorded a runaway incident the previous Tuesday under the headline 'Coal Train Crash at Pontnewynydd – Railwaymen's Lucky Escapes'.

'Commendable coolness and presence of mind was displayed by the engine driver of a runaway train at Pontnewynydd on Tuesday.

A train of 27 wagons on Blaenavon Top Line – nowadays used only for mineral traffic – got out of control and crashed into a stop block in a siding between Gwenallt signal box and Branches Fork, Pontnewynydd. The train had apparently started to run above Talywain, and signal boxes received the emergency bell. It was realised that the train had to be stopped at Gwenallt to prevent the risk of still further confusion if it went on to the junction with the main Blaenavon-Newport line at Trevethin Junction.

The driver, William Dauncey, of Capel Street, Newport, courageously remained on the engine throughout, but on his orders the fireman, John Lawrence, Brynton Road, Newport, jumped. Sydney Robert Perett, Phillip Street, Maindee, also remained at his post. Fortunately, the driver and guard did not sustain serious injury; the former was hurt in the right arm and left leg, and the guard was cut by glass splinters and was injured in the head. The fireman escaped with slight injuries to the head and legs.

More than 20 of the wagons piled up in a high mass of twisted distorted wreckage. The engine carried away the stop block and continued until it was embedded in a bank. While the down line was completely blocked with wreckage, obstruction on the up line was mainly capsized coal. Once this was cleared, the line was free. Most of the wagons were of the 20-ton type, and the train was carrying a load of hundreds of tons of coal.'

The loco was No 4233, and it was a train of loco coal destined for Taunton loco depot.

Another similar incident took place on Monday 3 January 1944, with engine No 4264, as reported in the *Free Press* the following Friday under the headline 'Valley Train Runs Away':

'Mr Edgar Charles, aged 43, is a patient at Pontypool Hospital, suffering from a fractured thigh sustained on Monday evening when a mineral train (of which he was driver) of 44 trucks ran away soon after leaving Blaenavon, and raced for several miles down the mineral line to Gwenallt signal box, near Pontnewynydd, where it was switched into the stop blocks and broke into three parts.

The fireman, Mr Edward George Ashman, 2 Chapel Lane, Pontnewynydd, and the guard, Mr John Timms, 168 The Highway, New Inn, were uninjured, although the latter is suffering from shock.

A few months ago a similar accident occurred on the line, when a mineral train had to be diverted into the stop block at Gwenallt.'

Many years later, on Monday 6 April 1970, I went to Blaenavon Furnace Sidings to take photographs, and the sidings shunter, Herbert Harrington, was there. I asked him, 'What time does this train go down?'

He replied, 'Why?'

I said, 'I want to photograph it coming through Varteg station.'

Herbert said, 'Have a word with the driver.'

When I told the driver that I wanted to take a photograph of his diesel going through Varteg station, he said, 'You go on down, and when I'm down a bit further I'll give a few toots on the horn to let you know I'm on the way.' That's how I got to know Gordon Secker, Bert Hardman, Bill Morgan, Albert Stopgate, Horace Morgan, Ted Preece and Gus McSheely, and the Macteer brothers, all drivers at Newport Ebbw Junction.

Edward Wyman hadn't been up to Blaenavon a lot with the diesel as a second man, but he was driving it back down. We'd just come through Blaenavon High Level station and his mate, driver Bert Hardman, said, 'You'd better put a bit of power on here to get around this curve.' We stalled at Cemetery Sidings, Blaenavon. We had to pick up a few brakes there to pull away, and that's why I took the photos there; this was before vacuum brakes were fitted to the wagons.

Gus McSheely would stop in Varteg station with a train of loaded coal from Big

Pit and pick up old blue edging slabs he'd purchased from British Rail (carved from quarry stone, around 2½-3 inches thick) and put them in the back cab of the diesel. They were about 3 feet long and 18 inches wide. He'd be stopped there for 15 or 20 minutes. He lived on the side of the main line between Newport and Severn Tunnel Junction and stopped on the main line near his garden to drop off the stones.

I would get on at Panteg Junction; sometimes you'd have a toot from the driver to have a ride up to Blaenavon. Terry Macteer drove the last passenger trip to Furnace Sidings on Sunday 13 April 1980, and I met him at Newport station. I got on the footplate when the train returned from Blaenavon Furnace Sidings; he would have given me a footplate ride if he had known I was on the train!

I photographed Ted Preece driving his diesel over Big Arch with *Islwyn* underneath.

One day I was visiting Rollei Kinnersley at Talywain signal box. Ted Preece had brought up a Class 08 diesel shunter for the opencast at Blaenavon with a train of empties, but I didn't have my camera to photograph it! From my diary I see that I got on the diesel at Coedygric Junction at 8.10am and arrived back at Coedygric at 11.20am. Rides from Talywain to Blaenavon would start at Talywain at 8.30am, or a later train at 11.25am. Engine numbers recorded on the Blaenavon branch during 3 September 1970 to 30 March 1972 were Type 3 diesel-electrics Nos 6969, 6959, 6997, 6982, 6991, 6958, 6906, 6987, 6918, 6939 and 6999.

The following footplate rides on the Top Line are recorded in my notes:

- Friday 24 July 1970: footplate ride given to sons Nigel and Philip Williams from Talywain to Panteg and Coedygric Junction.

Ted Preece drives a train of coal from Blaenavon south over the Big Arch at Talywain, while Andrew Barclay 0-6-0ST *Islwyn* waits outside on Friday 4 June 1971. *J. S. Williams*

- Thursday 3 September 1970: No 6969 from Panteg Junction to Furnace Sidings with Driver Bert Hardman and Secondman Edward Wyman.
- Friday 1 January 1971: Jeffrey Petty (the son of Pontypool Road Guard Ron Petty) and sons Nigel and Philip had a ride down from Blaenavon Furnace Sidings to Panteg Junction with Driver Gordon Secker on No 6976.
- Tuesday 1 June 1971: No 6918 at Talywain, departing for Blaenavon at 11.25am, Driver Terry Macteer, Secondman Glyn Powell.
- Wednesday in July 1971: Blaenavon, Talywain, Panteg & Coedygric Junction, Driver Gus McSheely, Secondman Huw Rees.
- August 1971: 'Baby Sulzer' from the New Sidings to Panteg Works, Driver Dennis W. Collett, Secondman Mostyn Richards (Severn Tunnel Junction) – see page 241.
- Friday 26 August 1971: 8.10am from Panteg & Coedygric Junction on D6939 to Blaenavon Furnace Sidings, returning about 11.20am, Driver Gordon Secker, Guard Bill Prowse.
- Wednesday 12 April 1972: trip to Blaenavon from Talywain (8.30am)

The last footplate ride I had was from Panteg & Coedygric Junction to Blaenavon Furnace Sidings on Saturday 22 March 1980 with my son Nigel on Class 37 No 37276; it was a light engine movement to check the condition of the track prior to an enthusiasts' special train, the 'Red Dragon', hauled by two Class 31 diesel-electric locomotives.

On 18 December 1982 Class 37 diesel-electric locomotive No 37099 is seen at Cwmffrwdoer, waiting to haul the last train from the Eastern Valley to Llantarnam Junction and on to Radyr yard. *Phil Williams*

On the same day No 37214 is seen at Cwmffrwdoer, at the truncated south end of the horseshoe curve. It is standing on top of the closed branch line to Tirpentwys Colliery. *J. S. Williams*

A Type 3 69xx diesel-electric locomotive enters Pentrepiod Halt with empties for Blaenavon Furnace Sidings on an unknown date. *J. S. Williams*

The Eastern Valley

North of Pentrepiod Halt, the RCTS Eastern Valleys Rail Tour of Saturday 8 May 1971 heads south. It left Newport at 10.20am, and arrived at Panteg at 10.47am, leaving Blaenavon at 11.46am. *J. S. Williams*

Pontypool Road memories

Charlie Hewlett was the shed master when I was teaching engineering at Pontypool College of Further Education in the 1960s. Brian Farr was a Ponty apprentice and one of our students, who was noted as being absent from lessons, so I had to go to the shed to discuss this with Charlie Hewlett. That's how I met Les Norkett. Some time later, Glyn Price, the College Principal, said there was a vacancy for a technician in the engineering department, and suggested that I go to the loco shed at Pontypool Road and ask around. (Glyn Price was the father of opera singer Dame Margaret Price.) I went to the shed and that's how I met Marcus Hunter, who had the job. I went there one day and Marcus said to me, 'Put this in your pocket.' It was a maker's plate from a 3,500-gallon Churchward tender.

In the mid-1960s I was wandering around Pontypool Road yard on my morning off from Pontypool College. The nameplate was still on the West Junction signal box, and a man from mid-Wales – Builth Wells or Radnorshire – was trying the cut through the rails by the West Box leading to the sand drag, using a burning torch. He couldn't get the torch to light. I showed him how, and was given some point rodding, which I now have stored in my garden, together with some point rodding from near B&Q in Cwmbran. I also have a notice from near the West Box, which I bought direct from BR.

In 1969 a 4,000-gallon tender was stored in the Northern Sidings against the stop block by New Road. It was later taken to the station and cut up at the end of the siding against the Civil Engineer's Office; somewhere I have a picture of it.

The Crane Street signal box nameplate was left on the side of the line at the station when the box closed. I went to see Roy Evans, the Permanent Way Inspector, at the offices at Pontypool Road station. I asked him if I could buy it. 'Oh no, don't touch that – I'll get it brought down,' he said. That was the last I saw of that. Mike Elvy was a Staff Manager at Pontypool Road station, and if I spotted a railway sign I would see Mike and ask if I could buy it. He'd say he'd look into it, and wanted to know the full details of where it was – and that would be the last I'd see of the sign!

'Westerns' and 'Warships' to Hafodyrynys

I made the following sightings of these diesel-hydraulics on the Hafodyrynys line:

- circa 5 June 1970: No D1000 *Western Enterprise* at Hafodyrynys Colliery
- circa 7 August 1970: No D1048 *Western Lady* at Hafodyrynys Colliery
- Thursday 9 April 1971: *Western Champion* passing over the Skew Bridge at Griffithstown.
- 25 April 1972: No D1053 *Western Patriarch* at Panteg & Coedygric Junction.
- date unrecorded: No D1007 *Western Talisman*
- Friday 17 July 1970: No D818 *Glory* at Hafodyrynys

Preservation

In 1971 the Eastern Valley Railway Company was formed with the intention of preserving the railway line from Llantarnam Junction to Big Pit, Blaenavon, and to haul coal trains to Llantarnam Junction using steam locomotives. This would be done by using restored engines from Woodham's Barry scrapyard. It was known at that time that British Rail wanted rid of the line and had offered it to the NCB, but they didn't want to have to maintain it.

My connection with this began when I saw a sticker in a car in Newport advertising the Eastern Valley Railway Company. A meeting was held early in 1971 in the village hall in New Inn. It was the brainchild of Maurice Shepherd and Graham Hanns, who both worked for the Post Office. Maurice was a former Pontypool Road fireman and is nowadays credited with saving *Duke of Gloucester* from scrap; in 1967, while working as a postman, he noted a tag on it in Cashmore's yard in Newport, stating 'Woodham Bros, Barry'.

There was great interest in the scheme, with locos Nos 9466, 7200 and 6960 being lined up. At the meeting there was opposition from the embryonic Dean Forest Railway, while Peter Rich, involved with restoring No 5322 at Caerphilly, feared such a scheme was too close and they would close. Peter is nowadays well known for his work in designing the 'Saint', 'County' and 'Grange' replicas, as well as the LMS 'Patriot' loco project. He sadly died from cancer on 1 February 2014 aged 73.

No 5643 had already been selected, and was painted green in Woodham's yard. Maurice Shepherd and Graham Hanns had selected suitable engines, for purchase by a Mr Pugh. The asking price was £2,200, and it was complete except for boiler fittings. Pontnewydd yard was chosen, as it was empty. However, there was no track, so four lengths of rail were dragged from the side of the BR line at Pontnewydd, and sleepers were bought from Pontypool Road yard; Graham Hanns transported them on his tractor and trailer. A buffer stop was bought from Godfrey Road, Newport. Dave Williams, a welder at Pilkington's glassworks, Pontypool, joined the project at this point.

No 9466 was the next engine for consideration. Myself, David Williams, a fellow railway enthusiast, and Phil Williams, a former driver at Pontypool Road loco shed, went to Woodham's to prepare No 9466 for removal. The loco was already stripped of parts, and there was no motion or side rods. Another pannier tank was selected with motion, but the wheels were in the wrong

The Eastern Valley

My old friend David Williams and the author are seen at Dai Woodham's scrapyard at Barry Docks in 1972. Ex-GWR No 6024 *King Edward I* is behind us. *J. S. Williams*

position to remove the inside motion. The outside rods were removed and a jack put under the crankpin and the wheel skidded to rotate the motion. The inside motion was then stripped, and placed in No 9466's cab. The loco was painted in red oxide. The asking price was £2,000.

In 1971 a group of youngsters arrived at Woodham's and started work on 'King' Class No 6024 – they were laughed at! Ex-driver Phil Williams left a big bag of my tools on No 9466 and they were never found again. In the event No 9466 was not bought, but is now a well-known loco on the preservation scene.

A stores van was required. Dave Fry had been the foreman loco fitter at Pontypool Road and was a friend of Phil Williams; he now worked for British Rail at Cathays depot, Cardiff. A coach van was looked at and it was full of locomotive water gauge glasses. It was £300, and was to be hauled by rail to Pontnewydd and jacked across to the loco. However, it wasn't bought. Graham Hanns had a tractor and trailer and went to Woodham's where a van body had been bought – but it was too big for the trailer, and was taken to Cwmbran by lorry.

No 5643 arrived at Cwmbran hauled by Wynn's Transport of Newport in September 1971. It was televised by the BBC, which had filmed various locations on the line to Blaenavon. These were early days in preservation. I made some replica number plates for the loco and Maurice Shepherd fitted a safety valve bonnet. Len Morgan, the well-known Abersychan photographer, took photos for a calendar. When it rained we sheltered in the cab. I had drilled out all the studs on the backhead and safety valve base, and made and fitted new ones. Ken Lewis, a blacksmith at Deep Navigation Colliery in Treharris and a member of my model

A 'Western' diesel-hydraulic passes ex-GWR 0-6-2T No 5643 at Pontnewydd Yard, Cwmbran, in 1972. *J. S. Williams*

John Williams's replica number plates and the safety valve cover made by Maurice Shepherd are seen in this publicity shot to publicise the Eastern Valley Railway Company preservation scheme. *J. S. Williams collection*

The Eastern Valley

Activity at Pontnewydd yard, with the Eastern Valley line heading south on the right. *J. S. Williams*

engineering class, had profile-cut the blanking plate for the safety valve ready for the time when the boiler would be hydraulically tested in the far distant future. Then there was some bad news. Rumours circulated that the loco hadn't been paid for, and interest in the scheme waned.

The stores van had been used for storing newspaper to raise funds, but kids burned it down. British Rail was demanding £6 a week rent for the loco as they hadn't given permission for it to be stored at Cwmbran. John Wynn, the haulage contractor, also hadn't been paid. Graham Hanns had given Wynns my number at Pontypool College, and they were demanding £150 payment. I took John Wynn to Graham Hanns's home and he paid the bill.

A little while later I was working on No 5643 when a car arrived at Cwmbran. It was Joe Greenwood from Carnforth – he was well known in the 1970s and 1980s for his involvement with Flying Scotsman Steam Services. No 5643 was subsequently moved to Carnforth, possibly within six months of leaving Woodham's. It was the only loco ever to leave Woodham's without being paid for.

As a footnote, a little later I was to meet Dr Peter Beet who had bought No 5643 – he was a GP in Morecambe (I had last met him in 1978 when I visited him with Ray Towell from Carnforth, later with the NRM, and recently retired). Peter called to see me and had a second-hand 10x injector from Swindon Works. He had two new castings and wanted them machined – but there were no drawings. These castings were for No 6960 *Raveningham Hall*, then owned by Brian Thomas, who worked for the International Paint Company. This was 1971, and getting boiler fittings machined for Barry engines was unheard of – it was before Hugh Phillips Engineering had started. I machined the injectors for this loco, as well as the safety valve, and the parts were taken to Swindon Works for setting on the safety valve rig; my friend, former Pontypool

Road driver Phil Williams, travelled with me.

In 1975 I travelled to Carnforth to fit the parts so that the loco could take part in the 'Shildon 150' celebrations in 1975 (we slept in a coach outside the shed and *Flying Scotsman* was being worked on at night – the corridor tender connection had been pulled off the back of the tender and welding repairs were being undertaken). A gentleman form BAe Warton also worked on No 6960, then would rush off and be involved in test flying of aircraft. I received a 'Castle' Class nameplate from Brian Thomas for doing this work. No 6960 is now owned by Jeremy Hosking.

At this time I was approached by Peter Rich at Caerphilly to machine the axle boxes for Ivatt tank loco No 41312, as they were short of money and couldn't afford to pay for the work (John Mynors owned that engine, together with No 7808 *Cookham Manor* and No 5322 – he was a surgeon living in Rhodesia). I have since been involved in machining parts, free of charge, for No 6990 *Witherslack Hall*, clack valves for Nos 4150 and 9681 at the Dean Forest for John Harris, injectors for Steve Whittaker for No 2857 at Bewdley, and the brake valve for No 4930 *Hagley Hall* at the Severn Valley. My last job was to machine compound firebox crown stays and nuts for *Nora*, for the Pontypool & Blaenavon Railway, in the late 1980s. All these jobs were done for nothing, in the days when volunteers would work on privately owned locos.

On some of these projects I was promised a footplate ride when the engine was steamed, as a thank you for my free work, but that never happened. Now of course you have to pay people a *fortune* to work on your engine!

No 7754 at Coedygric Sidings

The last steam loco to use the line was No 7754, which was brought under its own steam from Elliot Colliery, New Tredegar, in January 1969 to Coedygric Junction, Panteg, where it was stored in the sidings near the Coedygric Road Viaduct. It was driven by Len

The author's father, J. S. Williams, is seen with self-made aluminium cabside number plates for ex-GWR '57xx' Class 0-6-0PT No 7754, for use on the Dorset Railway Society rail tour, the NCB-loco-hauled Talywain-Blaenserchan Colliery special, on Saturday 21 March 1970. *J. S. Williams*

Jones, a driver on the NCB railway system at Talywain. The injectors had failed, so it was diesel-hauled to Talywain a day or so later. Coal Board engines would run under their own steam when transferred to another colliery, with a BR pilotman.

When diesel-hauled from Talywain in 1970 it was stored at Ebbw Junction diesel depot with a broken spring en route to NCB Mountain Ash. 'Austerity' *Llewellyn* was also diesel-hauled from Talywain to Hafodyrynys in 1970, making it the last steam loco to use the line. This was during the Whitsun miners' holidays.

I made number plates for No 7754 from

aluminium, for the trip to Blaenserchan Colliery on 21 March 1970. I borrowed the cabside number plate from No 7771 from ex-Newport fireman Cyril Goulding, who was a regular fireman on that engine.

12. Railway enthusiast Terry Jones

Blaenavon Bottom Line

'20xxs' worked the passenger services until 1932, when they were replaced by '64xx' tank engines, which had a lower tractive effort, but a larger wheel diameter.

A '20xx' would sometimes replace a '48xx' tank on the auto-train to Monmouth, if the '48xx' was being repaired; No 2041 was recorded on this route.

The Glascoed train is recalled as being hauled by two panniers, during the war and after, in the afternoon; it was in Abersychan station around 5.00pm. The train would pull up to Blaenavon, then the leading engine would run around to the back and take the train down; the train engine would run back down light engine.

Panteg Steelworks

I worked here from 1952 until the beginning of 1960 after undertaking National Service in the RAF. I looked after the Nominal Ledger for the steelworks. At the top end was the Fitting Shop, Foundry and the main steelworks, while the Sheet Works was the bottom end. Sid Foster was responsible for the Material Ledger, which covered the cost of materials, such as pig iron, while the Nominal Ledger held every account and covered everything from silica sand to loco costs. At the end of every month was stock-take time. When Sid was off, I would do it. Tins of aluminium shot were used for the electric furnaces, and worth a lot of money.

Panteg Steelworks' products were mainly sent out by road, but everything came in by rail – scrap, pig iron, etc – via Panteg sidings. The output was at the bottom end; the four-high mill was down there, producing steel sheet for the car industry in the Midlands and London, which was sent to Longbridge and to Ford at Dagenham.

Steel was categorised into two types

A pair of 68xx diesel-electric locomotives head south from Panteg station towards Sebastopol Halt on an unknown date. Panteg Steelworks in visible on the right, as well as the remains of the down line. *J. S. Williams collection.*

– carbon steel (known as acid steel) and stainless steel. There was a big demand for acid steel.

There were five open-hearth furnaces and three electric arc furnaces (for stainless steel, known as furnaces S, T and U – S and T had a 10-ton melt per shift, and furnace U had a 15-ton melt per shift). The open hearth output was carbon steel; when they tapped the 50-ton furnace it was teemed in a pit, into a ladle, and the ladles teemed it into ingots. Bars came out of these, which were taken to the bar mill and finished. The four-high mill at the bottom end cold-rolled steel sheets. Coils were also produced, for the car industry.

Furnaces were filled using 'chargers', machines on 4ft 8½in-gauge track, and these could travel outside to collect scrap steel for the furnaces. They had a big bucket on the front to collect the material, then a ram would come out and tip the bucket so its contents went into the furnace. Up to 50 tons of scrap for melting would be loaded into the furnace at a time.

All the basic slag that came from the steelworks after the melt was loaded onto wagons, and a loco took it down to the slag tip at the bottom end of the Sheet Works. Fisons, the fertiliser people, would use this.

Two new Peckett locos were bought when I was working there, and their cost came through on my ledger in 1954. The Coal Board was paying around £11,000 for a 'WD' 'Austerity' loco, but the new four-wheeled Peckett locos were £9,000 each, being regarded as costly. These replaced the locos *Italy* and *France*, which were left outside unused for years. Peckett No 1 is recalled being there. Panteg works had two locos working all the time, used for internal shunting off the works yard, and bringing in materials from Panteg sidings, or sending traffic out. Steel sheet mainly went out by road.

13. Wagon Examiner Andrew Atkins

I started on the railway in July 1961 as a wagon oiler at Hafodyrynys New Mine. I progressed to Wagon Examiner and moved to Pontypool Road, where I worked in all the yards. My mother died aged 47 in 1966 and I was offered a relief job, as an examiner and shunter. I have worked at all the collieries in Gwent, including Newport Alexandra Dock and Newport Mon Bank. I started at Oakdale Colliery in 1967 until 1989, when I was transferred to Ebbw Vale for 12 years, then to Llanwern Steelworks until 2007, when I retired.

At Hafodyrynys New Mine my first job was to oil empty British Railways 16-ton wagons at the tippler. There were four shunters at the mine – two at the top end and two at the bottom end. Three trains of empties would arrive in the morning from Hereford, Droitwich and the Hereford Pool, which was

Former Pontypool Road staff wait for a northbound steam special to pass through Pontypool Road station. Wagon Examiner and Shunter Andrew Atkins is on the left, with Firemen John Pike and Colin Polsom.
J. S. Williams

The Eastern Valley

a train of 50 empties. The empties were put in different sidings at the top of the screens for different sizes of coal – 'peas', 'beans' and small coal. Markham Colliery sent a lorry that was filled with small coal that wasn't washed.

The weigher put the wagon labels on and the examiner examined the wagons. To move an empty wagon forward once they'd tipped it, they would drop a loaded wagon against it. Tom Hewlett would say to me, 'Come on, sonner, I've made the tea.'

The Swansea vans came through about midday, for Manchester Docks. We had a cabin at Hafodyrynys close to the track; we'd see the train come through and get out of the cabin in case it derailed!

Wagon repairs

I worked at Hafodyrynys for a fortnight, and was then off for a fortnight for the annual miners' holidays. During the holiday in 1961 I was sent to work in the wagon repair shed at Pontypool Road. Everything was repaired here, including the wheels. Crippled wagons were sent for repair – there were so many that some were sent to Thomas Ward of Cardiff to be repaired. Any type of wagon was repaired. Every afternoon, after the staff had finished for the day, the repair shop would be shunted.

If we didn't have to go underneath, the wagon was repaired outside, but anything requiring lifting was repaired inside the building. You would often have a hot axle box on a train for Quaker's Yard. My first job was to fit a hammer head to its handle; I then assisted on wagon repairs.

Pontypool Road

I worked in all the yards at Ponty, working nights on 12-hour shifts, cycling to Ponty yard via the Black Ash Path.

The Loop cabin was between the wall at the Skew Fields and the South Sidings signal box, at the top end of the Loop Sidings. We used to break up our coal outside, and I was there one night when a pair of feet came by. It was a tramp. I said, 'Mate, why don't you whistle or do something rather that turn up unannounced?' We had a bench locker that we sat on, with a mirror so we could see who was outside. A couple of nights later a lot of police arrived, looking for Harry Roberts, from Blackpool, who had killed two policemen.

I was on Ponty station one night when a pigeon train arrived, and Charlie Reynolds, who was then a fireman, was relieving it. I asked, 'How far are you taking this?'

'It's nothing to do with you,' replied Charlie. So I turned my shoulder and left.

My mother passed away aged 47 in 1966. My boss said to me, 'Whatever you do, don't rush back. Before you come back, come and see me.'

I was off a fortnight, then he said, 'I've got a job for you.' I was put on relief work at Ponty.

I started at the station as an examiner, examining passenger trains and freight from West Wales that had relief at Ponty. I would examine the train on the Up Goods line by the North box. When examined, I would ring the signalman and say, 'OK, go, relief is on.' I don't think a train left on my shift without me examining it.

I once examined wagons in the Guest, Keen & Nettlefold's siding at Cwmbran, which had labels reading 'Panama Canal via London'.

Oakdale and Markham Collieries

When Ponty shut in 1967 I was offered three jobs; the first was Llanwern, and the second was Oakdale Colliery. I went to Llanwern first but didn't like the work, so I asked my boss if I could go to Oakdale Colliery instead.

I started in 1967 and worked there for 22 years until it closed in 1989. Coal was sent to three places in Margam, including Margam Yard and Margam Hump, as well as to Llanwern Steelworks. Oakdale had one train of empties in the morning, which went to Markham Colliery to pick up coal for washing at Oakdale, as Markham had no washery. The driver of the Markham train would leave the engine at Oakdale, and officially would catch a bus back to Ebbw Junction. However, a second Oakdale train would arrive in the morning, and the driver of the Markham would ride back with the driver of that train. The bus stop at Oakdale was by the Rock pub, which involved walking down a steep hill. However, getting a bus to Newport was difficult.

We travelled to Markham on the train, in the guard's van. The guard said, 'Sit down, Andy.' It was a rough ride! Instead of going up quietly the driver would open right up! You could hear the empty wagons bumping each other. Halfway between Oakdale and Markham was Llanover Colliery, which belonged to Abertillery Water Board. There was one of our wagons in their siding, and I took the red clip off it.

Driver Ted Preece was a former Ponty driver based at Ebbw. If Pontypool Rugby Club was playing at home we could look out and watch. One day we had a derailment at Oakdale, on our property. Ted come up with the breakdown vans and said, 'How long are they going to be?'

I said, 'I don't know, Ted – why's that?'

'Ponty are playing home,' replied Ted.

I said, 'Have a word with Control,' and was in the cabin when he rang. He said, 'Yeah, they're chock-a-block up here with coal wagons. You give me permission to leave the breakdown, and I'll give them some space up here.' And he did, and went home! Ted got away with it. 'Zapper Ted' we used to call him, and his son is the spitting image. In later years Gloucester men would work a train of coal from Oakdale for Scunthorpe Steelworks.

Chapter 2: Main-line memories

Pontypool Road station

Pontypool Road station was relocated and rebuilt in 1909. Shortly after opening, a GWR '3800' 'County' Class 4-4-0 is seen with a southbound passenger train.
J. S. Williams collection

Pontypool Road station is seen during the Edwardian era after reconstruction in 1909.

In this view looking north, carriages are seen in the South Bay on the left and the siding on the right. The photograph is taken circa 1911. *Kidderminster Railway Museum*

Left: Again looking north, carriages are seen in the carriage sidings on the left, and in the South Bay on the right. The photograph was taken circa 1922. *Kidderminster Railway Museum*

Right: Viewed from the end of the South Bay, an ex-GWR '41xx' Class 2-6-2T is seen on the up platform road, date unknown. *R. G. Nelson, Terry Walsh collection*

Main-line memories

Two GWR locomotives are seen on passenger trains in Pontypool Road station. On the left is 'Bulldog' Class 4-4-0 No 3424 *Sir N. Kingscote*, with 'Saint' Class 4-6-0 No 2905 *Lady Macbeth* on the right – the coaches in this siding were (generally) there for repairs. The short siding on the left was for changing engines, with the oil house for signals behind the buffer stop. Butt's Siding is not yet present – it will be on the right of the 'Saint', and was a short siding up to the Civil Engineer's Office. *Kidderminster Railway Museum*

Ex-GWR 4-4-0 No 3440 *City of Truro* and No 4358 are seen on the Down Main at Pontypool Road station on 18 May 1957 while working the 'Daffodil Express' from Gloucester to Neath, via the Vale of Neath line and Crumlin Viaduct. The photograph was taken by Driver Phil Williams's fireman. *J. S. Williams collection*

Pontypool Road Station Middle Junction is seen during demolition on Friday 4 December 1970. *J. S. Williams*

This is Pontypool Road South Bay, looking north. *R. K. Blencowe*

Main-line memories

Pontypool Road Ambulance Division are seen at the South Bay on an unknown date, with a shield that was competed for annually by Ambulance Teams within that Division. Donated by the Great Western Railway, it was presented by Joseph Shaw Esq KC. *J. S. Williams collection*

The Ambulance Division are seen again, outside the Refreshment Room, date unknown.
J. S. Williams collection

GWR '57xx' class 0-6-0PT No 9788 is in the bay platform at Pontypool Road with a train for the Vale of Neath line in August 1936. The water column and 'frost devil' are visible to the right, with 'Bulldog' Class 4-4-0 No 3308. *Kidderminster Railway Museum*

'45xx' 'Prairie' tank No 4593 acts as the Station Pilot, adjacent to the South Bay, on 4 November 1958. *D. K. Jones collection*

Main-line memories

1. Driver Tom Davis

Wartime memories

I was working the 4.29pm Bristol turn in June 1940. I am not certain of the date, but it was on the Thursday evening after the Sunday night when Bristol was bombed, and burned into complete devastation. We came off shed and were standing on the middle road at 7 o'clock when the sirens went, which meant to us a red air raid warning. The Traffic Inspector came to our engine and said, 'Driver, the air raid warning has just sounded and the signalmen have all switched out and gone to the air raid shelters, so there will be no movement until the all clear is given, so you and your fireman had best go to the shelter too.'

We closed down the dampers on the engine so that it would not make and blow off steam, and I sent the fireman to the shelter, while I remained on the footplate. I stayed there until a bomb dropped on the station and went right down the lift shaft, where it exploded, causing little damage, but that made it very necessary for me to go to the shelter too. We remained there until the night signalmen came on duty at 10.00pm and switched in; then the order came over the intercom for the crew of the Northern Pilot – that was us – and the crew of the Avonmouth to go to their engines, which we did. The air raid red was still on, but with the signals off, and no damage in front, the Avonmouth train left and proceeded to Stapleton Road, where they were stopped. They were warned that an unexploded bomb had dropped somewhere in the vicinity, and to proceed cautiously; this they did, but a few minutes later the bomb went off and killed both the driver and fireman.

We left at 10.15, still at the height of the raid, and although going very slowly we got away from Temple Meads and were nearing the huge gasometer at Stapleton Road when

Ex-GWR '57xx' Class 0-6-0PT No 7724 is the Northern Pilot, shunting loco coal for the Northern Sidings. It is seen just south of Pontypool Road station. This was the last engine to use Branches Fork loco shed, during the week prior to its closure. *Kidderminster Railway Museum*

a shower of incendiary bombs bounced off the gasholder, lighting everything up like daylight, but we kept going until we passed through Filton and down into the Severn Tunnel, which I may say I was very glad to enter, to get away from the inferno that was being caused by Hitler's bombs.

With a little silent prayer on our lips, we passed through Severn Tunnel Junction to the water troughs at Undy, where we scooped up a couple of thousand gallons of water from the troughs between the rails and arrived at Pontypool Road to be relieved by the men that would take the train on to Shrewsbury, then on its way to Crewe and Glasgow.

As we had more than 2 hours to go before completing our rostered turn's work – each turn was diagrammed for 8 hours – we booked to go to the engine shed, and take charge of a small tank engine to work a colliers' train to take miners to work on their night shift at Hafodyrynys Colliery, and bring back those who had completed their afternoon shift.

At one time the coaches of the colliers' trains had just plain, ordinary wooden interiors, but with colliery baths now being provided, the miners left their dirty working clothes at the pit, and travelled home in their nice clean clothes; therefore the railway company provided nice upholstered compartments for them, which was a little more amenable. Also, with further mechanisation and improved pay and working conditions in the coal mines, cars began to appear at the collieries, indicating a new affluence in an industry that had suffered over the years following its Trojan efforts to gain recognition for the valuable contribution being made to the country's economy. Unfortunately for the railways, the siding and platform that were once used for the colliers' trains were later removed, and the area became a car park for the new generation of coal miners.

Having now disposed of the coaches of the colliers' train in the sidings for cleaning by the carriage cleaners, ready for the next day's use, we took our engine to the shed and booked off duty at 11.30pm, which was a little more than our standard 8 hours, but was accepted by management and men in the interest of economics; this rostered working kept the engine crew fully occupied for a full turn.

Red air raid warning

During the Second World War, with the blackout and all the other complications, there were operational changes. Firstly, there were the emergency instructions that were issued for use during air raids. When the red warning went out from the central air raid point for that particular area to all signal boxes, every train was stopped by the signalmen and the drivers verbally informed that enemy aircraft were in the locality, and that the train could proceed under the air raid red precautions. They were able to continue at a speed of 15mph to the next signal box, and be prepared to stop at any obstruction that might be encountered. Well, this was all right in daylight when one could see any obstruction or damaged track that might be ahead, but it was in the dark that most of the raids took place, and that was a very different circumstance, so you just had to carry on and hope for the best. Furthermore, it was easy enough to carry out these instructions if it was a light train on an easy gradient, but when the train consisted of 14 eight-wheeled coaches and you had to stop at a signal box on a heavy gradient of 1 in 90, as was often the case, it was a little difficult trying to make a get-away and still conceal the light from the firebox that was created by the extra heavy blast on the fire when restarting.

On one occasion, having arrived at our destination with a mixed freight train from the Midlands, the Yard Inspector came over to the engine and said that the air raid red had just been given, and that all the staff had gone to the air raid shelter. At a local steel works a furnace had been tapped, and the white-hot metal running out of it was making it impossible to stop the light showing through the sides and roof of the works, making it a good target for enemy action. He also told me that on my train next to the engine I had nine vans of highly explosive TNT, destined for an ordnance factory nearby. With that information both the fireman and myself were quick to enter the air raid shelter. Fortunately the raid went over without dropping anything on what really would have been a devastation target.

Double home working

This kind of working started at 2.30pm on Monday afternoon and terminated at 11pm on Tuesday night, which meant that for the three turns you were booked to work you were away from your home for 94½ hours of that week – which is why any footplateman who liked the comforts of his own home intensely disliked double home work.

2. Fireman Derek Saunders

Local workings

No 349, an 0-6-2 tank, was the bad one. It was put on the Abergavenny banker, but was a bugbear and wouldn't steam very well. I had it on the Abergavenny banker with Driver Les Mathews. At Abergavenny Junction, when banking a train, it started to blow off.

'I take my hat off to you,' said Les.

I said, 'Wait till I put the feed on, it will be goodnight!'

It was a hopeless engine. Les was the only driver to take his hat off for me!

No 385 of the same class was a regular on the Little Mill Pilot, and was OK. Little Mill Sidings were used to store trains for

A general view of Pontypool Road Station South Junction, with the signal box on the right. The line going off to the right in the background leads to Crumlin and Neath, and that to the left to Newport. To the right of the signal box was the site of the former Admiralty Sidings. During the war, when Derek Saunders was a cleaner, he was walking between the two lamp posts in front of the South box at night when he was nearly run over by an Ebbw Vale train being propelled into the Northern Sidings. *Kidderminster Railway Museum*

Pontypool Road Station South Junction is seen again looking north on Sunday 19 July 1970. A Type 3 diesel-electric loco is seen on the Up Goods line, while on the right is the old station master's house for the original Pontypool Road station. *J. S. Williams*

Nos 4923 and 6433 are seen at Abergavenny Junction station, circa 1957. No 6433 is waiting with a passenger service for Merthyr. *Stan Brown, D. K. Jones collection*

Above: Pontypool Road's '56xx' 0-6-2T No 5659 is seen at Llanvihangel station in 1958, having banked a northbound train. *J. Chalcraft, Railphotoprints*

Cardiff and the Vale of Neath. A lot of trains would terminate there, coming down from Hereford. I don't recall Little Mill brickworks being shunted during my time.

A '45xx' 'Prairie' tank would be used to work empties into ROF Glascoed, and pull out an ammunition train. This would initially proceed to Pontypool Road yard, but was destined for Newtown, near Chester; it was worked by the Usk Pilot.

There was a train to Usk at 7.10am. The Usk Pilot would go to Usk, then to ROF Glascoed. When I was courting, my girlfriend would arrive at Usk

Ex-GWR (Rhymney Railway 'P' Class) 0-6-2T No 83 acts as the Station Pilot at the north end of Pontypool Road station, waiting on the Up Main, circa 1952. In the background, a northbound freight is seen on the Up Goods Relief line. On the right, on the Up Platform road, the old inspection pit is seen. This engine would stand on shed all day long; a pair of them from Aberbeeg would bring the workers' train to Glascoed, and one of the pair would return to Aberbeeg light engine to take the crews back, and the other would go back to Ponty and pick up the train in the evening. *Kidderminster Railway Museum*

On 16 July 1953 a double-headed Glascoed to Brynmawr workmen's train approaches the north end of Pontypool Road station on the Down Main, hauled by ex-GWR '4575' Class 2-6-2T No 5520 and '56xx' Class No 6672. Two flat cordon wagons carrying gas tanks to supply gas for carriage lights are seen stored alongside in the down carriage sidings. *Kidderminster Railway Museum*

station and have a ride on the pilot engine from the station into the goods yard; it would be a '46xx' pannier. Perishable traffic went into Usk goods yard, as well as wood from there.

Driver Jack Drayton would ask the footplatemen at Ponty, 'How long is the turntable?' A lot of them didn't know, but they would reply, 'About the same length as it is from the top of the bank to the stop block in Usk Yard!' Jack had run away down the slope in 1947 and hit the buffer stop, nearly landing up in the allotments. He had been into every catch point and sand drag there was!

Monmouth, Ross and Mitcheldean

There were two goods trains to Monmouth, one in the morning and one in the afternoon. The morning goods was the 7.50am working, while the afternoon Monmouth goods would require the footplate crew to travel to Monmouth to work back.

I had a few turns on this route. I have worked to Monmouth, Ross and Mitcheldean on the way to Gloucester. You ran round the train at Ross to go to Mitcheldean. This was a train of coal, and the loco would be a '45xx' tank engine. You would use a bunker of coal and come back via Ross. I never worked Monmouth Troy to Symonds Yat with steam, but worked the Class 37 diesels to Tintern Quarry when based at Severn Tunnel Junction diesel depot.

Main-line memories

Above: Ex-GWR '14xx' Class 0-4-2T No 1422 takes water in the North Bay with the Monmouth auto-train on 19 March 1955; the service was withdrawn in June of that year. *R. K. Blencowe*

Right: Another Monmouth auto-train is seen on 19 March 1955. *R. K. Blencowe*

Long-distance workings

The 'Marazion' was a cauliflower train to Shrewsbury and beyond from Marazion in Cornwall. Tomato trains from Jersey are also recalled. These trains were not very heavy.

Trains from Manchester and Crewe were split at Pontypool Road station; the first half went to Bristol, the second half to Cardiff, or vice versa. Trains of 14 coaches were typical, having a load of 450 tons, but 15-coach trains were rare.

I recall working the 4.48pm from Cardiff. On the Monday we had No 6000 *King George V*, in a blue livery, and all the kids were swarming around it. The following day we had a '63xx' tender loco and no one wanted to know!

Trains would sometimes have the Station Pilot on the front, but the load was only 450 tons.

One day a down express was running towards Abergavenny Monmouth Road and came under the bridge at the north end of the station. The signalman had set the distant for the down loop (in error) behind the down platform, and sent the express that way – it was a wonder it didn't derail.

Above: Pontypool Road's '53xx' Class 2-6-0 No 5388 is at Abergavenny Monmouth Road station having the brakes picked up, some time in the 1950s. *Stan Brown, D. K. Jones collection*

Right: '63xx' Class 2-6-0 No 6316 approaches the north end of Abergavenny Monmouth Road station, via the Down Goods Relief line, on 4 April 1951. *Stan Brown, D. K. Jones collection*

North to Hereford

At the top of Llanvihangel bank, about a train length south of Llanvihangel signal box, was a farm crossing and the stop board was situated there, on the down road to Abergavenny. We would always stop at the board and the guard would pin down brakes, unless the train was vacuum-fitted. There was a down refuge siding at Llanvihangel summit into which you could reverse you train to allow a passenger train to pass. If there was a passenger about, the signalman would ask if we would push back into this refuge siding – we would have overtime for doing this! Sometimes the signalman would say, 'Do you want brakes?' If we said yes, we would pull forward to the stop board to have the brakes pinned down. The brakes were picked up at Abergavenny Monmouth Road, either on the main line or in the down loop.

Occasionally I worked the branch from

Main-line memories

The first BR-built 'Hall', No 6981 *Marbury Hall*, passes through Llanvihangel station with an up express on 18 August 1962. *R. C. Riley*

Pontrilas to Hay, with No 5818. This was the one place where the fireman dropped the fire. Cyril Davis was the lighter-up at Ponty, and he would go to Pontrilas to light it up, otherwise there was no shed man there. I would finish my day pushing the fire through the bars; there was hardly anything to drop as the fire was so low, and you could push it through the bars with a pricker. You would work one trip to Hay and back, with shunting in between.

There was a munitions factory nearby. The boss would go there once a week and supply loco coal. One set of loco men was stationed there, who would also work the munitions depot.

Between Pontrilas and Tram Inn was St Devereaux, which had a goods shed where sugar beet was shunted.

Just after you cleared the main line at Red Hill Junction, Hereford, you had to put brakes down to proceed to Barton, the city's freight depot. This was where Driver Jack Drayton ran away with No 6872 *Crawley Grange* and smashed the front end. There was a train in front, standing at Barton opposite the loco depot, and Jack couldn't stop, so ran into the back of it.

We would work a train of cider apples to Hereford in steam days, relieving the train at Ponty station. We would have a '28xx', '38xx' or '68xx' on this job, and would work the train to Red Hill Junction and stop opposite Hereford loco depot, where we would be relieved by Hereford men. They would then work this train into Bulmer's sidings, which were known as Worcester Sidings, and were located opposite the cider factory.

In my time loco coal was taken to such depots as Tyseley and Wolverhampton only as far as Hereford, as double home working had stopped; before the war Ponty men had worked through to the Midlands with these trains. Double home working reappeared in the 1950s, and Newton Abbot men started to go through to Shrewsbury. When this happened, Ponty lost work.

Hereford men were known as the 'white-faced men', as Hereford cattle had white faces. They would deliberately run trains late, and would ask for relief at Ponty. I would go to the station in all weathers to relieve them and bring their trains into the yard and put away their engines while they were in the shed having food. Ponty men would also have to get the Hereford engine ready for the return working, yet Hereford was taking freight work from Ponty.

The Super came up there one day and watched the Hereford men at the loco shed. They put the bag in a full tank for 20 minutes, delaying the return working. Ponty got a few jobs back.

When I was on the Local Departmental Committee (LDC), which was the Union Committee, I got to know the diagram people at Paddington, and they discovered how Hereford was getting work from Ponty. A Hereford man called Mr Elliott, on the Hereford LDC, was friendly with a man in the Paddington Diagram Office, taking Ponty work to Hereford – this was in the 1950s and 1960s. I would play hell about this and put in suggestions, including working through to Birmingham on the 9.06am, but management wouldn't have it.

Working to Shrewsbury

We worked the 9.26am and the 8.27pm turns. We took water on the night 'Salop' at Ludlow water troughs. There was nothing on the side of the track to indicate where the troughs were. On one occasion a fireman didn't pull the scoop up quick enough and picked up part of a sleeper, which marked every crossing to Hereford.

The Bishop's Castle branch was marked by an abandoned railway cutting on the left-hand side just above Craven Arms, past the signal box and under the road bridge heading towards Shrewsbury. Older drivers I worked with could remember the rails being there, but they had been removed before I started on the railway. The branch was accessed via Stretford Bridge Junction, north of Craven Arms station. (Author's note: the branch closed on Saturday 20 April 1935, and the last demolition train left the line at Stretford Bridge Junction on 21 February 1937.)

You returned from Shrewsbury by way of Church Stretton, Marsh Brook and Marsh Farm Junction. There was a disused branch line at Marsh Farm, where the Royal Train was stabled when the Royal Family were visiting Shrewsbury. They would stop in the hotel at the Long Mynd. The branch used to go to Buildwas.

At Shrewsbury, at one time I worked to Crewe bank when driving, but never as a fireman. I also went to Cotton Hill on the Chester road. You rarely went to the shed as you had enough coal to come back, and would just shovel it forward.

Worcester

We went to Worcester, but not very often. We would go both ways – from Hereford via Shelwick Junction, and from Gloucester, on passenger and freight turns. We worked goods trains to Newlands near Gloucester.

Cardiff workings

The Little Mill Sidings to Cardiff Pengam goods ran at 6.55pm, and returned with mixed traffic for the Northern Sidings. One evening I was on this turn with a '72xx' tank working bunker-first to Cardiff. At Pontypool Road the engine stopped at the end of the platform, and I saw some Borstal boys on the platform and said hello to them. They got on the train, and I spotted them leaving it at Newport when the train stopped there. At Cardiff Pengam about a dozen police with flashlights were in the siding waiting for the train – the Borstal boys had escaped!

Main-line memories

The returning Ponty train started from the other side of the railway, at Pengam coal yard. A '42xx' would be the main engine on this job. On reaching Ponty, at Panteg Junction you would have a banker up through the cutting to the South Sidings.

We would use a tender engine on the Coleham Sidings to Cardiff turn, using the Old Monmouthshire line to go to Newport. Cardiff Tidal Sidings was a Ponty job, and we'd use any engine; it would branch off at Pengam.

Newport and Bristol workings

I was working a train of coal to Uskmouth at Newport, having left Ponty at 6.00am, and was moving from Sherbourne Road to New Inn. My driver was Jack Brisk from Cornwall, who wasn't very familiar with the road. He passed the signal at Uskmouth and said, 'Oh dear, there's a catch point up a bit further.' Our loco was a '72xx', working bunker-first. I had booked a removal van for 8.00am, and had visions of the last pair of wheels dropping off the track through the catch points. However, we came to a crossing instead of a catch point.

The 6.15am Exeter, later the 6.15am Severn Tunnel, worked from the New Sidings to Panteg Junction, then to Severn Tunnel. It consisted of clay empties for Truro and St Blazey, together with traffic for the London road. It was re-marshalled at Severn Tunnel Junction, for its onward journey, but I never worked it.

With a freight train you'd fire before entering the Severn Tunnel, then near the bottom of the tunnel the regulator would be opened. If the banking engine wasn't assisting as you wanted, you'd put some coal on to make some smoke – then the banker would begin to help!

We quite often worked to Temple Meads, with two or three booked jobs. We worked the 'seasons trains' (holiday trains) to Temple Meads via the St Philip's Marsh loop.

Loco memories

Sometimes an engine's reversing spring was not set right, and on locos with a lever reverse such as a '41xx', '42xx' or '28xx' the driver would have a job to pull the lever back and could damage his back. On one occasion I had to submit a report to support a driver who had injured his back in this way.

Hot axle boxes were not common. The only hot box on a loco I had was when I was a fireman to Bill Luxton, and we had a special passenger train working to Cardiff. Bill was driving the engine roughly, and I could smell that something was wrong. I levelled the fire on leaving Newport, and at Marshfield we had a hot box; the engine was declared a failure at Cardiff. Hot boxes were a regular occurrence on wagons that had grease axle boxes.

I worked on BR 'Britannia' 'Pacifics' to Shrewsbury. We learned by experience about the weak blower on these engines. You'd go through Dinmore Tunnel at nearly 70mph when coming back from Shrewsbury and to put the blower on full was useless; with the firebox doors open, flames would come back and burn you. You had to open the regulator when passing through tunnels, the blower was so weak.

You would relieve a crew at Ponty, and work the 'Britannias' from Cardiff to Shrewsbury, or to Cardiff. On one occasion I was with Dai James working the 4.20am from Shrewsbury. We relieved the crew at Ponty and worked to Cardiff. Dai would fire one day, and I would fire the next day. I drove from Newport, and discovered that both ejectors were open, the large and the small. We had relieved Bill Jancey, and upon leaving Newport I shut the large ejector, keeping the small one open. However, there was a leak in the vacuum, and in the tunnel at Newport the brakes were dragging. I therefore opened the large ejector and closed the small one. I questioned Bill about this. 'How would you manage if the emergency chord was pulled?' Bill hadn't given it a thought.

Of the other BR 'Standards', 9F 2-10-0s were used on freight trains.

Above: BR 'Britannia' Class 4-6-2 No 70023 *Venus* is seen at Newport High Street, working the up 'Capitals United' express on an unrecorded date.
Barry Foster

Right: Ex-GWR 'Star' Class 4-6-0 No 4049 *Princess Maud* runs light engine through Pontypool Road's down platform circa 1952. This manoeuvre is puzzling; maybe it is going the wrong way to couple onto the front of a mail train as a second engine, via the engine spur at the South Bay.
Kidderminster Railway Museum

The '30xx' 'RODs' would shake more coal off the footplate than ever got burned! They were run everywhere, and over the Vale of Neath line. Ponty had half a dozen or more, and No 3012 is recalled. They were known as the 'Ponty Castles'. They were all right when you were tired and wanted a 'doss' (a rest), as they had a long shelf alongside the firebox that you could stretch out on. They were an awful engine to work, but good engines in themselves. They would plod along – no matter how much steam you had, they'd still keep going. On one occasion at Newport I swept the tender clean and we had no coal on the main line! It may have been a light engine movement. We had to take coal at Ebbw Junction shed.

I saw one or two '78xx' 'Manors', but not many – they were not a patch on a '68xx'. *Frampton Manor* was at Ponty for a while.

I worked on '40xx' 'Stars' once or twice, but we had 'Castles' a fair bit in the top passenger link. You would relieve them at

Main-line memories

Pontypool Road station to Bristol or to Cardiff, only with Swansea passenger trains, or up to Shrewsbury.

The last of the 'Castles' were marvellous engines – they would run just like a watch. They were Top Link engines, and you would get them when you worked around the link. The Link lasted 12 weeks on 12 different jobs. I remember No 5005 *Manorbier Castle* (a rough engine), No 5008 *Rougemont Castle* and No 7023 *Penrice Castle*, which was a Worcester engine. The last named I regard as the best engine I ever had. I worked a 16-coach pigeon special from Pontypool Road to Bristol with this loco. The train had come down from the north, and I relieved it at Ponty.

'Halls' Nos 5975 and 5977 are recalled. They were used on

Ex-GWR '4073' Class No 5073 *Blenheim* shunts at Pontypool Road Station South Junction in July 1963. *www.britishrailwayphotographs.com*

'Castle' Class No 4076 *Carmarthen Castle* approaches the station on 17 June 1939. The oil house for signals is at the end of the North Bay, which contains a pit for oiling underneath and breaking up clinker using a sword pricker. *Kidderminster Railway Museum*

Ex-GWR '49xx' Class 4-6-0 No 4953 *Pitchford Hall* stands at Pontypool Road station, looking north on 28 September 1951. Note the freight trains on the left; freight going north would be for Little Mill, Chester, Shrewsbury, Crewe or Worcester depending on the time of day. *D. K. Jones collection*

Ex-GWR '68xx' Class 4-6-0 No 6829 *Burmington Grange* waits in the engine spur as stand-by engine, waiting to work a train northwards. Ex-GWR 0-6-0PT No 3609 waits in the platform with a Vale of Neath passenger service. In the background, ex-GWR '28xx' Class 2-8-0 No 2839 takes water on the Down Relief goods line. *ProRail*

freights. The 'Modified Halls' are also recalled – the '69xxs' weren't bad, but the '79xxs' were better.

The 'Granges' were regarded as being good. My fourth driving turn was on a 'Grange' to Shrewsbury, with a fireman who had never been out of the yard. Another driver tried to get me taken off the job, but the roster clerk said I had to do it as I was the nearest man for the job. All the time at Shrewsbury, standing for 3 or 4 hours, the engine never blew off at all. At Llanvihangel, coming back, the fireman said, 'Where are we now, mate?' I replied, 'You're almost finished now.'

As for the 'Kings', Ponty men would handle them like a 'Castle' and be rough with them. They would drive these engines using second valve and you'd be in trouble. They were used on the Shrewsbury jobs. No

6018 *King Henry VI* was a nightmare engine. I worked on it on the 8.27pm from Ponty to Shrewsbury, being the regular fireman, with Driver Bill Luxton. The engine wasn't steaming well. On this occasion, as a large number of complaints had been made about the engine, a Superintendent from Cardiff was riding on it when we relieved the Cardiff crew at Ponty station to take the train to Shrewsbury.

At Church Stretton we were low on water in the boiler. I was a passed driver at this time, and could do spare driving turns. Bill was driving, and as we topped the bank at Church Stretton I said to the Superintendent, 'If I was driving, I'd have stopped at Stretton and put some water in the boiler. If we go down to Leebotwood and the driver puts the brake on, the drop of water we have in the boiler will go the front and we'll scorch the fusible plugs.' Bill Luxton was looking daggers at me!

The Superintendent was a tall man and was knocking his head on the cab roof. We used a lot of coal on this job. The boiler tubes were clean, and No 6018 would make steam with the injector shut, but it was a poor steamer, and the previous fireman hadn't been doing his job when getting it ready. It was later discovered that the blast pipe joint was missing. When the smokebox door was opened you would see there were no ashes – they had all been blown out. The drivers would never think of it. 'Kings' also worked to Bristol.

In the spring of 1962, the year I went to Cardiff, I recall another outing with No 6018. After leaving Hereford station the next signal box was Brecon Curve and the signals were on. Creeping up to the signal, it came off, and the distant. My driver was again Bill Luxton. I shouted, 'Right away, distant off for Barr's Court,' and started to build up the fire, as it was a bad engine. Bill looked over the boiler and saw that the signals had gone back – there was a train in front of us, backing into a siding. If we had kept going, we'd have gone into it. Bill stopped the train and I went to the signal box.

The signalman said, 'I've made a mistake – will your driver say anything?'

I said, 'I don't know, we don't get on very well.'

The guard in the van was grinning. It was all hushed up. What had happened was that there were seven or eight permanent way men in the signal box and the signalman had become distracted. I couldn't understand it, however – if he had the home signal off as well as the distant for Barr's Court, he must had had his starter signal off as well. How could he have that signal at clear and dummy off for the train to set back? There must have been something wrong with the signals.

'43xx' and '63xx' 2-6-0s were used on coal trains, and were prone to slipping. No 6309 was used on the 7.45am Aberdare. No 6634 was a run-of-the-mill engine, and was later acquired by Pete Waterman. I can recall No 6666 on banking and passenger work; it was at Ponty all the time I worked there.

The '28xx' 2-8-0s were used on all the freights to Hereford. No 3833 is recalled. One day I worked with Don Willets on the parcels back from Hereford. I filled the firebox solid, put the tools away and washed my hands. Don said, 'What's coming off?'

I said, 'I've finished.'

Don laughed, but I never touched the fire until we got on the shed, and when I opened the firehole doors the bars were showing in places.

I would experiment with the injector. Coming through Pontrilas I would fill up the boiler to see how far we could go. The injector would next go on when passing the distant for Llanvihangel.

'28xx' Class 2-8-0 No 2863 heads a freight from the north, approaching Pontypool Road station on the Down Goods in 1963. The escaping steam indicates a leak from a joint at the exhaust injector grease box, between the frames. *ProRail*

I was with driver Tom Davis on a '28xx' to Hereford and had four wagons over load. There were 40 wagons of coal, and Tom said, 'Do you want a banker?'

I said, 'We'll be all right.'

The run up Llanvihangel was easy enough. I said, 'Try another four, Tom.'

Tom wouldn't try too many. It was a pleasure to go to work with him.

I worked to Aberdare with '28xxs'. No 2804 was the strongest. Driver Harold Good hit a landslide at Nantyderry in 1957 and I can remember seeing a bit of a tree on the front of No 2857, but not much damage had been done to the engine.

1961-62

A lot of turns on the Heads of the Valleys line are recalled, working on picking up the track from Ebbw Vale North to Abergavenny Junction in 1961-62. A pannier was used on this job. Track-lifting started at Ebbw Vale North, then to Beaufort and Brynmawr.

I was on a Blaenavon excursion to Barry in 1962, and on the way back we took water at Cardiff. My driver started away from there with a '41xx' tank loco, and it was priming, washing the lubrication out of the cylinders. I told him to put the loco one nick from mid-gear, and at Marshfield we caught up a train. 'Cor, he was going!' said the driver. I had learned about 30% cut-off at the improvement class.

3. Fireman Gwyn Hewlett

Runaway

In the 1950s I was firing to Wally McMale, an ex-Cambrian driver taken over by the Western Region, and he was hopeless! I was Secretary of the NAS, and instructing on steam and rules, and used to carry him about. We worked up to Hereford, and relieved Shrewsbury men at Ayleston Hill there in the early hours of the morning. We had a '59xx' 'Hall' loco, and a full train of coal. We were having water, and I was up on the tender. I saw the Shrewsbury driver give Wally a card of some sort, which he put in his pocket, and that was it. So I jumped the bag off, Wally blew up, and away we went. I said to Wally, 'What's in the card?'

He replied, 'I don't know – nothing really. It's nothing, I suppose.'

So away we went to Llanvihangel, where we had to have brakes down as we were a long train of non-vacuum-fitted wagons. I put the tender brake on, but it went too many turns and jammed, so there was no tender brake. I said to Wally, 'Get the brake in, Wally, there's no tender brake.'

But both vacuum needles were down to zero, so the Hiab band had gone. Now we were away and couldn't stop at the stop board – we were running away. I was blowing the brake whistle and the guard poked his head out, which made no difference whatsoever. We came down to the distant signal for Abergavenny Monmouth Road and went by all the signals. We went through all the signals at Penpergwm, and ran half way up the bank to stop at Nantyderry.

I walked back to the signal box at Penpergwm and said, 'Any damage?'

The signalman replied, 'You fellas are the luckiest guys ever! As you ran away and were blowing up at Abergavenny Junction, the "72xx" banker was in the platform having water, but the signalman had the presence of mind to ring the porters' room on the station. They shouted to the driver, who took the engine down through the crossover and into the other platform as you went by, otherwise you would have smashed into him.'

When we got to Ponty and back on to the shed, I said to Wally, 'Where's that card?'

It read, 'This engine must travel light only, no brake efficient at all.'

That was my worst incident, and was extremely frightening.

Collision at Ludlow

A call paper came up, and I had to travel to Shrewsbury as a passenger and make up with an LMS driver out of the Barracks (Coleham shed). We had an LMS 8F 2-8-0. I picked up the driver and we prepped the engine. Then it was tender-first to Harlescott to pick up the train.

The 8F was a good engine for steam. We went up the bank, over the top for Church Stretton, and dropped down for Craven Arms and Marsh Farm. The distant signal was on for Marsh Brook and we stopped. I could see a lorry had stopped on the level crossing. The signal protecting the crossing was on the end of the up platform, so I got off the engine and the signalman came to greet me.

'The lorry driver has fallen asleep, he's hit the signal at the end of the platform and broken it, and smashed his cab. There's enough room for you to go through on a green light.'

The driver was trapped in the cab of the lorry.

We proceeded through to Ludlow and the distant signal was off. The Penzance passenger was standing at the box at Ludlow with 14 coaches and two GUV vans (like parcels vans, but carrying Wills's cigarettes). It was hauled by ex-LMS 'Jubilee' Class No 45644 *Howe*. We then went round the corner and passed the Ponty parcels (Bristol parcels with Ponty men on), who were coming up. We proceeded down to Basin Hill at Hereford and had water. I went to the signal box to make a cup of tea.

The signalman said, 'That's a bad lot at Ludlow! The parcels has just run into the back of the express.'

I said, 'We passed him.'

But for 5 minutes we would have gone into the lot. The Ponty engine ended up inside the second GUV. It was ex-GWR 2-6-0 No 9306, hauling the 2.00pm parcels train from Penzance to Crewe.

The following night we worked the express, which normally worked up and down. I booked on at Ponty shed and my driver was Harry Robins. We walked to Pontypool Road station to relieve the Cardiff train to Shrewsbury, but had to go to Shrewsbury via Worcester because of the previous night's accident. The engine we had was *Spitfire*, one of Shrewsbury's 'Castles'. It was one of Shrewsbury's double home working engines to Newton Abbot – it was immaculate. While we took water at the top end of the platform the Bristol portion of the express came in. The Bristol men uncoupled their engine and the Station Pilot pushed the Bristol portion of the train onto the back of our train from Cardiff. We went to Hereford, then Ledbury, and had a pilotman at Worcester. We ended up at Wellington and went into Shrewsbury on the London line. We did a complete circle.

When we arrived at Shrewsbury they took the 'Castle' off us, and we walked to Coleham shed to find an old

Ex-LMS 'Jubilee' Class 4-6-0 No 45660 *Rooke*, working the 3.35pm Liverpool (Lime Street) to Cardiff train, takes water at Pontypool Road station on 6 June 1963. *R. H. Marrows*

On Sunday 11 April 1915 'Aberdare' 2-6-0 No 2604 overturned in the sand drag at Ledbury Tunnel after running away with Driver Frank Hazell of Pontypool Road. The engine is seen on the bank, with a pair of Dean 0-6-0 tender engines on the main line. *Terry Jones collection*

'49xx' already prepared for us. We backed onto the Post Office train to come back. We had picked up the express and left Ponty at around 8.30pm and arrived back there around 4.30am.

Other workings

There was a spate of work from Bristol at night, both coal trains and special trains. Other specials included banana trains, which were relieved at the station – they had worked in from Barry with a Cardiff man. They were trains of box vans, right away to Shrewsbury.

Cauliflower trains are recalled. These were heavy trains, using wagons like cattle wagons. You would have a 'Mogul' or anything, and would have bad trips and very little coal.

I liked to relieve the Weymouth trains at Ponty – these were trains of 14 wagons, full of flowers for Manchester or Liverpool. We worked these as far as Shrewsbury, then travelled home.

On a Saturday night or Sunday morning we would go to Marsh Farm to collect a train of coal stored there, returning bunker-first. A bad driver would say, 'We got a bad engine here.' We'd go into Shrewsbury, run round and back up so we come back head-first. But if you had a driver who wasn't very sure at Shrewsbury, they'd stick to bunker-first.

A '72xx' would rattle after it had been in service for some time – bolts would work loose, the bunker would move and also the cab. If you had it piled up with coal, there was dust everywhere going bunker-first. And they rattled like hell – a '52xx' didn't have this trouble.

The Dowlais tanks job came to Ponty, in the lower links. Jimmy Watkins worked it, and I worked it for relief from Ponty to Hereford; it was worked by a pair of Ponty '56xxs' through to Hereford, then another engine took the train northwards from there while the two '56xxs' worked back light engine to Ponty. You hadn't emptied the bunker, but a fair bit of coal was used.

Main-line memories

4. Fireman Charlie Reynolds Trips to Shrewsbury

The morning and evening 'Salop' jobs were one turn – to Shrewsbury. As the nearest fireman, you would go. I can recall working a week on the morning service with Driver Dick Everson. He was a very nice chap with chest trouble, but was a bit heavy with the regulator.

We went to the station to relieve the crew. The North Bay platform at Ponty was used for engine transfers going north, while the South Bay had a siding between the Vale of Neath line for the same purpose. The loco was a 'Hall' or a 'Grange', or maybe a 'Castle'. When we got to Shrewsbury we had to turn the engine. Then once you had hooked up against the train again, there was a 13-mile pull out of Shrewsbury. You would never let the engine blow off steam from the safety valves while you were standing in the station, as this practice was regarded as demonstrating bad firing skills.

On the return trip, coming towards Pontypool Road, Dick came across the footplate and said, 'That's your first trip over, Charlie. You've done very well. Have a hot bath when you go home and take things easy. When you get up in the morning you'll feel as though you are walking on air. Make certain you are in work on time in the morning. You come to work, and as soon as you are on the engine and get to Abergavenny tomorrow, the stiffness will go.' He was right, too.

On arrival back in Pontypool Dick caught the train to Clarence Street, as he lived in the town. I stayed with him to Clarence Street as his health was a bit under the weather, then I would take his ticket to the shed to book us off, to save him the walk. Sometimes someone would take my ticket back to the shed and Dick would catch the bus home from Pontypool Road. Otherwise he would book off himself, walk to Pontypool Road station to catch a bus or walk up to the Clarence, around the railway, depending what time of day it was.

Ten or 12 coaches were worked with one engine in steam days.

Ex-GWR '56xx' Class 0-6-2T No 5638 is seen on a freight train at Pontypool Road in 1963. *ProRail*

In this view looking south on an unknown date, Pontypool Road's North Bay is on the left, and on the right the up platform (with scissors crossover), Up Main line and carriage sidings. The Up and Down Relief lines are on the extreme right.
R. G. Nelson, Terry Walsh collection

Banana trains

These trains, heading north to Shrewsbury or Crewe, would use a '28xx', '38xx' or '53xx'. We worked them to Hereford, and Hereford men would take them to the Birmingham area. At one time the vans were all steam-heated, so you needed a passenger engine to put steam through. You would collect the train from Newport Docks. Fyffe's bananas were carried, using blue labels. The bananas were later loaded at Cardiff, then Barry, and Avonmouth Docks when Barry Docks stopped importing them. Newport Docks then imported Geest bananas, which had yellow labels. It was a good job to work – the train was braked right through and tight-coupled, so all the weight was moved at once.

The secret of the job was learning the roads. Working north from Pontypool to Hereford, upon leaving the station there was a 15mph limit, where you would pull out at the starting signal, and as a rule you could see the distant signal coming off at Little Mill. When you had done that, you opened up to reach the line speed for the train at Little Mill – freight trains required the couplings to be kept taught. You wouldn't shut off until you went over the top at Goytre, until all the train was over the bank; even if the signal was on, the driver would be easing down before you got there.

Once you got over the bank, the train would run all the way down to Nantyderry on a downhill gradient, and drop down steep to a dip over the river bridge at Penpergwm. Here the engine would be running flat out to get away from the train, keep the couplings taut and get around the corner. You then climbed all the way to Llanvihangel.. It wasn't so severe until you got to Abergavenny station, but from there going up it was a heavy pull with a freight train.

The engine would be opened up again at Pontrilas, then nothing at St Devereux.

Ex-GWR '36xx' Class 0-6-0PT No 3779 takes water while acting as the Station Pilot on 28 July 1963. *Rail-Online*

Main-line memories

Ex-GWR '66xx' Class 0-6-2T No 6693 waits in the engine spur while a train of parcels is sorted in the platform on 24 May 1960. *F. A. Blencowe, R. K. Blencowe collection*

Parcels on passenger trains

These were quite successful but disappeared. The station pilot at Ponty would be busy, with three or four trains coming in, and three or four trains to go out. Parcels for Bristol, Cardiff and Hereford were sorted on the platform – the Hereford parcels were placed on the up platform. A van would be emptied, and if it contained a lot of parcels it would be left there.

The parcel work finished when the railway started using DMUs. You would work to Shrewsbury, Cardiff or Swansea, or Bristol.

'Britannias' to the Severn Tunnel

Ponty men worked on 'Britannias' to and from Bristol, after the West Coast Main Line was electrified. They had a wide firehole door, and you fired them mainly in the back corners. They only had one damper, at the front of the firebox.

Consider working one of these engines from Bristol into the Severn Tunnel. There were two tunnels on the Bristol side – Patchway Tunnel and the Severn Tunnel itself. The first time you came over the drivers used to warn you, 'Whatever you do, close the damper and open the blower.' The engines were renowned for blow-backs, with flames shooting back into the cab when entering a tunnel. So you always closed the front damper and opened the blower hard on. It wasn't too bad at Patchway Tunnel as you didn't have the speed up, having come through a 30mph junction at the top of Filton Bank. The same applied for a Western engine, forcing flames and smoke back onto the engine.

Very often you wouldn't open the damper fully. When coming over the top from Bristol, when you hit the tunnels the effect was like a bike pump – as you pushed in, you pushed the air out. I didn't like running towards the Severn Tunnel with a 'Brit' – you had the blower hard on, shut the fire doors, drop the dampers and hide in the corner out of the way. The flames would shoot into the cab –

for a few seconds the air around the engine would come through the dampers and force the flames back, but after a few seconds things settled down. You ran with the back damper open, not the front, unless you had problems with the fire. There was a 2-mile descent on the bank, and with say 10 or 12 coaches they would start pushing you.

By the time you approached the tunnel, about a mile downhill further on, you were motoring. 'Britannias' had roller bearings and would run, while Western engines would stop – they were a lot freer running. On entering the tunnel the driver shut off steam, and the smoke and flames would ease up a bit. You wouldn't fire until you got to the bottom, but it was awkward. You would brake a bit in the tunnel to reduce your speed, but a lot of drivers didn't – it was a good bit of straight road. The engine would be opened up near the bottom of the tunnel, then you would open the front damper.

The tunnel had a quarter of a mile of flat track at the bottom, and there were warning lights telling you when you were approaching it. One light was located a quarter of a mile from the bottom, and there were two lights at the bottom, in both directions. Once you got by the first light, the driver would open the regulator to get away from the train (even more so with a loose-coupled freight) and to make getting out of the tunnel a little bit easier. If you ran to the bottom and then opened up, you would lose quite a bit of speed. You exited the Welsh end at about 50 or 60mph. You would 'have the boards' – a clear road – but the driver would ease down a bit for the crossovers at Severn Tunnel Junction, which you passed through at about 50mph.

When entering the tunnel from the Welsh end, you didn't notice it so much, as you passed over the crossovers at about 40mph, and didn't have as much speed up. But you opened up to get in and out as quick as possible.

If you required a banking engine through

Looking north towards Pontypool Road station, a North to West train hauled by an unidentified '4073' 'Castle' Class 4-6-0 No 5007 *Rougemont Castle* heads south. *Desmond Coakham*

the tunnel, it would be put on the front. You would be in one of the two goods loops at Severn Tunnel, where the booking-on point was. The banker would be in the bay at the station and attach onto you at the loop, or on the main line. You had a 45mph train, and were doing 45mph approaching the tunnel mouth. The bankers would take you through to Filton, where they would be taken off in the loop, or in a siding if going towards London. I never broke down in the tunnel.

'Castles'

Express engines had two shovels, in case you dropped one over the side or in the firebox.

Former GWR 'Castles' were used mainly on the northern trains. It would be a Cardiff engine, and you relieved the loco crew at Pontypool Road station, took the engine to Shrewsbury, turned it and came back.

Shrewsbury's 'Castle' No 5076 *Gladiator* was a Pontypool Road engine in the late 1950s. To work to Shrewsbury on a morning job you worked up and back down with the same engine. On the return you had relief at Pontypool. *Gladiator*'s booked turn was the 4.36pm to Bristol and back to Pontypool Road. This engine was got ready, and reversed to the station. The LMS engine would come off, be turned and taken to the shed for coal and water. The 'Castle' would then run to Bristol, where it was turned and returned from there at 7.15pm. Back at Pontypool Road it would couple up to the train from Cardiff; we were kept on the goods road to await its arrival. When the Cardiff train came in, the coaches were put in a siding, then the Cardiff engine would assemble the train and go to Shrewsbury.

The 'Castle' would then run to the north end of the station, drop back down to the West box and turn on the triangle, go into the loop by the Skew Fields, up to the station and drop back down and on to the ash pit and coal stage. The loco was kept out of the way on the

'Castle' No 5091 *Cleeve Abbey* heads a southbound vans on the Down Main on an unknown date; at this location a change of footplate crew would take place. *R. K. Blencowe*

ash road – it couldn't go through the shed or through the turntable – or it was kept against the stop block.

One week, Len Hough and Dick Everson had been heard saying they had done 100mph at the bottom of the Severn Tunnel. The speed limit on the bank into the tunnel was 75mph. I went through the tunnel in 3 minutes with this 'Castle'.

BR Standards

As already mentioned, the 'Britannias' went like hell, and were very free running. Coal was put in the two back corners of the firebox only – too much coal under the arch would kill the fire.

When the north was dieselised we saw more of them, in the last few months of steam. They were a free-running engine, but with boiler fittings in reverse compared to a Western loco. I would stand behind the driver to fire them.

The BR Standards were all very free-running, more so than Great Western locos. The '73xxx' 4-6-0s were weakish engines, but they would run! I was working with Driver Bert Hale on one of these on an excursion to Bristol. Bert would work overtime and was always looking for it. I had booked onto this job, and Bert played hell with me – he had been taken off a soft job, like working to Shrewsbury and back with a freight, especially on a Saturday when there were excursions about and you would be out a long time. The booked driver didn't know the road so Bert was requested to work the train, and the other driver was doing his job.

We left Pontypool Road and went over the top by the East box, then Bert let the engine go. By the Star Brickworks in Caerleon the loco went around the curve and kicked. I went up in the air and hit the side doors, bruising my ribs – without the doors I would have been over the side of the engine. Bert was all apologetic afterwards – it frightened him.

The 9F 2-10-0s weren't at Ponty very

Looking south on 4 November 1958, after changing engines BR Standard 4-6-0 No 73091 is in the platform, while a 'Castle' reverses back to shed on the Down Goods, and ex-GWR 2-6-0 No 6325 is seen on the Up Goods. *R. S. Carpenter*

long, and they would go too! They were used on the morning Chester and faster freights. They were not allowed on the Vale, but were allowed to Hafodyrynys. They were turned on the triangle at Ponty.

GWR engines

The 'Kings' were turned on the triangle by the West box, or were run to Newport to turn on the Maindee triangle, as they preferred to turn them on the main line. They were seen towards the end of steam, but not a lot. The last example I drove was preserved No 6024 in 1996 from Gloucester to Newport.

The '64xx' 0-6-0PTs were used to run to Blaenavon on the auto-trains. They were free-running engines, and Nos 6403, 6410, 6412, 6424, 6430, 6432 and 6435 are remembered. They were used on the Vale of Neath and to Monmouth. On the Blaenavon Low Level line you went up on the engine with the driver, but came down on the engine on your own, as the driver was in the auto-coach. Drivers were happy to have me work with them.

8F memories

I recall relieving the Briton Ferry tanks – a heavy train of chemical tanks – at Pontypool Road with Driver Bert Hale. We got on the engine at Pontypool Road station and got put in every loop. I said to Bert, 'We're getting low on coal.'

Bert said, 'We'll manage.'

We were in the loop at Bridgend and I got into the back of the tender by the water filler and pushed the coal from there into the front of the tender. Half way to Margam at Port Talbot the last of the coal went into the firebox. We dropped into the yard at Briton Ferry and the fire was quite low.

A shunter or foreman came up and said, 'Light engine to Llanelli.'

Bert shouted back, 'Light engine to shed!'

At the other end of the siding a shunter said the same thing. I put the pep pipe (used for washing down the coal and the footplate) in the tender and there was no coal.

Bert liked the money. Once past Port Talbot you would go to Margam for coal, but for Llanelli you wouldn't bother. At the shed at Margam I had never seen a tender like that before. You had to get to Neath station and come home to finish the shift. We had to get a ride to the station at Neath.

5. Fireman Terry Warwood

Banking turns

I booked on at 10.00pm to work on the Abergavenny banker. You would take a '72xx' to Abergavenny and bank the northern passenger, then go back to the shed and get home about 1.00am. My mother said, 'How many sandwiches do you want, son?'

I replied, 'About two, mother.'

One particular Saturday was different. I got to work and was told to work the Marsh Farm instead. Two Ponty '72xxs' were to travel north of Hereford, coupled together. My engine had a bunker full of coal, Midland 'snap and crackle', with another '72xx' coupled in front. Both engines were examined carefully before leaving the shed, and were bound for Church Stretton, where they crossed over and came back to Much Wenlock, picked up a freight train, and brought it back to Ponty. The rear engine had flats on the wheels, and kept me awake a bit.

Jack Drayton

I had Jack Drayton on the bankers and other odd trains. I worked up to Hereford when a train came in worked by an LMS 8F 2-8-0. Jack was driving, and wanted to show me the head codes on a Saturday afternoon.

I was soon to leave for New Zealand, and wasn't too interested in the job. I said, 'I'm not interested, Jack.'

Jack was a stickler for rules and regulations. You had to empty the fire iron trough on a tender before going off shed to stow the fire irons safely. He was going through the head codes, then the signal arm dropped off and

An ex-LMS 8F 2-8-0 heads south having reached the summit of Llanvihangel bank from the Hereford direction on 18 August 1962. R. C. Riley

we had to go. I got on the engine, the fire was clinkered, and there was small coal in the tender. I said, 'Jack, we won't get home to Ponty with this.'

'Oh, we'll be all right, mate, we'll be all right,' said Jack.

If I had taken a look at the fire straight away I would have failed it, but the signal was off, and we had to go. I immediately got the pricker in the fire, and got some steam in the boiler. Out of Hereford, whichever way you go, it's uphill. At Tram Inn we had to have a blow-up to raise some steam.

The signalman said, 'How long are you going to be there?'

I replied, 'When I have enough steam for it.'

It was really hard work with the pricker – it was like stirring porridge.

The signalman said, 'Hurry up – I've got the mails up behind you. We'll put you in at Pontrilas, and sort you out there.'

We struggled to get to Pontrilas, with a hot axle box on one of the wagons, but the engine was the problem. I got to the stage where I was hanging on the pricker in the firebox, and said to Jack, 'I've had enough, I can't do no more, I'm exhausted.'

It was like stirring porridge all the time. Jack had a go, but with no success.

The yard foreman at Pontrilas said, 'There's a light engine coming back off the Dowlais tanks to Ponty. Do you want him to back onto you?'

I said, 'Yes please.'

We would never have left Pontrilas otherwise, as we would have blocked up the whole lot. The light engine arrived bunker-first from Hereford, the driver saying to me, 'I'll remember you, boy.' The fireman was my mate, and was laughing. 'Stuck for steam again, Warwood?' The engine backed on and took us to Ponty.

Pontrilas, looking south. The saw mill on the left was later moved to the right of this photo. An Armstrong Goods 0-6-0 tender engine is seen shunting the station. *Phil Williams collection*

Bert Hale

A few weeks later I was on the 7.15am Chester freight, working on a 'Hall' from the Birkenhead Sidings. I didn't know who the driver was, but on the loco there was a clatter on the footplate from a 'double home' box. We got the engine ready and backed onto the train.

The guard gave the driver the tally and said, 'New fireman today, Bert.'

Bert said, 'Yeah – we might get to Hereford, we might not.'

I could fire a 'Hall' all day – they were the most wonderful engines to fire. Off we went, and Bert was looking at the clock and at the water all the time. When we stopped at Abergavenny I put some coal in the firebox. I thought we were going to take off, the speed we went up Llanvihangel, with the lever notched down. I had the injectors on, and Bert couldn't get the clock down. He was

'38xx' Class 2-8-0 No 3822 heads a southbound freight past Pontrilas signal box on 18 August 1962. *R. C. Riley*

'County' Class 4-6-0 *County of Monmouth* is seen on a southbound train, while '96xx' Class 0-6-0PT No 9650 enters the Neath bay on 16 April 1963. *R. H. Marrows*

looking at the water and the clock, with the regulator handle in the roof. When we got to Hereford we walked from Barton Hill to Barrs Court, where we relieved a train coming in.

It was a 'County', and I hadn't fired one before, but assumed it would be the same as a 'Hall', but only bigger. Off we went, and Bert didn't say a thing. Then he said to me as we crossed the bridge at Hereford over the River Wye, 'Boy, I'll take you anywhere.' I only ever worked with him once.

No 5322

I worked this 2-6-0 one day. We went to Hereford to relieve a crew and bring a train back. It was a train of ten glass-making sand wagons; we thought it was for Pilkington's glassworks at Pontypool, but it was sand for export. I got on the engine and there was a rough fire, and small coal in the tender.

We pulled into Pontypool Road station, thinking we were going to the New Sidings to drop the train off for Pilkington's, but the signal was set for Newport. I got steam up again, ready to work to Newport through the tunnels to the Eastern Valley Sidings.

At Newport I said, 'Light engine to Ebbw now is it?'

'No, light engine to Ponty,' said the yard foreman.

We were routed back to Ponty via the Monmouthshire line. I had three blow-ups to get to Ponty – in Newport, below Cwmbran, and again outside Coedygric signal box. We had enough steam to go past the engine shed and back on the ash pit. My driver was curious as to why the loco wasn't steaming. We took the baffle plate out, to find the tubes all blocked up – you couldn't see them for ashes. I was a young fireman and the driver would chastise you all the time. At this time in the early 1960s maintenance was getting less as diesels were coming in to replace steam, and you would get on engines without the tubes having been cleaned.

Battleship firing

I once blackened Abergavenny with smoke while working a freight train! It was an Abergavenny job, the fireman was on holidays, and I was linked up with another driver. The roster clerk said, 'You'll recognise the driver – he has a whopping big Roman nose.'

The driver said, 'They told you I had a big Roman nose.' His name was Mr Watts.

We went 'on the cushions' (by passenger train) to Cardiff Canton to pick up a '28xx' at Pengam sidings to work up to Hereford. We were going up Llanvihangel bank and the driver said, 'You ever done battleship firing, mate? Get a shovel full of small coal, keep the flap up while I notch the engine down, then trickle the small coal over the flap.'

You couldn't see Abergavenny! This technique was used on Royal Navy battleships as smoke screens.

We worked back again on the cushions.

A few weeks later I was on another job, going up Llanvihangel with a '28xx' and a different driver. I said to him, 'Have you ever done battleship firing, driver? Notch it down a bit, and I'll show you.'

My driver dropped the reversing lever down, and after seeing the smoke emitted from the engine he thought we would both be sacked!

Worcester loco depot

From Worcester we worked north to Kidderminster, south to Gloucester, west to Hereford and Malvern, and east to London Paddington, but I never worked to Hereford or Paddington. Other jobs were worked to Birmingham Snow Hill.

For the Malvern, I booked on at 4.00am, got a 'tanky' ready and took it to the bay in the station to work to Bromyard with a two-coach train. A train would arrive from Stratford-upon-Avon to Malvern, and we would relieve the crew; they would work our train to Bromyard and we would work theirs to Malvern, run round, and bring the train back into Worcester carriage sidings. We then

A '38xx' 2-8-0 heads south at Llanvihangel on 18 August 1962. *R. C. Riley*

returned light engine to the station to await the down 'Cathedrals Express'. This train was split at Worcester, one half going to Hereford, the second half to Kidderminster. We took the engine to Kidderminster, over the viaduct and down a slope to the shed, then walked up and came home on a railcar to Worcester. That was a nice job.

The first job I had was on afternoons for a fortnight on '22xx' tender engines on the Honeybourne banker. We only turned a wheel once – the decline was already starting. There's a triangle at Honeybourne for the Stratford-upon-Avon line, and we went up on the bank to put a fire out.

I never worked to Paddington, only the London goods, using a '28xx' as far as Honeybourne, where we were relieved by men from Kingham and returned with a train to Worcester. Once I worked on the return train and the engine was an LMS '46xx'. I said to the fireman, 'Is it OK?', to which he replied, 'It was fine.' I opened the firebox door to find all blue flames with clinker, and that the tender was full of small coal. The train had two wagons and a brake van. My mate that day was Pandy Bill (from Pandy), but my regular mate after the summer season was an ex-Abergavenny man called Bill Corr. Worcester loco depot had former LMS and Great Western footplate staff.

I said to Pandy Bill, 'Look at the state of this!'

'Don't worry about it, mate, well get home,' said my driver.

So I brightened up the fire and put in plenty of water. Coming to the city's outskirts and the home signal for Worcester, I said, 'The board's on, mate.'

My driver applied the steam brake, but it had no effect and we were still going. I was getting ready to put on the hand brake, but just as we were cruising towards the board it dropped.

6. Fireman Graeme Merryfield

'28xx'

The last time I worked a '28xx' 2-8-0 was with Driver Arthur Edwards. We were sitting in the canteen, in the Spare Link, at midday when the phone went and the foreman said, 'There's a "28xx" at the back of the coal stage – it's all ready, and the guard is ready for Hereford.'

We walked to the loco, checked the fire and oil, and pulled back down on to the train, which was all vacuum-braked, and on to the Relief line at the station, where we had water. The guard said, 'The banker will be waiting at Abergavenny.'

Arthur said, 'If we've got the road, we won't be stopping.'

At Abergavenny the distant was off, indicating that the signal at the end of the platform was also off, and Arthur opened the regulator wide. As we went through Abergavenny station the banker was dropping back down by the signal box, and Arthur blew the whistle, put his hand up and waved to it, as all the signals were off. We had a full load going up Llanvihangel. I didn't see any of the scenery as I was shovelling all the way, and left the exhaust injector on all the way up the bank. Arthur made his engine speed up the bank, and when we got to Hereford the guard said, 'You know what, we did that trip in passenger time.' Arthur was a cracking man to work with.

LMS 'Black Fives'

I was working with Driver Ernest Jones in the Spare Link on a Saturday afternoon, and we were again sitting in the canteen awaiting a job. The phone went and we were asked to work an excursion to Bristol Temple Meads, which required crew relief at Ponty station. We walked up to the station and watched the train pull up to the signal; it was 13 coaches hauled by a 'Black Five' 4-6-0. The tender doors were open, all the coal was at the back of the tender, and it was all slack. I was scratching for coal, and the fire was built up in

Main-line memories

the station. The lamps hadn't been lit for the Severn Tunnel, which was my job. We left the station and I got up into the tender to drag some more coal down. Running down the bank out of Ponty the engine began to blow off, and it took from Ponty to Caerleon to get the injectors to work; they had been reported as faulty. The boiler pressure had now dropped, which required to be built up, so on with the injector, and the pricker put through the fire. It was a struggle to get to Bristol.

7. Fireman Colin Polsom

Shrewsbury 'Castle' trip

I was living in Rowan Crescent, Sebastopol, at the time and, aged 17½, went to the dances at St Hilda's, where I met my wife. We used to meet at the gate of St Hilda's dance, have a few words, then she'd go in to the dance and I'd pedal my bike to the engine sheds.

On a Saturday night we worked a steam-hauled passenger train back from Shrewsbury; the rest of the week it was worked by a diesel. We travelled 'on the cushions' on the 8.05pm to Shrewsbury, and when we got there we walked down to the engine sheds, picked up a fresh engine, prepared it, went over to the chippy for fish and chips, came back over, and worked the 2.40am off Salop to Pontypool Road.

Bill Oakley was my mate. This night we had a beautiful 'Castle' to get ready.

'Get up in the tender, Colin,' said my mate.

I hadn't been on these jobs, only the Control Link, and I was a spare fireman.

'Throw the lump forward, and I'll fill the box up,' said Bill. So he filled up the box, but couldn't see a light in it. He said, 'It'll be all right – let's have our fish and chips.'

We returned to the station and coupled up, and coming past the prison I got the bar in the firebox and like magic the fire sprang into life. This was the best job in the world, on a 'Castle' out of Salop on a passenger train. A few hours earlier I had left my girlfriend, and was heartbroken. It was a frosty crisp morning, snow was just blowing across the ground and the stars were shining in the sky. At Dorrington I thought, 'What a fantastic job! Lovely driver, and the engine is steaming like a kettle.'

At Hereford the guard came up to me with a big coat on, and said, 'How's it looking? Can you put a bit more steam on there? It's freezing!'

I look at the Mason's valve – I hadn't put the steam heating on. I had a slamming coming back from Hereford to Pontypool Road – how I got up over Pandy I don't know, with the extra use of steam. I was sending steam back there to warm the train – I had to make that steam back.

'Black Five' to Salop

With the Control Link, in the summer with

'Hall' Class 4-6-0 No 5987 heads south past Pandy on 18 August 1962. *R. C. Riley*

excursions, you might have driver holidays or driver sickness, and a passed fireman made up to driver would have to found from one of us. We had a lovely driver from Abergavenny called Jack Griffiths, and we were on the 5.05pm Saturday Kingswear to Manchester train. We walked up to Pontypool Road station. I was a bit raw as I was only a young fireman. Jack went in the cabin halfway down the platform for a cup of tea, but I was a bit restless – I didn't do many passenger turns and hadn't worked with Jack before.

Under the bridge appeared our train, hauled by a 'Black Five'. 'I've never been on one of these before,' I said. The train had been hauled by a diesel-hydraulic up to Bristol, where the 'Black Five' had been put on to work through to Shrewsbury. Mike Lynch was the fireman, an ex-Abergavenny man. The footplate was pristine, and the tender was built up like a brick wall with 'snap and rattle' coal. These engines had a soft blast compared to a Western engine.

I said to Mike, 'What's she like, Mike?'

'Lovely, Colin!'

It couldn't have been handed over better – the fire doors were open and the boiler topped up.

We went down through Little Mill and were soon dropping down at Penpergwm. You had to get over the bridge at Penpergwm and start preparing there for Llanvihangel. It was no good waiting till you left Abergavenny – it was too late. You couldn't do it before Penpergwm bridge – if you were working hard before that point and a check rail threw out, it would throw you into the river. Once you got over the bridge you could open it up.

Approaching Hereford, Jack said, 'What are you like on the troughs, Colin?'

I replied, 'I've never done it before.'

We got into Hereford and I thought, 'What a beautiful engine!'

We had a packed train. Jack said, 'We'll pinch a drop of water,' so I raced up on top of the tender and, as I put the bag in, the guard was whistling and waving his green flag, so we didn't have any water. We raced through Leominster and into Dinmore Tunnel. All of a sudden this brick wall of 'snap and rattle' coal was gone; and behind it was left mediocre coal that had been left in the tender for weeks.

Coming towards Ludlow, Jack asked, 'All right for the troughs, Colin?'

I replied, 'Yes,' but my heart was in my mouth thinking of every eventuality. But Jack was looking after me.

'Right now, Colin, wind the scoop down.' Soon I could see the float rising in the tank, in super-quick time. 'Wind the scoop up,' says Jack. We were back at it now – we had a full tender, the train was going well, but we hadn't got much coal. We were still at Ludlow with a long way to go. Dust was flying everywhere. There was a pipe round the top of the tender as a coal watering system; however, when the tender was being filled with coal these pipes became clogged and bent, and the system didn't work. The cab was enclosed and dust was flying everywhere. But Jack had the engine purring along.

I was keeping the engine going using a 'Ponty splash'. If you had a tender full of rubbish coal, most of it small coal, when trying to maintain steam pressure it would kill the fire. We therefore bounced the shovel on the ring of the firebox to feed the fire in the form of a spray.

Was I glad to see Church Stretton! I was black, and looked at the steam clock. We were doing all right here.

The most difficult part was the 13-mile run downhill to Salop. The engine was rocking with a clean fire, but the trouble was that a high percentage of it was going into the ashpan. I couldn't 'Ponty splash' as such, as the regulator was shut. We ran into Salop, and the Crewe man was on the next road with a beautiful green ex-LMS 'Royal Scot'. I had to uncouple with three-quarters of a glass of water and 160psi steam pressure – you needed 160psi to blow the brakes off. I got down to uncouple and looked into the waiting room window – I was as black as Al Jolson from the dust on the footplate! But this engine was brilliant! We put it on shed, with pockets of warm ash in it, then went back 'on the cushions'.

Freights

A call boy came to my house one day when I was working with Les Evans. It was a Sunday turn, and had been cancelled, so we were booked to work the Barry banana train. They were heavy trains, fully vacuum-fitted. We went up to the station and sat on the platform, waiting to relieve the Cardiff man. It was an ex-Severn Tunnel engine, 'Hall' No 6965, and arrived with the blower hard on. A few weeks later we brought that engine back light – it was an Ebbw engine.

Looking north at Pontypool Road, an up freight is seen on the Up Main road, date unknown. *R. G. Nelson, Terry Walsh collection*

We got up on the footplate and the fireman was still firing, so the Cardiff man handed over his notes to Les. The blower was hard on and the water low. Coming from Newport to Llantarnam, it's all curves and a lot of firemen wouldn't fire until Llantarnam. But it's too late by then – you need to fire from Newport to get a full boiler and full head of steam for the long climb to Pontypool Road. They'd mistimed it and this is what had happened. We had water first, on the up main, using the water column opposite the top end of the platform. I got the bar in the fire to get an idea of its condition, then went into the tender to throw lumps forward, and put them in. Then I filled the boiler. It was a dirty engine, with flats on the wheels, and was drinking water, but it steamed like a kettle all the way to Salop.

On another occasion I went over to Bristol with Mo Thomas, to St Philip's Marsh shed. Mo went to pick up the details while I went to the engine board to find our engine. It was a 'Hall', immaculate, No 4949. But all that glitters is not gold! We left Temple Meads with a cold fire and struggled all the way up Filton. It was cold and I didn't have it right.

We worked it to Pontypool Road, where we had relief. It was a train of Wills's tobacco and Fry's chocolate.

The engine was later sent to Cashmore's in Newport for scrap. However, they had trouble with the new diesel-hydraulic locomotives and it was brought back into service, minus number and name plates; the number was chalked on the side of the cab.

One working was to South Sidings at Stourbridge. Sometimes it was the 11.55pm to Stourbridge, then for some reason it was changed to 12.05am. If it was 11.55pm you worked the Saturday night, but if it was the 12.05 you worked the Sunday night. We all preferred the 12.05am as you had the weekend off. I worked this with Dai James from Abergavenny.

Jack Jones was a passed fireman at the time, and his mate went driving the diesels, so I went firing to him. We had a '38xx' down to Margam. Fantastic!

One day I was on the Tap Road with an 8F 2-8-0. I used to swap turns with a friend of mine called Ron, and this day he was on the East Usk. I was very conscientious – I checked the firebox end, smokebox end and fire bars – but this particular day I didn't check the brick arch. Ernie Jones (Ernie

'Boot') was my mate. He was immaculate. We were going on the Cardiff road, so we went to the New Sidings for our train.

I thought, 'For a fresh engine off shed, it doesn't seem right.'

The Cardiff road was flat, so off we went, but before long we were struggling. I got the shovel in my hand and had a look around, and two bricks had fallen out of the brick arch into the fire. We had to put the engine on shed at Neath, put another engine on and drop the train off at Margam. It was partly my fault for not checking the engine.

8. Fireman Henry Williams

Abergavenny banker

One train come down Llanvihangel Bank with an axle box on fire. We hooked off the offending wagon from the down main into the siding used by the banking engine in between banking turns; they were afraid to move it too far in case the axle journal sheared off. When the banker came back down, it had to cross over and stop by the goods shed entrance and wait there.

We used to have seasonal trains on a Friday night, which came back on a Saturday or a Sunday. The drivers and firemen were from Hereford and Shrewsbury, and would work to Bristol and beyond. One day we had pannier tank No 9650 banking from Abergavenny to Llanvihangel, and were sent to Penpergwm as a train was doing rough. When it went past I had a look in the cab to see how the engine was doing for steam – I couldn't see the pressure gauge as the driver had covered it with his cap.

We pulled up to the starting signal at Penpergwm and the signalman crossed us over behind the train; we didn't hook on as we were running free. Whistles were blown and away we went. We had a go at banking him, but had just got past Trilley Mill near the summit when the train left us; once the train was over the top at Llanvihangel they were on their way. We had an inch of water in the boiler. My driver, Tommy Tamplin, said, 'There's nothing wrong with him, as he got away from us!'

Tommy had the reversing lever two notches off mid-gear – it was like being on a hobby horse, rocking back and forth. It was no good being at 45% cut-off as we wouldn't have kept up with it. We followed on behind, got to Llanvihangel, had water, built up our

'28xx' Class 2-8-0 No 2845 banks a northbound freight at Abergavenny Junction in 1958. *Stan Brown, D. K. Jones collection*

pressure and went back down to Abergavenny. On that moonlit night the white-painted church at Trilley Mill could clearly be seen.

In the opposite direction brakes were applied at the top of Llanvihangel bank, and released at Penpergwm. Most trains were run without pinning down brakes if the line was clear – you'd apply the brakes on the tender and on the guard's van and hope for the best. At Penpergwm there was a bend going over the River Usk. On one trip I had a driver who was a fool, and called me 'young George', after my Dad. 'Georgie boy,' he said, 'we're either going to go around that corner or you're going to have an early bath.'

Trips to Shrewsbury

I only had one trip on a 'Castle' to Salop and back. We got on at Ponty station. That engine would do high daily mileage, coming up from Cardiff in the morning, all the way up to Shrewsbury and back down at 4 o'clock in the afternoon, over to Bristol, back to Pontypool Road, up to the West box to turn, then back to Cardiff.

It's OK when the coal is near you – then it's all right. When you have to go and fetch it forward, and handle it again, and put it in the hole, you'd be surprised how much you move. Some of the old hands would tell you what to do: 'It's going to be heavy here – whack a bit in.' Coming back from Salop it was 13 miles uphill to Church Stretton. As soon as you backed onto your train you'd get as much coal in there as you could; in the end you had a little fire nearly out on the footplate!

We picked up one freight train that had come from Swansea, over the Vale, at night. We took it over at Ponty and had water at the station, opposite the North box. The driver was Bill Symes, and he said, 'We'll stop at Hereford for water.'

I said. 'Aye, all right.'

We went to Hereford Barr's Court and had our water. Soon after we left he said, 'Ever taken water at Ludlow before?'

I said, 'No.'

Looking south at Llanvihangel, an unidentified 'Hall' Class 4-6-0 approaches the station on 18 August 1962. *R. C. Riley*

'Oh, come on,' he said, 'I'll show you how it's done.'

We got to Ludlow where there was a big sign with a 'W' on it, for water. Then there was another sign at the far end to tell you that you were off the troughs. So we got the scoop down and picked up the water, but the sign at the other end wasn't lit. At the next level crossing – bang – off went the scoop. So we had to stop at the next box to tell them what had happened, and to tell the following train to watch out for the troughs.

I've gone over the top at Church Stretton with an inch of water in the boiler. Between Church Stretton and Shrewsbury was Leebotwood, which gave you a bit of a break, as it levelled out a bit there.

Pontypool Road Station North Signal Box, as seen in December 1970 prior to demolition. *J. S. Williams*

9.10am Manchester

This train was in Pontypool Road in the afternoon between 1.30pm and 2.00pm The engine never turned on the table at Pontypool Road. It was one of the 'Baby Scots', *The South Wales Borderer* maybe. Leaving the train, it went up around the West, back into the loop (by the old yard), back out to the Station South Junction signal box and onto the shed, where there was always a space left for it, because it had to be back out to take the 3.15pm. The fire was cleaned, ashpan and smokebox emptied and coal put on. The driver and fireman would be at the canteen having their food and the turners would look after it. There was a shed driver and passed fireman on the ash pit.

Double-headed expresses

If a '53xx' or '43xx' 2-6-0 was used with an engine with a four-wheeled front bogie, the latter had to be the pilot engine to avoid splitting points, a possibility with a loco with a two-wheeled pony truck.

Chapter 3: Aberdare loco shed memories

1. Fireman Terry Wilkins

The loco shed was at Robertstown in Aberdare. I started there as a cleaner in 1954, and was made a fireman in 1956; in 1958 I was made redundant and went to Southall. I was getting married, and my wife-to-be didn't want to live in London, so I transferred to Hereford and got married there. I was at Hereford until the end of steam. I qualified as a passed fireman on the diesels, and redundancy came again.

When cleaning I recall the 'RODs', the '30xxs' on the Swansea vans and the 8.10am Carmarthen, but by 1954 they'd gone.

The rostered work at Aberdare was poor. The majority of the freight work was to Severn Tunnel Junction, Margam, Neath and Swansea, and passenger trains to Pontypool Road and Cardiff Bute Road. Aberdare men never went into Cardiff General; we went to Queen Street, then Bute Road. On the morning turn we used to pick up coaches at Bute Road, go back out to Coryton, and fetch a train from Coryton to Bute Road.

Banking work

My first firing turn was on the Gadlys banker, on loco No 7213. We banked from Gadlys Junction to Gelli Tarw, and sometimes right through to Hirwaun station. The engine would mostly be a '42xx', '52xx', '28xx', '63xx' or even a '68xx', or a '49xx' from repair, for a week of running in.

The Mountain Ash ('Cresselley') banker shunted Cresselley Crossing and Nixon's Colliery at Mountain Ash, and banked trains from Mountain Ash to Quaker's Yard, had water and came back. When traffic was heavy, it was busy. We never coupled up.

When I was made a fireman, for the first six months I was afternoons on the Mountain Ash banker. One day Stan Bartlow was my mate. We went into Cefn Glas Tunnel and bang, we came to a stop! The signalman at Quaker's Yard had let a platelayer's trolley into the station, and the driver of the train engine had knocked the brake in.

An ex-GWR '28xx' Class 2-8-0 heads a coal train emerging from Cefn Glas Tunnel towards Quaker's Yard in March 1958. *D. K. Jones collection*

'46xx' Class 0-6-0PT No 4639 approaches Neath station with a westbound passenger train for Pontypool Road on 12 June 1964. *D. K. Jones collection*

Night banker jobs are recalled as being:

9.15pm Salisbury – usually a '28xx' train engine
10.10pm Pontypool – rarely banked
1.30am Severn Tunnel
3.45am Severn Tunnel
4.45am Severn Tunnel

The last two had a '42xx'/'52xx' as the train engine. The '28xx' worked the Salisbury via Machen, and we had relief at Basseleg. We left the Vale of Neath via the Sirhowy valley, to travel to Risca, then to Basseleg, or down the Taff, through Penhros Junction, to Caerphilly, Machen and hence to Basseleg, on the Pontypridd, Caerphilly & Newport line.

Passenger train memories

The first passenger train from Aberdare in the morning was the 6.35am Ystrad Mynach. It was a two-coach train, using Nos 8444 or 8445. It would travel to Ystrad Mynach, go back to Aberdare, Aberdare to Neath Riverside, then back to Aberdare.

The 11.15am Aberdare-Pontypool was a fair run. I was on this when I changed turns with an older fireman. I had an auto-engine, No 6410. We did Aberdare to Pontypool and Pontypool to Neath, then Neath Riverside to pick up schoolchildren. We stopped at all the small stations on the way back to Hengoed, where we ran round, then went back to Aberdare.

Pontypool jobs

We had to work a train from Little Mill, over the Vale. We went to Pontypool as passengers, if we didn't have a forward working, and got the engine ready there. I hated Ponty for getting an engine ready as there were never any tools. We mostly had briquettes; you couldn't put them in the firebox, but had to break them, and get dust and sulphur in your eyes. I'd have a '42xx' or '52xx', and the briquettes would block the view out of the back of the bunker.

Hereford memories

We worked over the Vale on a double home turn to Bordesley. We used to go down in the morning and relieve Birmingham men at Hereford, then work to Llanelli and get relief. We used to lodge, then work the Llandeillo back at night; this was a mixed freight and a D headcode. We normally had a 'Grange', and usually returned with the same engine. We left Hereford at 4 or 5 in the morning.

We regularly had the Gadlys banker up to Gelli Tarw, very often a '72xx', '42xx' or '66xx' – or an engine fresh off repair at Aberdare shed (a large one, maybe a '28xx' or a '63xx' before it went back to its home shed). On one job, on arrival at Gadlys Junction the guard said, 'I don't know why you stop – you have the road right through.' We had very good '68xx' on that job.

We would arrive at Llanelli around 10 or 11 in the morning, and would lodge at the hotel opposite the station – it had an Australian-sounding name. We had a cooked breakfast, then bed. We'd be called

Seen at Glyn Neath engine shed, looking north on 18 August 1962, ex-GWR '42xx' Class 2-8-0T No 4282 is acting as the Glyn Neath banker. M. Dart, *Transport Treasury*

No 4282 has been coupled as pilot engine to No 4668 at Glyn Neath station on the same day, ready for the 4-mile ascent to Hirwaun Pond. M. Dart, *Transport Treasury*

about 6.00pm to set up for a cooked dinner, then we walked down to the shed where an engine had been prepared for us; usually it was the same engine back. We'd leave Llanelli around 9.00pm and would be back in Hereford around 4 or 5 in the morning, to be relieved by Tyseley men. Very often we had a load on, so we had a banker at Glyn Neath, and also at Mountain Ash; the latter took us to Quaker's Yard.

We worked the Dowlais tanks from Hereford, via Talybont and Torpantau. The bank up to Torpantau was 1 in 38, the same as the Lickey. They knew in advance how many tanks were going to Dowlais, and coming back, so two engines were used. I was on this job two or three times. We had to change engines at Dowlais on one occasion as we had run out of coal.

2. Fireman Phil Marks

During the war years there were 140-odd sets of drivers and firemen at Aberdare. I was locospotting before I went on the railway, and saw trains from the Midlands (Birmingham) or London to Aberdare Park on a Sunday, as a lot of Welsh people lived in those areas.

I started on the railway in 1952, and was made a fireman at Reading in 1954. I did nine months there, then went into the Army, came back to Aberdare, was made redundant, went to Swindon for nearly two years, came back to Aberdare, was made redundant again, and left the railway.

Engine classes I remember from 1952 onwards are '56xx', '57xx', '66xx', '43xx', '52xx', '53xx', '63xx', '72xx' and '74xx'. We had one regular '63xx', No 6361, which was an Aberdare favourite, used mostly on ballast trains.

'28xxs' I recall are Nos 2808/10/13/28/31/36/57 for a spell, and 2860/61/63/73/74/76/80. We also had '38xxs'. We used the '28xxs' on jobs to Severn Tunnel.

Of the '42xxs', '52xxs' and '72xxs' I recall Nos 4228, 4257, 4246, 5263, 5237, 5258, 7213, 7214, 7221 and 7222.

Class '56xx' No 5649 was initially the only one we had, and was always used on the Ninian Park football passenger trains. In later years we had Nos 5649, 5624, 5644, 5633 and 5698. All the other engines were '66xxs'; we had Nos 6605, 6651, 6652, 6649, 6622, 6628, 6697 (with a cast-iron chimney), 6661, 6663 and 6665 (ex-Radyr).

We also had '84xx' Nos 8444 and 8445.

Taff Vale engines Nos 204, 208, 282, 284, 364, 362, 365 and 374 are recalled.

An ex-GWR '28xx' Class 2-8-0 is seen inside Aberdare engine shed in the 1950s.
D. K. Jones collection

Aberdare loco shed memories

Aberdare's '56xx' Class 0-6-2T No 5633 passes Mountain Ash (Cardiff Road) with a freight for Aberdare on 12 January 1960. *D. K. Jones collection*

Cleaning

The first engine I cleaned was No 65, an old Rhymney Railway engine, known as the 'iron lung'. It was a local yard engine.

The biggest disappointment I had as a cleaner was when I was booked to work the Rhigos passenger. We'd get a '56xx' ready and go from Aberdare to Rhigos Sidings light engine. We were coming out of the shed and the foreman shouted, 'Whoa, whoa! You've got to come off this job, Phil – the driver is refusing to take you. He's seen a qualified fireman on the Top Yard Pilot and wants you to go on that engine instead.'

All the Rhigos job entailed was to go light engine to Hirwaun, 4 miles away, and come back with six coaches. It was downhill all the way to Mountain Ash, then you started the climb up to Penrhiwceiber. I never spoke to that driver again!

There was a branch from Gadlys signal box on to the low level, to Bwllfa Dare Colliery. Only twice did I up there, once when I was a cleaner. One morning the foreman said, 'Who's the next oldest hand?'

I said, 'I am. Why?'

'Go with Wilf Rawlins now, get an engine ready and propel a train up to Bwllfa,' replied the foreman.

The next time I went there was on an '84xx' with low-loader wagons, picking up track on the way down, a bit at a time.

Working from Aberdare

For the Bottom Yard Pilot No 7423 was a regular. I booked on at 5.12am and got it

The 4.49pm train to Pontypool Road arrives at Penrhiwceiber High Level on 25 August 1959, worked by 0-6-2T No 6651. M. *Hale, Great Western Trust*

ready, then we'd go down to the Bottom Yard, do a bit of shunting in the goods shed and coal yard, and have a break. About 12.30-12.40pm we'd get relief and the afternoon shift would take over. The highlight of the day was to go up past Gadlys Junction to Aberdare Cables to pick up two box vans and take them down into the yard; they would go on the 8.00pm to Alexandra Dock, Newport.

One Saturday morning I had a passed fireman with me on No 7423. It was his first driving turn, and he was as proud as Punch. A phone message came through: 'You are required to bank the Pontypool Road to Hirwaun,' as it was overloaded. We coupled onto the train and banked it up to Hirwaun station – it was the longest run that engine had had for years!

Another day I was working with Ron Giles on No 4289 on the Gadlys banker, banking a '68xx' on the Bordesley, going up through Trecynon Halt. There was a dip at

'56xx' Class 0-6-2T No 5626 (right) is seen at Hirwaun station with the 6.50pm train to Merthyr. On the left is '46xx' Class 0-6-0PT No 4668 on the 6.22pm for Pontypool Road. The date is 18 August 1962.
M. *Dart, Transport Treasury*

Aberdare loco shed memories

An unidentified ex-GWR 0-6-0PT passes the former TVR Dare Valley Junction signal box in 1959, on the Bwllfa Dare. This signal box was closed and used as a shunters' cabin. Aberdare High Level station is on the right, and this view is looking east. *D. K. Jones collection*

the Creamery and the train engine pulled away from us – my mate was only buffered up against it.

I said, 'Ron, he's pulling away from you!' We had to go like hell in the night to catch up with him!

The worst job at Aberdare for a fireman was the 3.20pm Dare Valley Pilot. We used to go down to the Dare Valley and come off the Vale of Neath; the old signal box at Dare Valley Junction was used as a shunters' cabin. The highlight of the job was at 5.30-6.00pm, when we went down through the crossing gates where the North box was, down to Aberdare South, and he'd put you into Malvin Jones's builders' yard. You'd change a wagon of sand, do a few shunts, go back to the Dare Valley, and that's all you did all day – it was soul-destroying.

Other times we'd work a pilot engine at Nelson in the afternoon. We'd book on at, say, 3.15pm, and read the notices in the shed. Then me and my mate would walk to Aberdare High Level station and catch the 3.50pm Pontypool Road train. Nine out of ten times we'd pick up the pilot engine at Quaker's Yard when it was having water; the crew would return to Aberdare and we'd run light engine to Nelson. We'd do our shunting in the yard, then two or three trips to either Taff Merthyr or Deep Navigation Colliery (Ocean), and take the trains to Nelson yard.

We'd go engine and van to Taff Merthyr, but never went in as it was NCB track. The 8.40pm Rogerstone to Taff Merthyr was a train of 70 empties. The brake van would be braked and uncoupled, and the train would pull forward. There was a klaxon on the wall: one blast meant stop, three meant start. When we had the signal we'd push back into Deep Navigation.

At 9.30pm we'd form a train at Gadlys

Junction to work to Aberdare. They'd have moulds coming down from Dowlais Top, two at a time; they were a tremendous weight, and these would also be on our train. We'd shunt them off at Gadlys Junction; they were destined for Margam Steelworks, and would be sent there on the 3.30am down.

There were two pilots at Tower Colliery, and two trains a day. One pilot was at Hirwaun station, the other at Hirwaun Pond. The train would push you all the way down; if you were pushed too far you'd run away. You'd come down to Gelli Tarw Junction, where the signal on the right took you over towards Gadlys Junction, where the Merthyr line branched off from the Aberdare line. Many years previously there had been a connection to Cwmaman. You'd hammer the daylights out of the engine by putting it in forward gear if you were being pushed; the sparks and roar from the chimney were unbelievable when you were pushed down like that.

We had one job lasting 12 hours to work to Radyr, but it was only 18 or 20 miles at the most.

Working to Severn Tunnel Junction on a Saturday night, you came back as a passenger to Cardiff, but if you missed the last train to Aberdare you had to wait in the canteen for hours, until the 4.00am paper train was ready.

On the Mountain Ash banker I've banked to Quaker's Yard, coupled onto the front on a Monday morning only to work through to Maesycwmmer, when traffic was heavy coming out of the Phurnacite plant at Abercwmboi. We'd then come back light engine to Aberdare.

The 10.00pm Aberdare-Pontypool Road pick-up goods was a night job with a '55xx' tank engine. We booked on just after 9.00pm, picked up the goods train and left Aberdare at 10.10. We picked up everywhere, and were relieved by Ponty men half way at Hengoed. However, nine times out of ten they wouldn't be there and we'd be relieved at Penar, or the other side of Crumlin – they worked it to a fine art!

My favourite Vale of Neath engine was a Neath loco, No 8104, which was always on the 12.15pm passenger at Aberdare High Level, the 11-something from Pontypool Road.

The furthest I worked from Aberdare was from Penderyn Quarry to Hereford. We had a '28xx' on this job, and were relieved at Hereford.

We had one job to work over to Taff Merthyr with a workers' passenger train to Rhigos, using a '56xx' and six coaches. We'd get an engine ready at the shed, then go light engine to Quaker's Yard and couple on to the coaches in the sidings there. We'd then work up through to Rhigos, put the coaches in the sidings, run round and come back light engine to Aberdare. One night, me and mad Draker pushed the coaches into the sidings at Quaker's Yard ready for the morning.

I said, 'You've got the board, mate,' and crunch, we were off the road, first pair of wheels.

My driver said, 'I thought you said the board was off?'

I said, 'It is off – come and have a look.'

'What the hell's happened?' he asked.

We got the engine back on, went inside and came off a second time. We got it back on again, and went up to the signal box. The flanges on the front pair of wheels were thin and splitting the points. The points had now been clipped, and that engine was supposed to work the 11.00pm Radyr, but instead it went back to shed and over the inspection pit to get the flanges checked.

The Swansea vans

I came back from Swindon on compassionate grounds as my wife was expecting a baby. I was at Aberdare for three months, shunting the locos – I couldn't go off shed in case my wife was taken to hospital. One day the foreman came to me and said, 'Do me a favour. We are short of firemen – will you go with the Swansea vans to Pontypool Road?'

'Great,' I thought. 'Let's get out on the main line.'

I was hoping to have a 'Grange', as they were used mostly on the Swansea vans.

Aberdare loco shed memories

But when the train pulled in to Aberdare High Level it was a dirty old '63xx'! The fireman had broken his arm. The train came through here at about 10 in the morning, and I had relief at Pontypool Road. The driver asked, 'How are you going to get back?'

I said, 'I'll catch the train to Newport, catch the train to Cardiff, then the Cardiff to Aberdare.'

Between Newport and Cardiff a ticket collector came around. I was sitting in the corner in my overalls. He asked, 'Where's your ticket?'

I said, 'I haven't got one – I'm on duty.' I explained what had happened, that I had relieved a fireman at Aberdare, had worked through to Pontypool Road and was going back to Aberdare.

He asked again, 'Well, where's your ticket?'

I hadn't got it – the driver had the ticket. He asked me for my name and registration number, and told me that I'd be hearing more about this.

'Thank you very much,' I said.

I got back to Aberdare and the foreman said, 'You might have a query.' All the time I was working at Swindon, and travelling to Aberdare, I was never asked for a ticket.

An eastbound passenger train to Neath enters Aberdare High Level station on 18 August 1962, while a westbound passenger train headed by ex-GWR '66xx' Class 0-6-2T No 6605 is seen in the platform with a passenger train for Pontypool Road. M. Dart, *Transport Treasury*

3. Railway enthusiast Keith Jones

As a trainspotter I spent many, many hours at Cresselley Crossing. The beauty of the Vale of Neath line was that generally you never knew what engines were on trains – it was a spotter's dream! Freight could have anything from an 0-6-0PT to a 'Grange' or even an LMS 8F, while passengers again ranged from 0-6-0PTs to 2-6-0 'Moguls'. On odd occasions 'Granges' were used; these were regular performers on the Bordesley, and alternated with engines from 86G (Pontypool Road) and 87F (Llanelli). On only one occasion do I remember a 'Grange' coming through with a Tyseley engine – that was No 6879, with a 2A shed plate.

I was on Mountain Ash (Cardiff Road) station on 13 June 1964 when No 6836 *Estevarney Grange* came through on a Pontypool Road train at around 7.00pm. It was in an atrocious condition.

The first engine I remember as the Cresselley banker was 0-6-0PT No 5797; the only other engines I remember clearly were Nos 3627 and 3731. They were usually supplied by Aberdare, but they must have borrowed No 3731, which I photographed at Cresselley Crossing, as I can't find any record to show it was allocated to Aberdare – its home shed was Neath. I did see a photograph some years ago of ex-TVR No 204 as the

A GWR photo of Mountain Ash (Cardiff Road) station, as seen in 1922, with Nixon's Colliery in the background. The abutment of the bridge that connected the Taff Vale Railway (on the right) to the Vale of Neath line, across the River Cynon, is seen in the foreground. *D. K. Jones collection*

Cresselley banker; it was taken by Billy Harding, who was a signalman, but he passed away many years ago.

'Castle' sightings in the Aberdare area included No 5074 *Hampden*, which worked the Royal Train to Trelewis on 25 July 1958, taking the Duke of Edinburgh to Aberdare.

The driver was Hywel Butler and the fireman Ginger Williams.

No 4097 *Kenilworth Castle* worked on part of the Royal Train duty, and had worked to Aberdare shed; it returned a Taunton empty stock from Aberdare via Sirhowy, fired by Ronny Rees.

Ex-GWR '51xx' Class 2-6-2T No 5101 approaches Mountain Ash (Cardiff Road) with an eastbound passenger train on 12 January 1960. *D. K. Jones collection*

Chapter 4: A brace of Williams

1. Driver 'Full Load Phil' Williams: a tribute

Phil Williams was born in 1906, the son of an engine driver on the Barry Railway. He attended school in Griffithstown, and left school to gain employment in Pontymoile Iron Foundry. He joined the railway in 1923 to become a cleaner, and when Pontypool Road loco depot closed in 1967 he was transferred to Ebbw Junction diesel depot, retiring in 1968.

He was born at No 95 Stafford Road, Griffithstown, and looked over the wall on Stafford Road (when it was 6 feet high) to watch the first steam railmotor cross the Skew Bridge en route to Pontypool and Blaenavon Low Level in 1912.

The first engine he fired was the Cwm Glyn banker, on an old 0-6-0 saddle tank loco. Beames LMS 0-8-2T engines worked coal from Blaenavon High Level straight through to Panteg & Coedygric Junction, as the LMS had running rights through to Griffithstown.

The GWR Eastern Valley line to Talywain

Former Pontypool Road Driver Phil Williams (left) and former Blaenserchan Colliery Engineer Austin Jones (right) stand next to *Warwickshire* at Bridgnorth on the Severn Valley Railway on Sunday 11 October 1970. *J. S. Williams*

GWR 'Saint' Class No 2975 *Lord Palmer* with a South Wales to Birmingham train is seen on the Up Main at Pontypool Road station on 17 June 1939. *Kidderminster Railway Museum*

and Blaenavon was opposite his house. Before '42xxs' were employed on coal trains '31xxs' were used, and before that 'Buffalo' '1076' Class 0-6-0 saddle tanks. A well-known photo shows an Armstrong Goods 0-6-0 tender engine at the rear of a down goods train on Pontymoile Viaduct, attached to provide extra braking. At that same location, when banking a Blaenavon (Top Line) iron ore train with a '72xx', the train stopped on the viaduct on the up line, with the rear radial wheels overhanging a catch point at the south end of the viaduct.

When Phil started on the railway in 1923, Crumlin Viaduct was still double track, and when you were standing on the footplate you could step off and drop straight over the side!

Phil recalled seeing an accident at Pontypool Road West Junction in 1929, and someone was taking photographs from the three-legged footbridge. However, representatives of the Great Western Railway were present and the photographer was requested to stop taking them.

When cleaning 'Saint' Class engines, Phil recalled *Rob Roy* and *William Dean*. The foreman cleaner would put his finger at the back of the spokes of the wheels to check that they were cleaned.

As a fireman in the 1930s he would fire a 'Saint' Class light engine to Blaenavon Low Level. He would then work the 6.00am stopping train to Cardiff General, turn the engine and work the 7.25am West of England express to Bristol. The engine would be uncoupled to work the Plymouth express from Platform 9 to Shrewsbury, arriving there at 12.40pm. He then took the engine to the shed and booked off. He booked on again at 1.00am, prepared the same engine and worked the 2.25am mail and passenger train back to Pontypool Road.

During the Second World War Phil saw LMS 'Princess Coronation' Class *Duchess of*

Hamilton pass through Pontypool Road after returning to Cardiff from the USA. In May 1941 Prime Minister Winston Churchill travelled over Crumlin Viaduct via Pontypool Road on a train hauled by a pair of 'Castle' Class locomotives, one of which was No 5038 *Morlais Castle*. The train had been diverted from travelling into Cardiff because of bomb damage at Pengam. One night during the war Phil gave a US serviceman a footplate ride on a GWR 'Hall' from Bristol Temple Meads station (he had missed his train) and dropped him off at the Maindee curve in Newport.

Phil remembered the auto-train to Brynmawr, using No 4820 (now No 1420 and preserved), stopping to pick up passengers at Six Bells Halt, Garndiffaith. The next stop was Varteg, where the platform would be full on a market day, with passengers waiting to travel to Brynmawr Market.

In the snow of 1947 he drove No 7206 with a snowplough through Pontypool Crane Street to clear George Street road bridge of snow.

On one of the author's visits, Phil showed me his driver's log for No 5322, for working a trip to Shrewsbury; over several days this was recorded as SOS – short of steam! He was the last person to drive it before it was withdrawn.

An unusual memory was that of working a train back to Pontypool Road with an engine (possibly a 'Hall') that had a bolt missing from the driver's-side cabside number plate, and the plate was swinging back and forth. Arriving at Pontrilas down loop he had had enough, so he unwound the nut on the remaining bolt and pushed to bolt out of the cabside, enabling the number plate to fall to the floor!

No 5043 was always a flyer!

The outstanding run by No 5043 *Earl of Mount Edgcumbe* on the Settle-Carlisle line in 2010 reminds the author of a similar run on the North-to-West route in the early 1960s between Shrewsbury and Pontypool Road.

Phil was at Shrewsbury station with his fireman in a coach of the Manchester to Cardiff train one summer's evening, returning 'on the cushions'. The train was hauled by a 'Warship' diesel-hydraulic. The tannoy announced that the diesel had failed and a steam crew was required to work the train south. Phil arrived at Shrewsbury shed to find an unusual sight – a green 'Castle', different from the usual uncleaned example, bearing the number 5043. The train was worked to Pontypool Road, reaching speeds of 80 to 85mph en route. On arrival Phil dropped off the fireman's side to oil up, and upon returning to the cab saw a gentleman in a suit with a briefcase walking away from the loco; his fireman told him the gentleman had been delighted that a steam engine could keep up with diesel timings!

During the Suez Crisis of 1956, Phil relieved a 'Castle' on an ammunition train originating from Southampton; it was returning the ammunition north, as it had been supplied at the wrong size. He was with his fireman outside the North box at Pontypool Road when the struggling 'Castle' could be heard in the cutting adjacent to the loco sheds; it arrived on the Up Relief line at Pontypool Road station short of steam and stopped a few times before drawing up short of the water column opposite the North box. The crew got off complaining that it was the wrong engine and that the load was too much.

Phil worked the loco to Shrewsbury. At the top of Llanvihangel bank the train was stopped and he and his fireman climbed down to break up some fence posts to pin down extra wagon brakes for the run down past Pandy. The train was late, and upon arriving at Pontypool Road a report had to be presented to Inspector Jack Kersley. On it Phil wrote: 'Had to stop at Llanvihangel to break up fence posts to pin brakes on train; if I hadn't the loco and half the train owned by the Ministry of Defence would be in a field owned by the Ministry of Agriculture'!

Phil Williams was known as 'Full Load Phil' as he wouldn't take a loco out without a fitter testing the brakes, as 'We will have a full load tonight.' On one occasion he was in the locomen's cabin at Cardiff Canton, and a former Pontypool Road fireman, who had worked in the banking link, was re-telling stories of working trains to Paddington from Cardiff, and the tales were getting thin. Phil then stated that it was harder to work a train of 36 coal wagons from Talywain (on the Trevethin Junction-Blaenavon Top Line) to Pontypool Road on a dark, dirty night! To start a stationary coal train from Talywain required full regulator, as most of the brakes on the wagons were pinned down.

Phil remembered the 'Kings' being introduced. 'They wore them out on the London road, then we had them on the Salop road.'

In 1964 he drove No 7029 *Clun Castle* on the Shrewsbury route heading a Stephenson Locomotive Society special, and brought it back from Shrewsbury light engine to Pontypool Road shed. He was given a 10-bob note as a tip by the organisers on this occasion. Cine film exists of him oiling the engine at Abergavenny (Monmouth Road) on the trip to Shrewsbury.

In 1971 Phil was reunited with No 5043 in Barry scrapyard and lamented its condition, when No 5643 was being prepared for preservation at Cwmbran. He would have been thrilled to read of its recent exploits.

'Full Load Phil' by David Williams

Phil's first job at the loco sheds, as a cleaner, was to light up and turn off the shed gas lamps. He was cleaning in 1926, and recalled the foreman threatening a fellow cleaner with instant dismissal when he stopped for a cigarette break; unemployed men would be looking expectantly over the wall of Coedygric Road viaduct.

The Nelson passenger is remembered. Returning with the Nelson auto-car and a '14xx' tank loco one day, having passed Hafodyrynys, the water was running too low for comfort. Upon arrival at Pontypool Road the train passed the up platform and ran straight up to the North Bay for water before dropping off any passengers! This was a regular occurrence, as it was uphill to Hafodyrynys from Crumlin, and once through Cefn Crib the remaining water was in the front of the tank and couldn't be picked up by the injectors. The only places to take water coming back would be Hengoed High Level or Crumlin Junction (where there were two water columns, one before the signal box when travelling west, and the other at the top of the branch line leading to Llanilleth).

When he was a fireman Phil worked a night train up through Glyn Neath Tunnel, on the Vale of Neath line. Every time they entered it the driver would open up the engine and cinders would fill the tunnel; upon leaving the tunnel he would slow down and laugh his head off. This happened for a few nights, then one night a cinder bounced into the driver's pocket, setting fire to some oily waste!

In the 1930s, to gain seniority as a fireman, Phil was transferred to work trains in the Rhymney Valley. He would often tell me about working in and out of Ogilvie Colliery.

Phil moved again to Worcester to gain seniority, by which time he had just been made a driver. One day an engine was being prepared for a turn to London – a 'Star' Class loco, *Swallowfield Park*. The fireman hadn't turned up as his child was ill. The foreman therefore didn't have a fireman for this job, so Phil volunteered, saying that he hadn't long come off firing to take up driving.

He once had a runaway above Pontypool Clarence Street station with the Hafodyrynys colliers' train. By the destructor (a refuse disposal site with a big chimney, now the football field), just west of Clarence Street station, he applied the brakes and nothing happened. He applied the brakes again, then made a full application, just managing to keep the last coach on the platform at Clarence Street. Colliers were jumping down on the track and shouting things about learner drivers! The train was examined at Pontypool Road – only one of the coaches was braked. The coaches were stored at Pontypool Road station.

He recalled working nights and having a banking engine – a 'Hall' – parked in the North Bay at Pontypool Road station, for banking trains north or south from Little Mill. He went to the porters' cabin for a chat, and a little later a call came through to bank a train north. He returned to the engine to find his fireman asleep on the bucket in the corner of the cab. He woke him, and on opening the firebox saw a wheelbarrow load of embers under the door! The train arrived and they just managed to keep up with it. Upon returning to Pontypool Road station the engine was declared a failure; a loco from the shed arrived and pulled it back to shed.

At Abergavenny Monmouth Road Phil would leave the Abergavenny banker – a Webb 'Coal Tank' – behind, before the banking engine had got to the starting signal!

2. Dave Williams's trainspotting memories

I first went trainspotting in Bath for the day, and the first three engines I saw were 'Granges', all in the first half a dozen of the '68xx' number series. *Bucklebury Grange* was one. When spotting I never used to put the year down, only the date. My friend Mervin Price would note the year, but not the date.

I would walk across the Black Ash Path to the East box, cross the main line and go into the round shed. The south end of the shed was never visited from the viaduct. You tapped on the foreman's office and asked if you could have a look around the shed, please – but you had taken down half the numbers on the way in. Towards the end the foreman was glad to see you – 'With pleasure'! he would say. The signalman at the East box would scoot you off.

You visited in the evening after school. I saw the turntable working once or twice. The shed would be full – particularly the straight roads, when boiler washing was undertaken. A new stationary boiler arrived on a wagon before the shed closed – it was never used, but stored on a low wagon in the yard.

The first diesel shunter is remembered – it was stuck in the front of the shed, on the same road as the smashed-up No 5218 was later stored (the Coal Stage road). I remember my friend Mervin Price saying, 'Ponty got a diesel, Ponty got a diesel!' I also remember seeing the steam crane moving boiler ashes, and the coal stage working, and seeing engines having their fires dropped.

'Austerity' 2-8-0 No 90192 was stored in the yard for a long time in 1963, between the coal stage and the triangle at the West Junction.

Plymouth trains are recalled coming through Panteg station from Llantarnam Junction and being diverted through the yard and past the shed two or three times.

Pontypool Road station was the place; in the evening or on a Saturday you walked down to the canal basin, down the Black Ash Path and up to the station. I would go mostly on Jones's bus – 2½d. You could sit on the embankment and see the steam at Little Mill. Or you could sit on the fence on the station approach, or buy a platform ticket and go on the station. The Relief lines were used by trains from the Glascoed 'Dump'; two trains are recalled, one double-headed with a pannier tank and a '56xx' tank, the other with one engine, maybe a pannier tank.

The 1.42pm Swansea would change engines, from an LMS to a Western engine. The Ponty engine would take the train to Cardiff, where another engine change took place before the train proceeded to Swansea. Anything would be used at Ponty to take the train onwards to Cardiff – tank engines, '28xxs' and pannier tanks. Neath trains used the South Bay, sometimes the platform road, with normally a '56xx' tank loco or a pannier tank.

I recall seeing glassworks wagons, but no shunting; that was undertaken using the internal diesels. 'Castles' are recalled on the North-to-West trains, while 'Britannias' would arrive at 4.30pm in between the London turns, to Salop and back. Newton Abbot crews wore white polka dot neckerchiefs – 'They were the kiddies!' A regular engine was 'Jubilee' *Prince Rupert* on a Saturday.

The refreshment room was very busy. In the evening a train from Cardiff and one from Bristol would join at Ponty to go north. The Bristol train would come in second, up the Relief line, and cross over in front of the Cardiff train; the station pilot – a '56xx' or a pannier – would then shunt the Cardiff train behind it. Sometimes the pilot would drag the coaches out if the train was too long; then the train from Bristol would run into the platform road, and the Cardiff train would be pushed back in. There was a 'backing board' (a subsidiary signal arm with two holes in it) to allow this reversal. The station Middle box is recalled, as well as the North and South boxes (two signalmen worked there), and the East and West boxes.

Pontypool Crane Street

A '72xx' is recalled most mornings in 1963 when I was going to work at Pilkington's glassworks. I would see it when catching the bus at Park Terrace, Pontypool, with not many wagons, going towards Crane Street. I remember the goods yard when I was little; you went up the pathway from Crane Street and over the footbridge.

Pontypool Clarence Street

I remember 8Fs on the Vale of Neath, hauling freight trains. A pannier would pull the train out of the yard at Pontypool Road, and would end up almost in Pontypool Road station when this manoeuvre was complete. At Clarence Street the banker would be pushing only half a dozen wagons, with the engine making a lot of noise! Mervin Price tape-recorded trains leaving Clarence Street from his bedroom window.

Chapter 5: Later years 1965-1988

All photographs by J. S. Williams unless otherwise credited.

1. Pontypool Road shed closure

Below and following pages: On the last day of steam at Pontypool Road shed, 31 May 1965, Nos 3708, 7210, 4285, 4639 and possibly 5208 await firedropping. Nigel Williams and my cousin Allan Jones are seen on Nos 3708, 4285 and 4639, and my father, brother and cousin had a ride on No 4639 through the shed.

Later years 1965-1988

Below and following page: British Rail route closure transfer workings to Ebbw Junction as a result of the proposed closure of Pontypool Road yard, as supplied to ASLEF in 1966/67. *Derek Saunders*

```
                    PROPOSED CLOSURE OF PONTYPOOL ROAD YARD

                                                              APPENDIX 'D'
                                                              Page 67

PONTYPOOL ROAD

TURN NO. 906

        DRIVER AND SECOND MAN
                        On duty  05.10. MO
                                 04.30. MX

Prepare 1750 DE. CTN. 800
Pontypool Rd. S.Pt.             06.00 EBV. MO.   J.44.
Llanwern          06.50.
Take diesel left by Turn 614 MX.
Pontypool Rd. S.Pt.             04.45. LD MSX.
Pontypool Rd.     04.50.        05.00. Cl. 9.            EBW.
Llanwern          06.15.

Pontypool Rd. S.Pt.             05.10. LD. SO.
Pontypool Rd.     05.15.        05.25. Cl. 9.                    Not Required
Llanwern          06.40.

Llanwern
Furnace Sdgs.     09.15.        07.20. Cl. 9.   M-S

Furnace Sdgs.
Pontypool Rd.     11.55.        10.20. Cl. 9.   M-F.

Relieved by Turn 911.

Furnace Sdgs.                   10.20. Cl. 9.   SO.
Pontypool Rd.     12.00.        12.05. LD.
Pontypool Rd. SPt. 12.10.
                                Off duty 13.10 )  8H.OM.
                                         12.30 )
```

PROPOSED CLOSURE OF PONTYPOOL ROAD YARD

APPENDIX
Page 76

PONTYPOOL ROAD
TURN NO. 932
DRIVER AND SECONDMAN   On duty 08.10 M-F 06.10 SO
                       S/Man   08.40 SX, 06.40 SO

Prepare Diesel (350 H.P. EBBW 832)
Stabling Pt.   08.55 LD M-F (J.48)
Pontypool Rd.   09.00
Old Yard Pilot
Pontypool Rd.   13.00 Cl.9
Panteg Works   13.15   14.00 Cl.9
Pontypool Rd.   14.15
Old Yard Pilot
Relieved by Turn No.935 at 16.30
Stabling Pt.   06.55 LD SO
Pontypool Rd.   07.00
Old Yard Pilot (J.48)
Pontypool Rd.   14.00 LD
Stabling Pt.   14.05

                 Off duty 16.45 SX 8H.35M.
                          14.25 SO 8H.15M.

Ebbw V.

NOT REQUIRED

PONTYPOOL RD.
TURN NO.933
          DRIVER ONLY   On duty 12.40 M-F

Prepare Diesel Ebbw 822 (D.95XX) SX
Stabling Pt.   13.15 LD (A)
Pontypool Rd.   13.20   13.30 Cl.9
Abergavenny Mon.Rd. 14.00

SHUNT Monmouth Rd. berth traffic at Brecon Rd. and
SHUNT Abergavenny Jcn. as necessary.
Abergavenny M.Rd.   19.00 Cl.9
Pontypool Rd.   19.30
Relieved by Turn 935 at 19.45
                 Off duty 20.40 8H.0M.

Ebbw X

NOT REQUIRED

(A) Pontypool Rd.Gd.105 as Second Man
    30 Mins. P/N Break between 15.40 and 16.10

PROPOSED CLOSURE OF PONTYPOOL ROAD YARD

APPENDIX 'D'
Page 68

PONTYPOOL ROAD
TURN NO. 907
                DRIVER & SECONDMAN
                              On Duty 05.25. SO.
                                      06.40. M-F

Relieve Turn 931 at Panteg & G. at 07.00 (Ebbw 812 'C').
Panteg & G.   07.00.   07.10. Cl. 9. M-F (J.46)
Pontnewydd   07.25.
SHUNT Branches Fork, Return with Opencast coal
to Pontypool Road. 09.00.

Pontypool Rd.   09.25.   09.45. Cl. 9.
Cwmbran   10.05.
   Shunt Coal Yard.
Cwmbran   11.10. Cl. 9.
Coedygric   11.30.   11.55. Asst. (11.15. Talywain).
Trosnant Jcn.   12.00.   12.05. Asst.
Hafodyrynys   12.25.   12.35. LD.
Trevethin Jcn.   13.05.   13.45. Asst. (13.10. Talywain)
Trosnant Jcn.   13.55.   14.00. Asst.
Hafodyrynys   14.20.   14.25. LD.
Pontypool Rd. S.Pt. 14.45.
Relieved by Turn 601.

Prepare diesel (1750) (Ebbw 812)   SO
Pontypool Rd. S.Pt.   06.00. LD
Pontypool Rd.   06.05.   06.50. Cl. 9.   (J.46)
Panteg   07.00.   07.10. Cl. 9.
Pontnewydd   07.25.
   SHUNT Branches Fork until:-
Pontnewydd   11.00. Cl. 9.
Panteg   11.20.   11.30. LD.
Pontypool Rd. S.Pt. 11.40.

                 Off duty 13.25. SO. 8H.0M.
                          14.55. SX. 8H.5M.

EBBW. S

Not Required

Pontypool Road depot is seen from the Eastern Valley line at closure, 4 April 1967. *R. H. Marrows*

This view of the depot was taken during the winter of 1967/68, with demolition in progress. *Robert Hall*

The south end of Pontypool Road shed, looking north on Sunday 19 July 1970.

The filled-in turntable pit, photographed on the same day. In the background, the wall at the edge of the Skew Fields was the location of the Middle Junction signal box.

2. Vale of Neath: Crumlin and Hafodyrynys

Above: Crumlin Viaduct saw its last passenger train in 1964, and had been demolished by the end of 1967. Here are my mother and brother on the Kendon Valley section of the viaduct, looking towards Crumlin Junction after track-lifting had been completed.

Right: This is Crumlin Navigation Colliery, as seen from the catwalk beneath Crumlin Viaduct.

Below: Mike Jones (left) and John Williams (right), Engineering Lecturers at Pontypool College of Further Education, stand with a *South Wales Argus* journalist beneath Crumlin Viaduct, adjacent to Crumlin Navigation Colliery.

Looking east towards Crumlin Junction in late 1965, with the decking partly removed.

The closest a train could get to Crumlin Viaduct in the 1970s on the Vale of Neath line was the eastern portal of Hafodrynys Tunnel; a short spur of track west of Cefn Crib was used by the NCB for wagon storage in the late 1970s. West of the level crossing at Cefn Crib in 1972, a weed-killing train is seen in action.

Later years 1965-1988

No D1000 *Western Enterprise* is seen in June 1970 at Hafodyrynys with coal for washing.

Activity at Hafodrynys New Mine and washery in August 1970. No D1048 *Western Lady* has delivered empties and waits to collect a train of washed small coal, while a Type 3 diesel-electric waits to head south for Llanwern Steelworks with a train of washed small coal.

Driver Gordon Secker of Ebbw Junction heads for Hafodyrynys New Mine washery on 30 June 1972 with No 6922.

Below and top right: On Thursday 3 September 1970 Type 4 diesel-electric No 1917 awaits departure from Hafodyrynys washery sidings with a train of washed coal. On the right is former Tirpentwys Colliery 'Austerity' 0-6-0ST No 3810 *Glendower*, seen in close-up in the second picture.

Later years 1965-1988

In the early 1970s a DMU rail tour visits Hafodrynys New Mine. This view is looking west.

3. The Top Line

Driver Bert Hardman has arrived at Blaenavon Furnace Sidings with Type 3 diesel-electric No 6969 and train of empties for Big Pit on Thursday 3 September 1970.

Secondman Edward Wyman and Driver Bert Hardman flank an unknown railwayman, again with No 6969, at Furnace Sidings on Friday 27 August 1971.

Driver Gordon Secker stands with Furnace Sidings shunter Herbie Harrington and Guard Bill Prowse.

Below and following page: In about 1973 No 6969 is seen again, having arrived at Furnace Sidings, with Lyon's Sidings on the left of the first view. In the third picture the driver and secondman pose for their photograph.

Later years 1965-1988

The washery and muck tip (removed in 1979) at the Big Pit, Blaenavon.

An Andrew Barclay 0-4-0 ST is seen at the weighbridge.

No 6969 is ready for departure.

An enthusiasts' rail tour visits Furnace Sidings in the early 1970s.

A Type 3 diesel-electric locomotive approaches Furnace Sidings with empties on an unrecorded date.

Below and next page top: Rear cab views leaving Furnace Sidings and passing Big Pit Colliery on Friday 27 August 1971 with Driver Gordon Secker.

The rail tour seen earlier is captured again at Tyre Mill, Forgeside, Blaenavon.

Later years 1965-1988

Right: Another footplate ride, this one on Thursday 3 September 1970 and viewed from the front cab looking north. Cemetery Sidings were on the left, and the remains of Blaenavon High Level station are at the north end of the railway bridge at Varteg Road. The train is about to stall.

Right: A view of the stalled coal train at Cemetery Sidings. The locomotive stalled due to lack of power being applied on the journey to the sidings; brakes were picked up to allow the train to proceed. Behind the platelayer's cabin was the LNWR branch line to John Vipond's Colliery. It was from this location that both of the Blaenavon runaway coal trains began their journeys during the Second World War, being halted at Gwenallt Loop.

Below: Ebbw Junction Driver Terry Macteer is on No 6987 on Tuesday 1 June 1971. The secondman was Glyn Powell.

Right: The Oxford Publishing Company's 'Gwent Valley Invader' rail tour approaches Furnace Sidings on 11 March 1978.
J. Chalcraft, RailPhotoprints

Bridges at the snail creep and Varteg, photographed on 28 November 1982.

At Varteg station on 5 December 1982 all-welded rails from north of the Incline Bridge are seen alongside the platform awaiting recovery by train.

North of Varteg station on 28 November 1982, the remains of the track pass beneath John Vipond's Incline bridge (stolen after BR track recovery operations).

Crew changeover at Varteg on Wednesday 8 December 1982, during the all-welded rail recovery operations.

The all-welded rail is still in situ at Jackdaw Quarry, Cwmavon, looking north on 28 November 1982. *Terry Target*

The end of the all-welded rail section prior to recovery, north of Jackdaw Quarry, photographed on the same day. *Terry Target*

A view looking south during the all-welded rail recovery at Cwmavon, north of Varteg station.

A platelayers' cabin at Jackdaw Quarry, with my father John Williams alongside, in December 1982. *Phil Williams*

A southbound train of coal passes the site of Six Bells Halt, Garndiffaith, and heads towards Garndiffaith Viaduct on 10 April 1969.

Track removal north of Six Bells Halt on 16 July 1983 – note the remains of the signal post.

Garndiffaith cutting, south of the former Six Bells Halt, is seen from the front cab of a diesel locomotive, with Driver Gordon Secker, on Friday 27 August 1971.

In early 1980 a number of rail tours visited Furnace Sidings, Blaenavon, but as the track was by then out of use, on a number of occasions a few hours earlier a light engine movement was made to inspect the track. Here Class 37 No 37276 has stopped at the south end of Garndiffaith cutting for John Williams to photograph it. In March 1980 Nigel and John Williams had a footplate ride from Coedygric Junction to Furnace Sidings and return prior to a pair of Class 31 diesel-electrics using the line later that day.

Garndiffaith cutting, looking north on 13 March 1982.

Later years 1965-1988

The north end of Garndiffaith Viaduct, as seen from the front end of a diesel locomotive, date unknown.

A train of empties for Blaenavon Furnace Sidings heads north across Garndiffaith Viaduct circa 1972.

The Oxford Publishing Company's 'Gwent Valley Invader' rail tour, hauled by Class 37 diesel-electric locomotives Nos 37233 and 37269, is seen on the horseshoe curve at Wain-ddu near Pentrepiod and Garndiffaith Viaduct on 11 March 1978. *J. Chalcraft, RailPhotoprints*

The road bridge at Booth's Lane on the horseshoe curve, photographed on 18 October 1981, was supported underneath by lengths of rail. *Both Terry Target*

Later years 1965-1988

A trackless Garndiffaith Junction on 16 July 1983.

Alastair Warrington, a member of staff at British Rail Newport Civil Engineer's Office, is seen in the rear cab of Class 37 No 37281; he was the last person to travel across Garndiffaith Viaduct by rail. *Terry Target*

The last complete train of coal from Blaenserchan Colliery leaves Talywain at 1.15pm on Tuesday 31 March 1970.

Viewed from the top of the Big Arch, all the remaining Blaenserchan engines were unofficially pulled outside to be photographed by my father on 2 April 1970.

Andrew Barclay 0-6-0PT *Illtyd* (No 2331 of 1952) is seen outside the loco shed at the Big Arch with, from left to right, Jack Roden, Ernie Jones and Len Luter in March 1970. The author can just be glimpsed on the right.
J. S. Williams

Ex-GWR '77xx' Class 0-6-0PT No 7754 is diesel-hauled across the Big Arch to NCB Mountain Ash on Wednesday 29 April 1970. It spent a sometime at Newport Ebbw Junction awaiting a replacement broken spring, said to have been obtained from Woodham's scrapyard at Barry.

The Engineer's Inspection Saloon is in the loop at Talywain hauled by Type 4 No 1907 (Driver Albert Stopgate) on Tuesday 13 October 1970, waiting to change the single-line staff with a southbound coal train behind No 6982.

Shunters Eddie Evans and Herbie Harrington and Signalman Rollei Kinnersley are seen inside Talywain signal box in August 1971.

A train of Blaenavon coal heads south through Talywain, circa 1972.

The southbound coal train passes the stop board where wagon brakes were adjusted for the journey to Pontypool Crane Street.

An enthusiasts' rail tour is viewed from the NCB Big Arch site circa 1973. It is passing over the Big Arch with the house coal yard in the foreground.

Travelling down from Talywain, we see Cwmbyrgwm Colliery and the British Ironworks site in the background. The former double track was singled in 1966, and the best parts of the up and down main were used; here the up main skews over to the down main. The Big Arch is out of view on the right.

Later years 1965-1988

On top of the Big Arch looking towards Talywain on 23 May 1983. *Terry Target*

Looking south towards Abersychan & Talywain station on 13 March 1982. *Terry Target*

Castle Pond Sidings looking north, viewed from a signal post on 5 December 1982. *Terry Target*

Abersychan & Talywain station buildings, as seen on 10 April 1988. *Terry Target*

A train of coal passes over Powell's Arch at Pentwyn in June 1971.

Looking towards Talywain, a train of coal passes the reclaimed Abersychan Ironworks slag tips on 30 August 1972. Powell's Arch is to the right of this view.

Class 37 diesel-electric No 37196 is seen at Pentwyn station during scrap rail recovery between January and March 1980.

Pentwyn station site looking south on 9 October 1982. *Terry Target*

The 'Big Pit Special' is seen at Pentwyn station on 30 October 1982. This was the first half of the train, which had been split at Gwenallt due to excessive undergrowth. *Terry Target*

The Cwmavon track recovery train passes Pentwyn, crossing Powell's Arch on 8 December 1982.

This is the site of Cwmffrwdoer Halt, looking south on 5 December 1982. *Terry Target*

Class 37 No 37214 heads the track recovery train at Cwmffrwdoer Halt on 18 December 1982.

Right: The reverse curves at Gwenallt, looking south on 17 October 1982.

Below: The 'Big Pit Special' of Saturday 30 October 1982 has stalled at Gwenallt, due to excessive vegetation on the track. The train was split and transported to the Big Pit in two journeys.

Above right: While the special is stalled at Gwenallt, BR officials and loco crew pose for a photo with Class 37 No 37243. These photos were taken by Gordon Carter, Permanent Way Supervisor in charge of the office on the ground floor at Pontypool Road station.

Right: No 37243 passes Gypsy Lane on the horseshoe curve from Big Pit to collect the second half of the train. *Terry Target*

Gwenallt looking north on 5 December 1982. *Terry Target*

No 37243 waits to leave Gwenallt with china clay wagons forming the final train to Big Pit.

Later years 1965-1988

The underbridge (since demolished) near the Little Crown pub, Wainfelin, photographed on 16 June 1983.

Merchant's Hill road bridge, Pontnewynydd, looking north on 8 January 1983.

My old friend, the late Brian Harris, is seen cutting the deck on Merchant's Hill railway bridge on Saturday 18 January 1986. *Phil Williams*

The site of Trevethin Junction, looking north from George Street on 16 April 1983.

Later years 1965-1988

The site of George Street Sidings, looking south.

George Street road bridge. The Fountain Inn is on the right.

An English Electric Type 3 loco passes the site of Pontypool Crane Street.

Another coal train passes the stop board south of Crane Street on Friday 1 January 1971. The driver is Gordon Secker, with No 6976.

The site of Pontypool Crane Street is seen from the railway bridge crossing Albion Road, Pontypool, on 16 April 1983. *Terry Target*

The reverse curves north of Crane Street on 9 April 1983.

Trosnant Junction, with the former Ash Siding on the left.

Trosnant railway bridge, crossing the Vale of Neath line.

Later years 1965-1988

The last recovery train is seen at Trosnant on Saturday 18 December 1982, with Class 37 No 37214.

A Type 3 loco passes the site of Blaendare Halt with empties for Big Pit, Blaenavon, date unknown.

In April 1979 track-lifting is in progress on the former up line at Blaendare Road, which was used as the route for Hafodyrynys washery via Trosnant Junction.

The site of Blaendare Halt, looking south in April 1979. *J. S. Williams*

Above: Blaendare Halt and road bridge looking north on 16 April 1983. *Terry Target*

Right and below: Class 52 diesel-hydraulic No 1053 *Western Patriarch* passes the Vicar's Cottages at Maesderwen, en route to Coedygric Junction in April 1972.

Driver Gordon Secker passes the same location en route to Hafodyrynys New Mine on 30 June 1972, with No D6922.

In 1978 a scrap recovery train and breakdown crane were photographed at the south end of Pontymoile Viaduct.

Later years 1965-1988

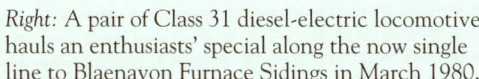

In Maesderwyn cutting the up line from Hafodyrynys washery is being lifted in April 1979.

Right: A pair of Class 31 diesel-electric locomotive hauls an enthusiasts' special along the now single line to Blaenavon Furnace Sidings in March 1980.

Below and below right: The remaining track is lifted.

The south end of Cwmnyscoy Viaduct at the Cwm. *Terry Target*

4. Pontypool Road

Pontypool Road station down platform, looking south at the North Bay, is seen during demolition work on Friday 4 December 1970.

Staff of scrap metal merchant W. J. Harris pose at the North Bay of Pontypool Road station during demolition work – I am on the extreme right. W. J. Harris dismantled the Monmouth line for scrap after closure, and dismantled Pontypool Road loco sheds.

In June 1979 a train derailed at Llantarnam Junction, causing the diversion of main-line traffic down the Eastern Valley Line via Pontypool Road South Junction to regain the main line at Llantarnam Junction. The next three pictures were taken one Saturday morning; the first shows the view looking south from Pontypool Road station.

Looking north towards Pontypool Road station.

A southbound train approaches Pontypool Road Station South Junction.

At the South Junction a Class 31 diesel-electric locomotive waits to propel a train of vans northwards through the New Sidings to Pontypool Road station south and Pilkington's fibreglass works via Panteg Junction Down Loop.

A train of vans from ROF Glascoed heads south on the main line, viewed from Coedygric Road Viaduct.

A DMU passes the site of the East Junction on Sunday 19 July 1970.

The New Sidings are seen from the points leading to the sidings' shunting spur. The reception road on the right is from the East Junction, and continued, in a truncated form, to Panteg Steelworks.

Later years 1965-1988

Looking north, the Down Goods Relief line is seen near the East Junction in October 1979. Ebbw Junction Driver Gordon Secker was working on this turn on a Sunday morning, removing signals from the up platform and outside the signal box.

A Type 3 diesel-electric locomotive is seen at Pontypool Road Station South Signal Box with a train of rail on Sunday 19 July 1970.

A southbound train waits in the New Sidings for a northbound train to go by, then passes the South Junction.

A train of concrete sleepers is seen at the South Junction, also on 19 July 1970. The Black Ash Path subway ventilation guard is seen in the foreground, and where the photographer is standing is the start of the triangle towards the West Junction.

The Station South Junction signal box was removed in June 1980 by being set on fire, then demolished using a mechanical digger.

5. South of Pontypool Road

'Warship' Class No D818 *Glory* (from Severn Tunnel Junction), with a brake van, approaches the skew bridge in Griffithstown on Friday 17 July 1970; this was a Severn Tunnel Junction-Hafodyrynys New Mine working.

In September 1971 a train of coal is seen between the skew bridge and Coedygric Farm in Griffithstown, with the disused gasworks in the background.

In 1978 a scrap recovery train is seen at the skew bridge. Dick Bassett is on the right, and Brian Toddle to his left.

This is the curve below the skew bridge over the Monmouthshire & Brecon Canal at Griffithstown, looking towards Maesderwen on 16 April 1983. *Terry Target*

Track removal at Coedygric Farm in May 1983. *Phil Williams*

Below and top right: Looking south, then north, at the skew bridge, also in May 1983. *Both Phil Williams*

Track-lifting at the north end of Stafford Road, Griffithstown, in May 1983.
Phil Williams

Viewed from Panteg & Coedygric Junction signal box on Thursday 3 September 1970, diesel-hydraulic No D1009 *Western Invader* arrives with empty wagons for Hafodyrynys New Mine, to be stored at the New Sidings.

Another 'Western', No D1007 *Western Talisman*, approaches Panteg & Coedygric Junction with empties for Hafodyrynys washery on an unrecorded date.

Later years 1965-1988

In another undated picture a 'Hymek' diesel-hydraulic locomotive approaches the junction with washed coal from Hafodyrynys washery.

Approaching Panteg & Coedygric Junction on 3 September 1970; this is the view from the cab of a Type 3 locomotive with Driver Bert Hardman. The remains of the Down Loop are on the left. By the time of a similar trip with Driver Gordon Secker on Friday 27 August 1971 this loop had been removed.

Changing the single-line staff, also recorded on 3 September 1970.

On Monday 14 December 1971 Type 3 No 6914 ran away from the second stop board below Cwm Glyn at Mynydd Maen, and was diverted into the catch points at Panteg & Coedygric Junction. The Cardiff Canton steam crane is seen from the New Sidings shunting spur during removal of the damaged wagons the following day.

The Hafodyrynys runaway locomotive has been recovered to the New Sidings, where the accident damage can be seen.

'Western' Class No 1053 *Western Patriarch* approaches Panteg & Coedygric Junction in April 1972, as viewed from Station Road.

Inside Panteg & Coedygric Junction signal box, looking north. The pheasant in the roof was a souvenir from the winter of 1947, having been obtained from the cutting for the Down Goods line to Panteg Junction. During track removal in October 1979 the bird was discarded outside the front of the signal box.

In 1979 Rollei Kinnersley, the former Talywain signalman, arranged a footplate ride from Panteg & Coedygric Junction to the Down Loop at Panteg Junction, via Pontypool Road South Junction, where vans were dropped off for Pilkington's fibreglass works. The return journey was by car!

Panteg & Coedygric Junction on 16 April 1983.

The Blaenavon weed-killing train heads south through Panteg & Griffithstown station on Saturday 20 May 1972.

Station Road, Griffithstown, and the railway bridge opposite the Mason's pub on Station Road are seen looking south in May 1983.

This train has travelled from New Sidings to the former Panteg Junction to collect a train of coils from Panteg Steelworks in July 1971, with Severn Tunnel Junction Driver Dennis Collett and Secondman Mostyn Richards.

This is the line north of Sebastopol Halt on 16 April 1983, with Panteg Steelworks on the right. *Terry Target*

The view south of Panteg sidings and goods shed on the same day. *Terry Target*

Panteg looking north, again on 16 April 1983. *Terry Target*

6. Aberdare and Quakers Yard

Aberdare High Level station, as seen in 1972. *Phil Williams collection*

Quaker's Yard High Level and Low Level stations, also seen in 1972.

Aberdare High Level station and goods shed, with the station nameboard, in 1973. *Phil Williams collection*

7. Childhood memories

Right and top right: The final photos in this book remind me of the many childhood hours spent at Abersychan & Talywain signal box in the early 1970s with my father. Here Type 3 diesel-electric No 6932 heads north through the station towards Garndiffaith Junction with empties for Big Pit, circa February 1972.

Below: Conversation piece: Type 3 diesel-electrics Nos 6969 and 6971 meet at Talywain circa 1973, with the 1940s Blaenserchan Colliery waste tip visible in the background. No 6971 is heading south with a train of Blaenavon coal.

Nigel Williams, myself (in the driving seat) and an Ebbw Junction driver are seen with Type 3 No 6602 having enjoyed a footplate ride from Blaenavon Furnace Sidings circa August 1971.

A weed-killing train heads south through Talywain, with Nigel Williams and myself in the foreground, on Saturday 20 May 1972.

Index

Bankers
Abergavenny 119, 132, 141, 167
Cwm Glyn 163
Gadlys 153, 155
Honeybourne 146
Little Mill 167
Llantarnam 12
Llanvihangel 121
Mountain Ash (Cresselley) 153, 160, 161

General
Air raids 118-19
Auto-trains 13, 14, 16, 51, 52, 57, 65, 123, 165, 166
Banana trains 136, 149
British Ironworks 64, 94, 202
Eastern Valley Railway Co 102
Monmouthshire Railway & Canal Co ('Old Mon' line) 10, 45, 60, 63-65, 127
Pontypool Road Ambulance Division 115
Railmotors 72-74
Weston's Biscuits 18

Locations
Aberdare High Level 159, 160, 161, 243-44; loco shed 152ff
Abergavenny (Monmouth Road) 88, 123, 124, 132, 137, 145, 148, 166, 167
Abergavenny Junction 120, 132
Abersychan & Talywain 10, 15, 16, 20, 36, 40, 41, 45, 47, 55, 58, 59, 60-62, 86, 91, 94, 95, 98, 166, 198, 200-04, 244-46
Abersychan Low Level 49, 51, 59, 60, 65-66, 74, 86, 94

Barry Island 53, 57, 76, 85, 132; Woodham's scrapyard 102, 103, 105, 199
Big Arch, Abersychan 25, 34, 46, 47, 61-62, 94, 95, 96, 98, 198, 199, 202-03
Big Pit Colliery 47, 59, 74, 102, 183, 185-86
Bishops Castle branch 126
Blaenavon High Level 40, 47, 48, 55, 58, 62, 93, 187
Blaenavon Low Level 13, 14, 49-50, 51, 53, 55, 67, 72, 94
Blaendare Road Halt 13, 15, 16, 32, 46, 57, 57, 71, 85, 217-19
Blaenserchan Colliery and branch 20, 23, 24-25, 26, 27, 28, 94, 107, 198, 245
Branches Fork Junction 20-23, 24, 56, 62, 70, 85-86, 89, 97; shed 21, 22, 25, 33-34, 41, 44, 117
Bristol 117, 127, 134, 138, 140, 147, 149
Brynmawr 16, 44, 54, 57, 165
Caerleon 13, 15, 85, 141
Cardiff 126-27
Castle Pond Sidings 204
Cefn Crib 166, 176
Cefn Glas Tunnel 153
Cemetery Sidings, Blaenavon 36, 39, 44, 47, 97, 187
Church Stretton 148, 152
Coedygric Sidings and Viaduct 15, 35, 43, 45, 46, 55, 62, 82, 89, 90, 225, 232
Cresselley Crossing 161, 162
Crumlin and Viaduct 164, 166, 175-76
Cwmavon Halt and Reservoir 63, 67, 72, 94, 191

Cwmbran and Junction 17, 19, 29, 44, 49, 61, 65, 71, 103, 105, 109, 145; Girling factory 50-51
Cwmffrwd Halt and Junction 49, 50, 53, 66-67, 73, 94, 95
Cwmffrwdoer Halt 24, 35, 74, 99, 100, 208
Cwmnyscoy Viaduct 222
Dare Valley Junction 159
Dinmore Tunnel 127, 148
Elled Colliery 33
Furnace Sidings, Blaenavon 35, 39, 40, 41, 42, 44, 45, 47, 54-55, 58-59, 62, 63, 89, 97, 180-85, 187
Gadlys Junction 155, 157, 158, 160
Garndiffaith Junction and Viaduct 36, 37, 58, 62, 72, 96, 192-93, 194-96, 197
Gellydeg Sidings 26, 27
Glascoed Ordnance Depot 50-51, 54, 90, 107, 122, 167, 225
Glyn Neath 155, 156, 166
Golynos Junction and Ironworks 63, 64, 94
Graig-ddu brickworks 23, 24, 26-29
Gwenallt loop and Colliery (Jack Pit) 22, 23, 24, 27, 28, 29, 40, 45, 47, 55, 70, 97, 209-10
Hafodyrynys Colliery 15, 16, 26, 35, 44, 89, 90, 91, 106, 108, 109, 118, 166, 178-79
Hay-on-Wye 125
Hereford 124-26, 131, 132, 136, 142, 143, 144, 145, 148, 152, 155, 160
Hirwaun 153, 155, 157, 158, 160
'Horseshoe curve', Pontnewynydd 20, 35, 45, 58, 74, 100, 196, 209
Jack Pit *see* Gwenallt Colliery
Jackdaw Quarry 62, 63, 75, 190-91
Ledbury Tunnel 134
Little Mill 35, 90, 127, 136, 154
Llanelli 155, 156
Llanerch Colliery 25, 26, 27, 28
Llantarnam and Junction 17, 18, 19, 49, 71, 74, 102, 149
Llanvihangel and bank 121, 124, 125, 130, 132, 137, 142, 144, 145, 150-51, 165
Ludlow 133, 148, 152
Maesderwyn 64, 219-21, 231

Maesglas 58, 60, 62
Malvern 146
Margam 76, 109, 141, 160
Markham Colliery 109-10
Marsh Farm Junction 126, 133, 134, 141
Mitcheldean 122
Monmouth 122, 123
Mountain Ash 153, 156, 157, 161, 162
Mynydd Maen Colliery 15, 16, 89
Neath 154
Nelson 166
Newport, Dock Street 12, 20, 44, 45, 62
    High Street 65, 128
    Mill Street 10, 44, 59, 62
    Pill 58, 60
Oakdale Colliery 109-10
Panteg & Coedygric Junction 43, 98, 106, 145, 163, 234-35, 236-39
Panteg & Griffithstown 12, 15, 16, 17, 20, 46, 49, 51, 55, 60, 61, 62, 74, 77-82, 85, 230, 231, 233, 239-40
    Hospital 16, 46
    Sidings 12, 34, 35, 39, 43, 61, 242
    Steelworks 12, 43, 78, 79, 107-08, 241
Penpergwm 136, 148, 151
Penrhiwceiber High Level 158
Pentrepiod Halt 36, 45, 72, 100, 101
Pentwyn and Junction 34, 47, 205, 206-07
Pontnewydd, Lower 18; Upper 49, 104, 105
Pontnewynydd, Junction and yard 16, 21, 24, 26, 41, 45, 49, 51, 56, 62, 63, 67, 70, 71, 74, 89; Merchant's Hill bridge 68, 75, 211-12
Pontrilas 142, 143
Pontymoile 64, 65, 164, 220
Pontypool Clarence Street 64, 89, 90, 135, 166-67, 168
Pontypool Crane Street 13, 15, 16, 24, 30, 31, 32, 33, 46-47, 49, 54, 55, 56, 58, 62, 64, 65, 68-71, 74, 85, 86, 89, 102, 168, 214-15
    George Street bridge and sidings 67, 74, 213
Pontypool Road shed 53-54, 169-74

Index

Pontypool Road station 86-88, 90, 111-16, 167-68, 222-24
   Black Ash Path 75, 109, 167, 229
   East signal box 35, 75, 84, 167, 168, 226-27
   Fish and Chip Siding 57-58
   Middle Junction 114, 168, 174
   New Sidings 46-47, 78, 80-84, 226
   North Bay 88, 123, 129, 135, 167, 222
   North signal box 109, 152, 168
   Skew Fields/Bridge loop 13, 15, 56, 140, 174, 230-31, 232-33
   South Bay 88, 112, 114, 115, 116, 144, 167
   South Junction signal box 35, 76, 84, 88, 119, 120, 129, 168, 224-25, 227-29
   Wagon repair shed 109
   West signal box 75-76, 101, 141, 164, 168
Pontypool Town Forge, Pontnewynydd 27, 33, 56, 57, 67
Porthcawl 53, 85
Powell's Arch 205, 207
Quaker's Yard 160, 243
Rhigos 157, 160
Ross-on-Wye 122
Sebastopol Halt 15, 86-87, 147, 241
Severn Tunnel 127, 137-39, 140
Severn Tunnel Junction 139
Shrewsbury 126, 134, 135, 147, 148-49, 151-52
Six Bells Halt 93, 94, 165, 192-93
Snatchwood Halt 51, 64, 67, 72, 74
Swansea 160
Taff Merthyr 159
Talywain *see* Abersychan & Talywain
Tirpentwys Colliery and branch 20, 23, 25-26, 56, 91, 178
Trevethin Junction 16, 57, 58, 59, 61, 69, 86, 212
Trosnant Junction 13, 15, 89, 216-17
Tyre Mill 40, 41, 44, 47, 54-55, 58, 62
Uskmouth 16, 127
Varteg 36, 37, 38, 62, 63, 74, 95, 165, 188-89;
Varteg Hill Colliery 36
Viaduct Colliery 27, 28, 29
Vipond Colliery and Incline 36, 38-39, 61, 96, 187, 188-89
Waenavon 47, 54, 57
Wainfelin 47, 68, 72, 75, 211
Worcester 126, 146, 166
Ystrad Mynach 154

Locomotives and units, diesel
Class 25 80-83
Class 31 221, 225
Class 35 'Hymek' 235
Class 37 15, 38-39, 84, 99, 100, 107, 120, 177, 178, 180-82, 184, 185, 187, 192, 194, 196, 197, 206, 207, 208, 209, 210, 214, 217, 236, 237, 244-46
Class 42/43 'Warship' 102, 165, 230
Class 47 15, 77, 83, 178, 200, 228
Class 52 'Western' 102, 104, 177, 219, 234, 237
DMUs 49, 84, 85, 184, 186, 202, 226

Locomotives, steam
'14xx' 0-4-2T 123, 166
'20xx' 0-6-0PT 107
'22xx' 0-6-0 146
'28xx' 2-8-0 125, 127, 130, 131, 132, 136, 145, 146, 153, 154, 155, 156, 167
'30xx' 'ROD' 2-8-0 128, 153
'31xx' 2-6-2T 164
'36xx' 0-6-0PT 136
'38xx' 2-8-0 125, 136, 143, 150, 156
'41xx' 2-6-2T 15, 112, 127, 132
'42xx' 2-8-0T 20, 41, 127, 153, 154, 155, 156, 164
'43xx' 2-6-0 15, 131, 144, 152
'45xx' 2-6-2T 121, 122
'46xx' 0-6-0PT 154
'48xx' 2-8-0 107
'51xx' 2-6-2T 162
'52xx' 2-8-0T 32, 134, 153, 154, 155, 156
'53xx' 2-6-0 124, 136, 152
'55xx' 2-6-2T 160
'56xx' 0-6-2T 121, 122, 135, 156, 157, 158, 160, 167, 168
'57xx' 0-6-0PT 116, 117

5MT ('Black Five') 4-6-0 146, 147, 148
'63xx' 2-6-0 131, 153, 155, 156, 161
'64xx' 0-6-0PT 13, 16, 107, 141
'66xx' 0-6-2T 15, 33, 137, 155, 156, 158, 161
'72xx' 2-8-2T 34, 35, 36, 40, 42, 55, 62, 63, 126, 127, 132, 134, 141, 155, 156, 168
'73xxx' 4-6-0 (BR) 140
'77xx' 0-6-0PT 199
'84xx' 0-6-0PT 157
8F 2-8-0 132, 141, 142, 150, 161, 168
'94xx' 0-6-0PT 14
9F 2-10-0 (BR) 54, 58, 128, 141
'Aberdare' 2-6-0 134
Beames 0-8-2T (LMS) 163
Beames 0-8-4T (LMS) 48
'Britannia' 4-6-2 (BR) 76, 127, 128, 137, 168
'Buffalo' 0-6-0ST 164
'Bulldog' 4-4-0 113, 116
'Castle' 4-6-0 76, 128, 129, 131, 133, 139-40, 147, 162, 165, 166, 168
'County' 4-6-0 76, 111, 144
'Grange' 4-6-0 125, 130, 153, 155, 161, 167
'Hall' 4-6-0 125, 129, 130, 132, 134, 144, 147, 149, 151, 153
'Jubilee' 4-6-0 133
'King' 4-6-0 76, 123, 130, 141, 166
'Manor' 4-6-0 76, 128
'P' (Rhymney) 0-6-2T 121
'Saint' 4-6-0 77, 113, 164
'Star' 4-6-0 128, 166

People
Ashman, Edward 94, 97
Atkins, Andrew 108
Attwood, Arthur 68, 85
Attwood, Mrs Margaret 32, 68

Badham, Bert 65
Bailey, W. L. 71
Baker, Billy 31
Bartlow, Stan 153
Batley, Alf 27-28
Beet, Dr Peter 105
Benfield, Ken 65
Bigham, John 33, 34

Birch, Les 15, 66, 86
Brisk, Jack 127

Canning, Bill 27
Carter, Wilfred 94
Charles, Edgar 94, 97
Charles, Vince 67
Collett, Dennis W. 79, 99, 241
Corley, Mr (station master) 68
Corr, Bill 146

Dale, Bill 21, 27
Dauncey, William 97
Davies, Tom 10
Davis, Bill 50
Davis, Cyril 125
Davis, Mike 67
Davis, Tom 117, 132
Deakin, Chris 89
Drayton, Jack 122, 125, 142

Elvy, Mike 102
Evans, Dick 31
Evans, Eddie 200
Evans, Graeme 62
Evans, Les 149
Evans, Roy 102
Everson, Dick 135, 140
Eyeball, Arthur 68

Fletcher, Alan 68
Ford, Bryn 68
Foster, Barry 75
Foster, Sid 107
Fry, Dave 103
Fry, Eric 28
Fry, Hector 70

Giles, Ron 159
Godsall, Walter 68
Gollop, George 65
Gollop, John 94
Good, Harold 132
Goulding, Cyril 107
Grave, George 13

Index

Greenwood, Joe 105
Griffin, Mrs 32, 70
Griffiths, Jack 148
Griffiths, Mrs 45

Haddigate, Mrs 89
Hale, Bert 140-41, 143-44
Hales, Stan 31
Hanns, Graham 105
Harding, Billy 162
Hardman, Bert 97, 180, 235
Harper, Will 95
Harrington, Herbert 39, 40, 97, 181
Harris, Bob 32, 85
Harris, Brian 75, 212
Harris, John 106
Harris, W. J. (scrap merchant) 223
Harris, Walter 68
Harvey, Edgar 25
Hewlett, Charlie 53, 101
Hewlett, Gwyn 53, 132
Hewlett, Tom 109
Horton, Alec 31
Hough, Len 140
Hughes, Jack 68, 85
Hunt, Norman 34
Hunter, Marcus 101
Hurn, Ray 31

James, Dai 127, 150
Jancey, Bill 127
Jones, A. E. 71-72
Jones, Arthur 93
Jones, Austin 163
Jones, Ernest 147, 150
Jones, Ernie 199
Jones, Jack 150
Jones, Keith 161
Jones, Len 106
Jones, Mike 175
Jones, Rollei 33

Kersley, Jack 13, 165
Kinnersley, Rollei 94, 98, 200, 238

Lawrence, John 97
Leek, Owen 67
Lewis, Ken 103
Luter, Len 199
Luxton, Bill 131

McMale, Wally 132
McSheely, Gus 97, 99
Macteer, Terry 97, 98, 99, 187
Marks, Phil 156
Mathews, Les 119
Morgan, Bill 97
Morgan, David 94
Morgan, Horace 97
Morgan, Len 103
Morgan, Rob 45
Mount, Miss 86
Muldoway, Andrew 67

Newcombe, Larry 62
Nicholas, Ben 91
Nicholas, Norman 91
Nicholls, Jack 41
Norkett, Les 101
Nutt, Derek 31

Oakley, Bill 34, 147
Oates, Frank 96

Parry, Mr 95
Paton, John 91
Pearce, Tom 57
Peppin, Mr 86
Perett, Sydney 97
Petty, Jeffrey 99
Polsom, Colin 62, 147
Pope, Danny 65, 66, 71
Powell, George 31
Powell, Glyn 99, 187
Preece, Ted 97, 98, 110
Price, Glyn 101
Price, Mervyn 167, 168
Probert, Ken 68
Prowse, Bill 99, 181

Rawlins, Wilf 157
Rees, Huw 99
Rees, Ronny 162
Reynolds, Charlie 15, 109, 135
Rich, Peter 106
Richards, Mostyn 79, 99, 241
Roberts, Harry 109
Robins, Harry 133
Roden, Jack 199

Saunders, Derek 10, 119
Secker, Gordon 97, 99, 178, 181, 185-86, 193, 220, 227, 235
Shepherd, Maurice 104
Slade family 90
Smith, Jack 94
Stanley, Fred 12
Stone, Bill 54
Stopgate, Albert 97, 200
Sullivan, Jim 31
Sylvester, Ivor 65, 66
Symes, Bill 62, 152

Tamplin, Tommy 151
Target, Terry 63, 85
Taylor, George 32, 68
Thomas, Bob 62
Thomas, Brian 105, 106
Thomas, Mo 149
Timms, John (Jack) 94, 97
Toddle, Brian 93
Towell, Ray 105
Tuck, Mrs 45

Warrington, Alastair 74, 197
Warwood, Terry 58, 141
Waters, Tony and Hazel 68
Watkins, Jimmy 134
Whittaker, Steve 106
Wilcox, George 65
Wilkins, Terry 153
Willets, Don 131
Williams, Cliff 91
Williams, Dave 167
Williams, David 103
Williams, 'Full Load' Phil 103, 105, 163-67
Williams, Harry 90-91
Williams, Henry 56, 150
Williams, Horace 91
Williams, John S. 106, 191
Williams, Ken 70
Williams, Stanley 91, 92
Williams, Thomas 90-91
Williams, Will 91
Wyman, Edward 97, 180

Young, Harry 33

Pilots
Alexandra Dock 62
Dare Valley 159
Little Mill 121
Northern 117
Old Yard 43
Panteg 13
Pontnewynydd 29, 30-33, 34, 56, 57, 70, 71
Pontypool Road Station 50, 121, 123, 136
Tower Colliery 160

Further reading

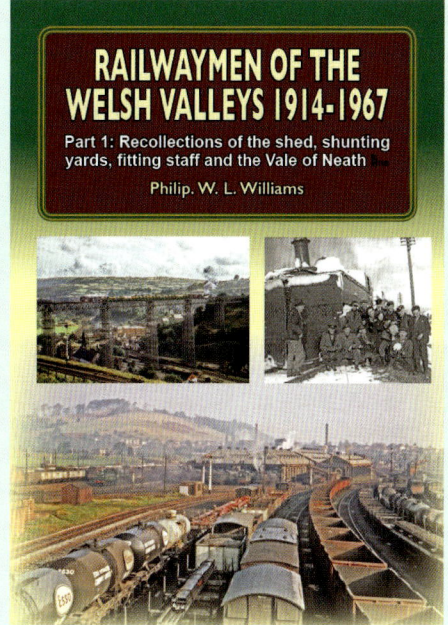

RAILWAYMEN OF THE WELSH VALLEYS 1914-67

MEMORIES OF STEAM WORKING FROM PONTYPOOL ROAD SHED AND FAR BEYOND!

This book, published in two parts, is dedicated to the memories of all those people who once worked for the Great Western Railway in South Wales, at Pontypool Road loco depot, the Eastern Valley and the Vale of Neath railway, as well as to those people who worked in the industries once served by the railway in those locations. In 2016, the UK coal mining industry is extinct, and the future of the steel industry is in doubt.

This book serves as a reminder to future generations as to what a fantastic place the South Wales valleys once were for heavy industry and transport infrastructure, and also as a tribute to the pioneering 19th-century railway builders.

Local railway enthusiast, the late Phil Williams, was a contract structural engineer in the aerospace industry. His father's uncle, Harry Miles, was a Swindon-trained locomotive fitter at Pontypool Road in the 1930s. His family have interesting links to the mining industry. His great-grandfather was Thomas Williams, the colliery engineer at Tirpentwys Colliery from before 1902 up to 1912; then at Crumlin Valley Colliery, Hafodrynys and the Glyn Pits from 1915 until he died in 1925 aged 76. His father's great-grandfather, Joseph Harper, was one of the 1890 Llanerch Colliery disaster rescue team; he worked at the British Top Pits. His father's uncle, Williams Harper, was the foreman of the wagon shop at the Big Arch Talywain.

Author: Phil Williams
Imprint: Silver Link Books
Category: Railway
ISBN: 978 1 85794 488 4
Format: Hardback
Pages: 280
Published: February 24, 2020
£35.00

RUNNING ON RAILS
A JOURNEY THAT INCLUDES UNUSUAL INDUSTRIAL AND PASSENGER RAILWAYS OVER 150 YEARS

This new title from the authors of A World of Rail – John Legg and Ian Peaty – takes us on a fascinating tour of Britain's rail-borne transport system, or rather systems, as it covers a wide variety of locations and gauges. The variety of rolling stock is a feature, including both passenger and freight vehicles. Locations range from London's Underground to the Bass Brewery in Burton-upon-Trent and from Ford's Dagenham plant to the whisky distilleries of Scotland.

This is a book that takes the reader off the beaten track, over many years, to provide a wide variety of images from all sorts of unusual and rarely seen passenger and freight services the length and breadth of the country.

Images from the earliest days of railways right up to the modern day scene are accompanied by informative text and detailed captions. This is a book that is sure to provide variety.

The authors, John Legg and Ian Peaty, have been close friends for more than 50 years and have shared their enthusiasm for railways both at home and around the world. During this time they have accumulated photographs, technical data and books on vast numbers of industrial and passenger railways and some interesting events that surround them.

To date Ian has had eight books published that include his interest in brewing and railways with the last book, A World of Rail, being a joint effort covering many countries the authors and families have visited around the world. Although they are the 'older generation' they are still very enthusiastic and keep on travelling!

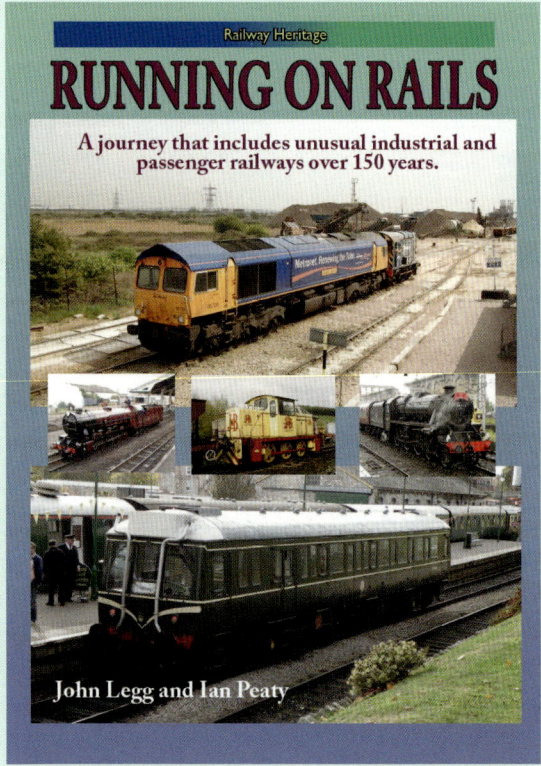

This book, Running on Rails, covers many areas around the UK and highlights not just a few well-known standard and narrow gauge railways, but some of the lesser known and written about industrial and passenger lines, events and locations that extend over the last 150 years up to today's continually modernising railway network.

Authors: John Legg and Ian Peaty
Imprint: Silver Link Books
Category: Railway
ISBN: 978 1 85794 548 5
Format: Hardback
Pages: 192
Published: February 24, 2020
£25.00

Further reading

DEVON AND CORNWALL RAILFREIGHT

Although today's railway in the South West is principally a passenger operation, an exception is china clay traffic, which has been a feature of the area's railways for much of their history and today is the main reason for railfreight managing to retain a toehold in the peninsula.

This wide-ranging survey of the history of freight traffic in the two counties commences with a brief look into the past, when the railway was a 'common carrier' hauling all manner of goods, largely by the wagonload. It then chronicles the ultimately unsuccessful 50-year-long fight to retain at least a portion of such traffic on the railway, including the initial development and final demise of the 'Speedlink' and 'Enterprise' services. Other commodities that have been handled over the last 40 or 50 years are then considered in more detail, particularly where there is or has been a trainload operation, and more detailed consideration is given to traffic that is especially distinctive to the area.

In the era of the privatised railway system, today's railfreight companies have to be nimble in their dealings with customers and quick to respond to both opportunities and problems, something that British Railways often had a reputation for being poor at - it is quite probable that there would be even less freight on rail today if we still had a nationalised system.

Nonetheless, railfreight activity in the South West appears to be hanging on by a thread, but it is still doing what it is good at and hauling commodities such as china clay, aggregates and cement in bulk, although increasingly freight operators are having to pin their hopes on a continued growth in intermodal traffic.

David Mitchell has maintained an interest in railways for 60 years and has been an active photographer for much of this time. Having spent his early years in Cornwall before moving to Devon, he has a particular interest in the railways of the South West and has had many photos published in books and magazines, including contributing more than 25 articles and features to different periodicals. He has also authored or co-authored 11 titles in Silver Link's long-running British Railways Past and Present series.

He has travelled over most of the UK's surviving railway network from the 1970s and also has a strong interest in the railways of the US and Canada. He has crossed the Atlantic on 14 occasions on photographic expeditions to these countries.

Author: David Mitchell
Imprint: Silver Link Books
Category: Railway
ISBN: 978 1 85794 473 0
Format: Hardback
Pages: 208
Published: September 24, 2019
£40.00

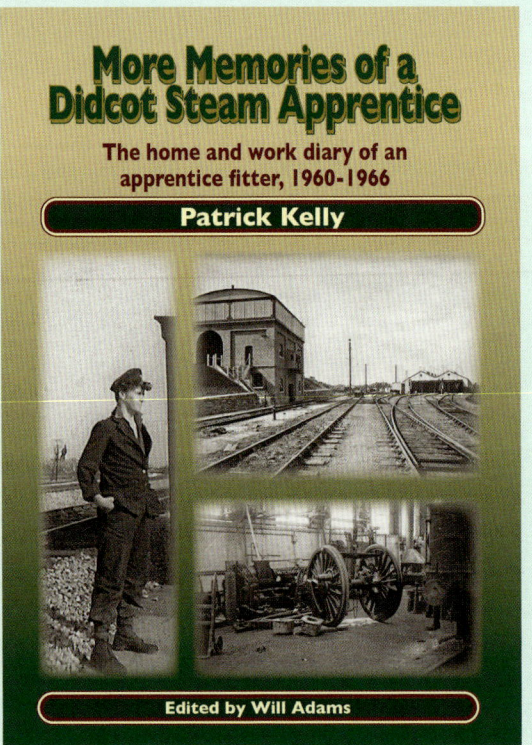

MORE MEMORIES OF A DIDCOT STEAM APPRENTICE

The first volume of Pat Kelly's memoirs of his time with British Railways in the early 1960s, *Didcot Steam Apprentice*, was published in 2008, and found an enthusiastic audience. Since then Pat has felt the need to dig deeper into his memories, and reveal much more detail about his day-to-day life at Didcot shed on BR's Western Region in the dying days of steam, as a young inexperienced 15-year-old thrown into the tough, uncompromising world of working men. His new book, hugely expanded, describes in detail some of the perilous and dirty jobs they did on and beneath the steam locomotives, long before the days of 'Health and Safety', and how he perfected his skills at the shed's forge. It also covers daily routines, initiation ceremonies, and his assorted workmates, some friendly, and some whose greatest pleasure was trouble-making and back-biting. In particular he describes his warm, encouraging and almost father-and-son relationship with his mentor, lifting shop fitter Jim Tyler, and with the running and maintenance foreman, Arthur Brinkley. Almost novelistic in its breadth, Pat's book also tells of his difficult home life, his close friendships and his girlfriends, the latter strongly disapproved of by his domineering mother.

Here then is the enthralling story a boy learning to hold his own in a man's world, revealed in fascinating detail and told with great honesty. Featuring not only Didcot shed, but also spells at Swindon, Reading and Old Oak Common, it will appeal to anyone who has ever found themselves in a similar situation, as well as railway historians and enthusiasts.

Author: Patrick Kelly
Imprint: Silver Link Books
Category: Railway
ISBN: 978 1 85794 572 0
Format: Softback
Pages: 288
Published: March 25, 2022
£35.00